IRISH THUNDER

THE
HARD LIFE & TIMES
OF
MICKY WARD

D0110002

BOB HALLORAN

LYONS PRESS
GUILFORD, CONNECTICUT
AN IMPRINT OF GLOBE PEQUOT PRESS

The Library of Congress has cataloged the hardcover edition as follows:

Halloran, Bob.
  Irish thunder : the hard life and times of Micky Ward / Bob Halloran.
    p. cm.
  ISBN-13: 978-1-59921-220-3
  1. Ward, Micky. 2. Boxers (Sports)—United States—Biography. 3. Irish American boxers—Biography. I. Title.
  GV1132.W24H35 2007
  796.83092—dc22
  [B]

                                        2007034176

ISBN 978-0-7627-6986-5

CONTENTS

CHAPTER ONE

A dozen bellies cozy up to the bar. Shots and beers for a small group of men. It's nine o'clock in the morning, and drinking seems like a good idea. It had been this way at the Highland Tap for the better part of three decades, and if it stayed that way for three more, that would suit these men just fine.

The Tap was their comfort zone. It was dark, and it was quiet. The faces were as familiar as the conversations. The tap was no-frills with a handful of tables and enough wooden stools to surround a small, oval bar. Pictures of fighters hung from the walls, local boxers whose images filled these patrons with a sense of parochial pride. If you grew up in Lowell, you were tough, because Lowell made you that way. There were times in Lowell's history when it had been a good place to raise a family. The rest of the time, it was a good place to raise a little hell. Most of the men who ventured into the Highland Tap had done both.

"This used to be one helluva tough town," one man says to no one in particular. The speaker turns out to be Manny Freitas whose picture hangs on the wall only a few feet away. The photo was taken some thirty years earlier when Freitas was still able to pick up a few bucks fighting in small New England venues from Providence to Portland.

Freitas had had the privilege of being knocked out in the first round by the great Marvin Hagler in Portland, Maine, in 1973, when Hagler's career was just getting started and Freitas's career was much closer to its end. Freitas reminisces humbly, "I'd seen him in the amateurs, so I knew he was a good fighter, but he surprised me with his hand speed. I never even saw the punches." Hagler was supposed to fight a tomato can by the name of Curtis Phillips that night, but Freitas was the last-minute replacement. Freitas makes no pretenses about his boxing skills, never really thinking of himself as a boxer anyway. He never trained as a boxer. He was just a guy who got into a lot of fights. One of those fights was against a man with a machete, knocking Freitas into jail at MCI-Concord and a few more years in a work-release program in Lancaster. He had hoped to open a boxing gym with his brother, but he works behind the counter at the liquor store down the street instead. It's a job, and Manny is in no hurry to get to it this morning.

Freitas finished his boxing career with a record of 20–27–2. Besides losing to Hagler, his greatest achievement in boxing may have come when he broke Tommy Dragon's jaw in Providence. Probably the best legal punch he ever threw.

Freitas commands respect because, here, a man earns respect simply by stepping into the ring.

"It's still a tough town," Freitas hears from across the bar. He thinks about some of the kids from Lowell, like himself, who regularly took beatings to make money.

There was Roy "Baby Face" Andrews, who went the distance with Willie Pep for the World Featherweight Title in Boston in 1950. Andrews lost to a man who entered the ring that night with a record of 145 and 2.

There was Blonde Tiger who lost more than 100 of his 155 professional fights in the 1930s and 1940s.

There was "Irish" Jim Mulligan, the light heavyweight who wouldn't retire until he had lost fifteen of his last eighteen fights.

And there were so many more, including some who had enjoyed varying degrees of success, such as Larry Carney and "Irish" Beau Jaynes. Carney was a former New England middleweight and light heavyweight champion. He lasted longer than a lot of tough kids from Lowell, but like many of them, he was beaten by the drink. Carney died at the age of fifty-eight, on New Year's Day 1992, after he fell down a flight of stairs and cracked open his head.

Jaynes is the only man in history who ever held five New England titles at one time. He was the featherweight, junior lightweight, lightweight, junior welterweight, and welterweight champion, gaining and losing weight for each title fight. He grew up in the Acre, the toughest part of Lowell. He was eight years old the day he came home from school to hear his father say, "It's time you learn how to fight. Tomorrow you're getting in the ring."

That was 1955, and he stayed in the ring for the next twenty-five years. He started fighting at the Immaculate Conception CYO and in the Silver Mittens, moved on to the Golden Gloves, and kept his hands up until he was punched out. It took him 160 amateur fights and 95 professional fights, including 43 pro losses, to get there, and then he stayed there, in Lowell. He married Donna Eklund, a pretty young girl from a large Lowell family, and started working for the Lowell Department of Public Works some thirty years ago. Oddly enough, Carney had also married into the Eklund family, hooking up with Gail, the one known as "Red Dog," the one with the long red hair. Without those marriages, Carney's and Jaynes's brothers-in-law Micky Ward and Dickie Eklund might never have been introduced to boxing, and many lives would have been very different.

"It ain't as tough as it used to be," Freitas says as much to himself as anyone who might be listening. "Kids around here used to know what it was like to throw a punch and what it was like to take one in the chops. They used to choose boxing over drugs. Now, the gyms are empty, and you can spit in any direction from where you're standing and you'll hit somebody who's ready to sell you some drugs."

Cleo Surprenant, the owner and tender of the bar at the High-land Tap, listens to Freitas and nods his head in agreement. Cleo, a white-haired, thin man in a red shirt buttoned all the way up, has the face of many a New Englander, friendly and worn. He knows that the pride of Lowell has taken some hits in recent years because of its failure to produce a boxer of any magnitude. In fact, the West End Gym on Middlesex Street, the gym that opened in 1970 and put up signs such as THE MORE YOU SWEAT, THE LESS YOU BLEED was gaining a reputation as an opponents' gym. That meant that box-ers from other parts of the state, such as Brockton or Southie, would come here looking for a kid who didn't have much chance of win-ning. Opponents were just club fighters. The other kids were the contenders. Lowell kids climbed the wooden stairs to Art Ramalho's two-ring, dusty gymnasium on the second floor of an abandoned textile mill and trained in isolation.

Still Lowell had the occasional hopeful. Folks thought for a while that Jackie Morrell could have been a contender. He was one of the West End Gym's top prospects in the early 1980s, but after losing his last eight fights he started to worry he'd end up like Ding Dong, the old fighter who was either punch-drunk from boxing or shell-shocked from one of America's wars. The Lowell kids on the school buses used to taunt the old man, yelling "Ding Dong" when-ever they drove by him. Ding Dong would chase the bus and hit it with his fists. His knuckles would bleed. Other kids would throw rocks at him. He would turn around and chase them. And this rit-ual continued for years. That was not the future Morrell wanted for himself; he hung up his gloves and passed the speed bag on to the next kid who thought he might be tough enough to climb through the ropes and up the ranks. But that kid hadn't shown up in years.

The days when there were thirty-five professionals fighting out of the West End Gym were long gone. Morrell quit soon after he was knocked out by Kevin Rooney and Marlon Starling. Another Lowell kid, a heavyweight named Don Halpin, fought some big guys with big names like Mike Tyson, Jimmy Young, Tex Cobb, and Tony Tubbs, but Halpin lost to all of them. In fact, he lost twenty-three of his thirty-two pro fights, getting knocked out fourteen times. He was a prison guard at the Concord Reformatory and only fought on the side for the five hundred bucks of easy money.

Morrell was the same way. His real job was laying track for the Boston and Maine Railroad, but he'll never forget the day he got the call from the West End's owner and trainer, Art Ramalho. Ramalho, who had trained his own son David to become the New England featherweight champion, was known as the "Lowell Connection" because he had been delivering fighters from Lowell for the better part of three decades. If a boxing event needed four fighters, he produced four fighters. Usually they lost, but promoters knew that they could count on him to produce game, competitive fighters.

So when Marlon Starling, the young up-and-coming welterweight out of Hartford, Connecticut, was scheduled to make his first appearance at Madison Square Garden and his opponent canceled on him the day before the fight, Ramalho got a call asking about Morrell. Morrell, who hadn't been training, took the fight for four thousand dollars, and was stopped in two rounds. When he regained consciousness, he gave Ramalho his cut (one-third) and then bought a 1982 Corvette.

But Morrell and Halpin stopped fighting in the 1980s, along with other promising young West End kids—Roberto Colon, Ricky Camaro, and Tom Ignacio. All of them eventually succumbed to injury, limited skills, or hard living.

"We got no contenders here," Morrell would explain. "Anyone who thinks he is goes down to Marvin Hagler's gym in Brockton."

True, when the Petronelli brothers, Goodie and Pat, opened up their gym, the West End ranks were decimated. The last fighter with any real promise from Lowell was Micky Ward, the brother-in-law of Beau Jaynes and Larry Carney, but Ward had retired in 1991. That was three years ago.

"Did you hear Micky's coming back?" Cleo asks.

"Micky Ward?"

"Yeah, Micky's coming back."

"He never left. I see him paving the streets all the time."

"I don't mean he's coming back to Lowell. I mean he's making a comeback—to boxing!"

That didn't surprise Freitas, who attempted his own ill-fated comeback nine years after he retired, only to be knocked out in the first round again.

"Yeah, I hear that cop, Mickey O'Keefe, has him in the gym, and they're looking to get Micky on a card somewhere," Cleo says while drawing another beer.

Freitas knew about O'Keefe. They were friends, good-enough friends so that when Freitas was training for a fight, he'd use O'Keefe as a sparring partner. And when O'Keefe split Freitas's eye open during one of those sparring sessions, there were no hard feelings. Their friendship continued even when Freitas was an inmate at the Billerica House of Correction and O'Keefe was a guard.

Freitas could still remember the day O'Keefe was closing up the weight room by himself. Only four men were there at the time: O'Keefe and three inmates, Freitas, Joey Andel, and Eddie Fielding. Freitas watched as Joey and Eddie approached O'Keefe, intent on persuading him by any means possible to keep the room open a little longer.

Joey started with this: "Fuck you, asshole! We're not leaving!"

O'Keefe, knowing that his job and, by association, his life depended on how he handled situations such as this, wouldn't back down. Eddie threw the first punch, and Joey jumped right in. A real donnybrook ensued. O'Keefe was doing the best he could to fight off both of them, but he started to lose the battle when he was cracked over the back by a cue stick. That's when Freitas joined the fight to protect his friend. Freitas the street fighter was accustomed to taking on two and three guys at a time, and he already knew the pain of being stabbed and shot, so he let his instincts take over.

"O'Keefe is good people. He'll take good care of Micky,"

Freitas said. Then he added. "But isn't it kinda strange for Micky to be working with a cop? I mean, after what happened and all."

Everyone knew the story, and nobody seemed to mind hearing it or telling it again, least of all Mike Lutkus, who was sitting on the other side of the bar. Lutkus looked up from his beer to recount the events of May 9, 1987. "I was there that night," he says.

Mike Lutkus was there pretty much from the beginning. He was Micky Ward's cousin, and he and his brothers Jerry and Gary used to hang out with Micky and his brother, Dickie. Micky was the youngest, but even at the age of five, Mike remembers that Micky could hit pretty hard. He'd tell people, "We used to take him down to our house in the backroom, and we'd put the little gloves on him, and he used to come right at us. We used to bang each other good."

When the five boys weren't shining shoes, they were in the gym or sneaking into Boston on the T. They got to know the conductor, Red, and if they didn't have enough money, Red would give them five dollars, which was enough to get them to Fanueil Hall to hang out. They'd make their way over to the Garden Gym, the one up the street from Boston Garden, and they'd watch guys like Johnny Dunn, Marvin Hagler, and Vinnie Curto. Those were the days when it was still safe for five kids under the age of fourteen to walk the streets by themselves. Besides, it was a lot safer in Boston than it was in the Acre where they all grew up.

"Boxing saved us," Lutkus has said many times. "The Boys Clubs saved us. We were there all the time. That's how Mickey O'Keefe found us. He's the one who kept us out of trouble. None of us ever got arrested. At least not as kids."

That changed for Micky that night at the Cosmopolitan Café, a well-known danger zone that attracted all kinds of rough characters: druggies, bikers, transvestites, you name it. Micky had won his first thirteen pro fights. In the fight just prior to the Cosmo incident, he had beaten a kid named Kelly Koble at Caesars Palace in Las Vegas on the undercard of the Hagler–Sugar Ray Leonard fight. Hagler lost a twelve-round split decision, but Micky knocked Koble out in the fourth round.

A month after giving Koble a beating, Micky was on the receiving end of a beating from the Lowell police. Micky tells the story this way:

"I was out with a friend at some bars in Lowell, and we ended up at the Cosmo. I saw my brother, Dickie, in there, and some other guys. It's a wicked bad bar, very violent, real bad. I was with my friend Mike Lapointe. His mother had gone out with this Puerto Rican guy and the guy had hit his mother. So, when my friend saw him in the bar, they started arguing. They took it outside and started fighting, beating the Puerto Rican guy up. Dickie comes out, and Mike Lapointe has this Puerto Rican guy on the ground, and he's hitting him. And Dickie comes over and tries to help the guy out, saying, 'He's a friend, I know him.' As Dickie's picking the guy up off the ground, the cops show up and think Dickie's beating him up. They tackle Dickie and now he's arrested. Nothing you can do, and they're walking him back to the wagon. That's fine. Then they take him and pull him down, throw him on the ground. That's when I went over and yelled, 'What the hell are you doing?' Boom! They must have thought I was gonna do something to them.

"They dragged me, and got me on the ground. One cop was yelling, 'Break his fucking hands! Break his fucking hands!' I don't know who it was who said it. I was cuffed at the time. They split my head wide open. I got seven stitches in my head, and I got my hands busted up."

The police account of the story isn't much different, though the report filed by Officer Edward Dowling failed to mention Micky's injuries or the fact that twelve other officers had responded to the Cosmopolitan Café on Market Street that night.

Dowling details arriving at the scene and witnessing Dickie punching and kicking twenty-nine-year-old Angel Rosario. Several police officers attempted to subdue and arrest Dickie, but he punched Dowling several times and attempted to escape. Suddenly, Dickie's older sister, Gail Carney, rushed from the crowd that had gathered and attacked Officer Dowling from behind. She kicked and clawed and threw a few punches that demonstrated she'd been around the fight game for a while, but after a brief struggle she was cuffed and led to a patrol wagon. Meanwhile, Dickie was finally captured and cuffed as well. Dickie continued to thrash around and was crying out for help. This time it was Micky who emerged from the crowd, throwing himself into the mix. He tackled Dowling, forcing him to the ground, and another man kicked Dowling while he was down.

"It wasn't me," Lutkus claims to this day. "When the cops showed up, I was getting ready to run."

But Micky didn't run. He never did, not in the ring and not in the streets. All he wanted to do was to get the cops off his brother. Once he had accomplished that, he was prepared to accept the consequences, but he had no idea what the extent of those consequences would be.

"Crack!" Lutkus blurts out, pausing long enough to make sure his audience is properly startled.

"Crack!" he says again, louder.

"They banged Micky a couple of times with one of those long flashlights they carry around."

Those blows opened a cut on Micky's head. Blood oozed down into his eyes, blinding him while a policeman's knee was in his back and the cuffs were being slapped on his wrists.

"Then somebody yells, 'Hey, don't do that! That's Micky Ward.' And one of the cops yells back, 'Fuck Micky Ward,' and another one says, 'Yeah, break his hands so he can't fight again,' and then they cracked him again."

This time they delivered a crushing blow to his hands.

"My hands were behind my back, and they were hitting them, a bunch of times," Micky says. "I just feel as though I was gonna do something with my life, and they said, 'Fuck this little punk.' You know? I had just come back from fighting in Vegas. They probably didn't like me, because I was having some success."

Or maybe it was because of who his brother was.

Micky's success would have to wait. His night at the Cosmo occurred ten days before he was scheduled to fight in Corpus

Christi, Texas, on national television against a contender named Joey Belinc. Micky would have made twenty-five thousand dollars for that fight—by far his biggest payday to date. Instead, he had to cancel the fight because of a broken left hand and a swollen right hand. Micky's replacement won a unanimous decision over Belinc.

Micky never got as far as the hospital the night of the Cosmo melee. He sat in the patrol wagon while his brother and sister were arraigned for assault and battery, disorderly conduct, and marijuana possession. Dickie was also charged with assaulting Rosario, although Rosario never claimed that Dickie had struck him.

"It wasn't Dickie's fault," Lutkus tells the bar. "He really was just helping the guy up, but when the police arrived, Dickie was holding the guy, and I'm sure it looked to the cops like Dickie was involved. It's not like Dickie had made himself any friends on the police force."

For his part, Dickie treated the incident as if it were just one of those things that happen in Lowell. He was not his brother's keeper, and he took no responsibility for what happened to Micky that night or the impact it would have on his boxing career.

"I was there and Micky just came on his own," Dickie told the *Boston Globe* at the time. "Everybody blames me, but I didn't take Micky down to the Cosmo. . . . He's twenty-one years old. I can't follow him around with a chain. He hits too hard."

With that, Dickie laughed.

Though this was Micky's first arrest, Dickie had already been hauled down to the police station on twelve different occasions. On a hot August afternoon the previous summer, a police officer was questioning Dickie on a street corner when another officer drove up in a cruiser. When Dickie spotted the cruiser, he sucker punched the first cop and took off. From petty larceny to public drunkenness and now his fourth assault charge, Dickie had established a reputation.

So it wouldn't come as any big surprise that the police would presume Dickie was the instigator of the brawl, or that they would use aggressive force to deal with him. And Micky? Guilty by association.

"Oh yeah, it was a confrontation," said Superintendent John Sheehan, though he denied his officers were unnecessarily violent. "I've seen it many, many times. Guys get together after the fact and tell you what you want to hear. Their recollection of the event breaks down. I'm here to tell you there was a confrontation. It was like most confrontations. It starts off probably verbal, and it tends to get physical."

"I don't know what he was doing there that night," Cleo says. "It's one of the toughest bars in New England. It's just a shame. Micky had a chance to go all the way."

By the time he got to the hospital that morning, the blood had already begun to calcify in the joints of his left hand, causing tendonitis that would bother him for the rest of his life.

The next morning, Top Rank boxing promoter Teddy Brenner called Micky's mother, Alice Ward, just to see how Micky's training was going. Alice, who had taken over managing Micky's career, had to explain that Micky would be unable to take that fight.

"They were helping a fellow up from the ground," she said, "and the guy was telling the police that Dickie and Micky were helping him. The fellow who beat him up went back in the bar and wasn't there when the police showed up. They arrested Dickie, and Micky tried to calm things down and was arrested, and they beat him up, too."

Micky's fight was canceled while the Wards considered a civil suit against the Lowell Police Department.

"The family never did sue, did they?" Lutkus asks. Cleo shakes his head. But he wonders if they should have.

"One thing's for sure," Cleo says emphatically. "That Micky Ward always put on a great show."

"Tough kid," they all agree.

But that was to be expected. After all, he grew up in Lowell. This is the kind of town where boxers breed. Boxers go to the West End Gym, and any number of similar cold, dark places with a scant number of speed bags, heavy bags, jump ropes, and mats for sit-ups. Just the basics. Boxers come without moms, or with working moms, and they walk or run to the gyms several miles away. More often than not, boxers grow up in poverty, and in ethnic communi-ties such as Lowell's Acre section, with its numerous Irish and Greek immigrants.

Certainly, if a person had a choice, he wouldn't choose boxing. But Micky really didn't have a choice, not if he wanted more for himself than to be working on a crew paving the streets of Lowell. And he did. He wanted more than that.

Cleo looks up at the photograph of Micky on the wall. He was a teenager when that picture was taken. He was simultaneously frail and sinewy. "Maybe someday," Cleo thinks, "I'll be hanging a pic-ture of Micky wearing a championship belt." And that makes Cleo smile.

Mike Lutkus looks down at his watch and realizes that it's ap-proaching 9:30 a.m.

"Shoot, I've got to get to work," he says, as if that realization surprises him. He looks at his newly drawn beer and says, "It's yours, buddy," and then he bolts out of the Highland Tap. Some of the other men take notice of the time and quicken the pace of their conversations. They throw back their shots and drink their beers and also race off for work.

Manny Freitas doesn't watch them leave, but he hears the door slam behind him. He has time to sit a while longer. So, he simply stares at what's left of his beer, and thinks about his days in the ring, the ones he can remember. Those were good days.

"Good luck to Micky Ward," he thinks. "Here's hoping that boxing treats him better than it treated the rest of us."

He raises his glass to the skinny teenager on the wall, and throws back his beer. "Hit me again, Cleo. Hit me again."

CHAPTER TWO

As Micky was planning a comeback, his brother, Dickie, was losing his battle with drugs. He had become a crack addict with an eighth-grade education and nothing to show for all the time he had spent in the gym.

Dickie knew *exactly* when it all went wrong. It started several years and several armed robberies ago when his friend Chico offered him part of his kilo of cocaine. As a popular fighter known for his thunderous left hand to the body, Dick Eklund commanded respect when he walked through the streets of Lowell. This was his town, and everybody was either his friend or wanted to be. So this was not the first time he'd received such an offer, but it was the first time that he accepted. He grabbed the stash from Chico, chalked off a little bit, and was instantly hooked. The fighter stopped fighting and surrendered to the coke habit.

The boy who had grown to be a man much faster than most became a boy again. Forgot his mom and dad. Forgot his little brother and his seven sisters. Sure, he loved them all. But drugs were his new master. Boxing would have to wait. All the hours of intense training, all the years of sweating, all the times he hemorrhaged from his nose or his eyes were swollen shut by the vicious attack of another muscular warrior—it all meant nothing. "He should have been a champ," his mother laments.

"He was a natural," says Johnny Dunn. "He couldn't miss. We should all be swimming in money right now. Believe me when I tell you, he should have been champ."

Dickie concurs, "If I did everything the right way, I would have been champ."

But Dickie did very little the right way. When he was just twelve years old, he was already lying about his age and his name, just for the opportunity to fight jockeys. That's right—jockeys.

Still not weighing as much as a slender jockey himself, Dickie would tell his mother he was going over to a friend's house, and instead he would sneak down to Rockingham Park for amateur boxing night. Rockingham was a popular racetrack in Salem, New Hampshire, and boxing night at "The Rock" was heavily populated by jockeys. Dickie remembers vividly going up against one particularly strong twenty-six-year-old on two separate occasions, losing both times. But even if records of such events were kept, they would never show that Dickie Eklund ever fought there. When duking it out with the jockeys, Dickie went by the name of "Dick Huntley." A trainer at the gym, who was looking at a poster of an old fighter named Def Huntley from the Bahamas, gave him the name.

"He says to me, 'You're Dick Huntley tonight,'" Dickie remembers. And the name stuck well into his professional career.

Dickie had been a frail-looking little boy, with a whiffle haircut, who occasionally had to ward off the bigger kids who wanted his milk money, but he learned early that he had a talent inside the ring. For example, when he was only nine years old, he began winning organized brawls. Ouchie McManus, a popular trainer at one of the Lowell gyms, would give about a dozen kids one glove each and throw them into the ring just to see who would be the last man standing.

"They'd have a big battle royal," McManus says. "They'd all whack it out. One kid would get slugged, and he'd come out holding his face. Pretty soon there'd only be two left, and it would really be a battle. He was the king, Dickie was."

But to Dickie, the king was Larry Carney. He stared with his mouth wide open whenever he got a chance to see his idol and brother-in-law fight. He also took some tips from his other brother-in-law, Beau Jaynes. He was always throwing punches, looking to spar, shadowboxing, and squaring off with his cousins, the Lutkus boys. And Dickie trained hard down at Ramalho's gym.

When Dickie was thirteen, he won the New England Silver Mittens, the precursor to the Golden Gloves. At age fifteen, he was still eligible for the Mittens, but he was too good and therefore potentially dangerous, so the tournament officials bumped him up to the Golden Gloves. His opponent in the finals was a defending champion at 126 pounds, but Dickie beat him pretty easily.

"I didn't get hit that much when I was a kid," Dickie says. "I was fast."

He was also a natural southpaw in the ring, the nontraditional style in which a boxer leads with a right jab. Dickie was encouraged to switch to the orthodox stance, however, because it was sometimes difficult for lefties to get fights. There weren't enough of them, so nobody wanted to fight them.

Without school to take up six to ten hours a day, Dickie took various jobs in construction, trained as he saw fit, and daydreamed about one day being a world champion. There was, however, time left in the day for other activities. So, when he was sixteen, he came home and told his mom that his girlfriend, Debbie, was pregnant.

"I couldn't believe it," his mother would say. "When could she ever have gotten pregnant? He was always home by nine."

Dickie and Debbie got married in a hurry, and their daughter, Kerry, arrived soon after Dickie's seventeenth birthday. By then, he had turned pro, determined to follow his dream and provide for his new family. Instead, divorce was around the corner, and the Cosmo incident was just a little further up the road.

"Fighters have been going [to the Cosmo] from day one," the police chief at the time, John Sheehan, says. "I remember kicking Dickie out of there when he was sixteen. He'd just won the Best Fighter Award at the Golden Gloves. He was given a bowl, and he was drinking beer out of it. I sent him home, and I told Alice to keep him out of there."

Alice, who didn't know that Dickie was slugging it out with jockeys at twelve and taking his five-year-old brother Micky by train into Boston and then by bus to Randolph to see his friend Bubbles Morcioni at thirteen, had no control over Dickie. Nobody did, not even Dickie.

In his youth, he seemed to have a single-minded devotion: he wanted to be a world champion. That dream was able to lift him out of the streets of Lowell and across the Atlantic Ocean before his twentieth birthday. After building up a 10–1 record as a professional fighting exclusively in New England, Dickie took a fight in Copenhagen, Denmark, against a Helsinki fighter of little or no reputation named Erkki Meronen. He went six rounds with Meronen, losing on points because of a disputed head-butt.

"He head butted me, so I butted him back," Dickie claims. "There's no way I was going to win a decision in his backyard."

Two years later, Dickie was back across the ocean in Wembley, England, taking on a former European welterweight champion, Davey Boy Green. Dickie lost that fight, too, but he was going places. Unfortunately, he always ended up back in Lowell, back in trouble, and oftentimes back in jail.

Folks who thought he might be the next champion from Lowell had to reconsider their optimism. Nothing underscored that point more than his fight with Sugar Ray Leonard in 1978. Sandwiched between the Davey Boy Green and Erkki Meronen fights, Dickie's loss to the future champion and Hall of Fame boxer signaled the beginning of the end for Dickie.

"I said if I can't beat Leonard, I might as well quit," Dickie tries to explain to no avail. It's nonsense. Losing a ten-round decision to an Olympic Gold medalist who was undefeated in his first twelve professional fights isn't an indicator that you're worthless as a boxer.

"I should have just kept going," he continues. "I didn't know I was as good as I was."

Maybe he just fought Leonard too soon. He was only twenty years old, and he didn't have the benefit of the Olympic experience. He'd only had fourteen pro fights at the time and was coming off a loss, the third of his career. But Dickie's mother was managing his career, and how could she pass up a chance to fight Sugar Ray Leonard? Everybody knew who he was, and soon everybody would know who her son was as well. Dickie wanted it, too.

"I wasn't scared of him," he says.

A month before the fight, scheduled for July 18 at the Hynes Auditorium in Boston, Dickie and a bunch of his friends took the short ride up to Hampton Beach in New Hampshire. Not surprisingly, he went to a bar and started drinking. It was the serious kind of drinking, the kind a man does when he wants to have so much fun that his troubles will disappear. It was also the kind of drinking a person doesn't do just prior to climbing onto a motorcycle. But Dickie did it.

"I was the lead motorcycle," he recalls. "Everyone was following me, and I saw this girl in a bikini. I just turned for a moment, and then *Boom!* I hit a curb. The motorcycle stops dead, and I went flying over, landed flat on my back!"

While lying in the back of the ambulance, Dickie began thinking about the fight that could make or break his career, the one he was supposed to be training for. He now had a built-in excuse if he didn't fare too well inside the ropes against Leonard. Dickie showed up for the pre-fight press conference a few days later on crutches.

"I'm fighting him?" Leonard asked.

But Dickie was very fit when he stepped into the ring wearing shiny blue trunks and blue sneakers. He bounced around with a lot of life, but five thousand people watched Leonard win all ten rounds, nine of them unanimously. Still, Dickie has always been able to brag that he went the distance against one of the greatest.

After all, Davey Boy Green didn't make it the distance. Some eighteen months after his dance with Dickie, Leonard knocked Green out in four rounds.

It took many years, but Dickie finally stopped bragging that he had knocked Leonard down during the fight. He never did. He was throwing his jab, but not with the intention of making effective contact. He was just trying to keep Leonard at arm's length. As Sugar Ray started to land a few shots, Dickie appeared to lose his balance, and while accidentally stepping on Sugar Ray's foot, Dickie shoved him to the ground. Dickie stood over this great, undefeated fighter, apparently unsure of what had just happened. Dickie bounced nervously into a neutral corner, while the referee notified the judges that it was not a knockdown. It was ruled a slip, but Dickie's original version of the event was always aided by the memory of Leonard with his ass on the canvas. That allowed for a re-creation of the truth for several years, until the entire town, in an unspoken show of unanimity decided to forego the fabrication. Everyone always knew the truth anyway, so what was the point of retelling each other the same old lie?

"No, I didn't knock him down," Dickie now says. "That was bullshit. He slipped."

Leonard told the *Boston Globe* six years later that his fight with Dickie was "One of my most disappointing fights. I had a problem with my weight, and it was my first experience with racism—the crowd. Dick and I were friends, but it was the crowd."

Dickie took the next year off from fighting, finally making his return at the Lowell Auditorium thirteen months to the day after the Leonard fight. He went up against Fernando Fernandez, a tough kid from Pawtucket, Rhode Island. Fernandez had beaten none other than Beau Jaynes, Dickie's mentor and brother-in-law, on the undercard of Dickie's fight against Leonard. And Fernandez would go on to beat Jackie Morrell for the New England welterweight title. But that night he lost to Dickie.

That tells you where Dickie could have been headed. He had risen past the aging Beau Jaynes who was now fighting on Dickie's undercard. He outboxed a talented kid who would go on to win a regional title. He had been to Europe twice. And still, he couldn't keep his eyes on the prize. He lost a rematch to Fernandez in Boston a year later, and his career was completely rudderless.

He started grabbing fights wherever he could find them for whatever money he could make, nothing more than three thousand dollars. In the summer of 1981, he drove up to Halifax, Nova Scotia, to fight Allen Clarke. It turned out be Dickie's most violent fight.

"It was the eighth round. I went *bam* with the right hand in the jaw, and he winked at me on his way back to the corner," Dickie begins. "And I thought, 'Oh my God! You've got to be kidding me.' So, the ninth round comes. I went *bang* into his side. Once I hit him with that shot, I knew I had him."

With just a hint of jealousy, Dickie stops his story to point out that they call that hard left to the body the Micky Ward body shot, "but that's my shot," he says. Then he continues.

"I could have backed up after that shot, but I remembered him winking at me, so I chased him to the other side of the ring, and I hit him, *bang! boom! boom!* One, two, three, four, five, six, seven, eight, nine, ten! Ten big shots! And his eyes rolled into the back of his head."

This time with just a hint of pride, Dickie explains that the Halifax news station that night introduced the boxing highlights by saying, "This is not for the faint of heart."

Dickie claims to have put Clarke into a coma, but the records show that Clarke fought for the Canadian welterweight title only five months later. Quick recovery.

After knocking out Clarke, Dickie fought only nine more times in the next four years. Training became difficult for him because his trainer, Johnny Dunn, was in Boston. Dickie had a falling out with Ramalho when he turned pro. Ramalho had given him full use of his gym, trained him, and nurtured him through the Silver Mittens and Golden Gloves. Ramalho assumed that when Dickie turned pro, he'd still be his trainer, but Dickie had other ideas. He and his mother wanted someone with more connections, so they passed over the "Lowell Connection," and went with the sixty-eight-year-old Dunn.

"I trained Dickie myself for nine years," Ramalho says. "He was a great, great fighter. But he kind of broke my heart, because he came to me and said he was going pro, but his mother wanted him to go with this other trainer in Boston, Johnny Dunn. Dickie was like one of my own kids. I expected to be training him when he turned pro. I just got so mad, I didn't want nothing to do with him. We're good friends now, though. He's told me a thousand times his biggest mistake was leaving me, but you know how parents can be sometimes."

The decision to go with Dunn was a sound one. Dunn was one of boxing's true characters. Born John D. Donarumo, Dunn had worked with former champions, such as Terry Downes and Bob Foster, but he spent most of his time working with the local hopefuls, Jaynes, Eklund, and Ward. He was a bit of a family caretaker in that way. When Dickie was about to fight Sugar Ray Leonard, Dunn told him in the locker room: "We'll beat this fucker!"

He promised both Dickie and Micky at different times that he would make them champions, but he died of heart failure in December 1990 without ever making good on those promises.

"Johnny always had something to offer," Dickie says. "He knew more than the trainers you hear about now, but he never got the recognition. We had to help him into the ring, but just having him around was like having someone around who was eighteen years old." Dunn trained fighters up until one month before his death, but he was of little help near the tail end of Dickie's career. Dickie began training in his own basement, but he was unable to find sparring partners and suffered from a swollen left knee that he hurt while jogging. He grabbed a three-thousand-dollar payday against a part-time fighter named Mark Harris in April 1982, but the fight fell through. He ended up facing a lesser fighter, Cesar Guzman, for less money. Guzman lost twenty-four of his twenty-seven professional fights, but his specialty was going the distance. Like many others before and after, Dickie couldn't knock him out either.

Dickie won the decision, and a year later, in 1983, he won the New England welterweight title in a split decision over James Lucas up in Portland, Maine. He beat Lucas again nearly two years later. And that was it. He hung up his gloves with an unimpressive 19–10 lifetime record. It means he was better than some, worse than others. But nobody knows if he could have been the best, or at least one of the best. Dickie was just another one of Lowell's "should have beens." Instead of raising a fist in victory and becoming a world champion, Dickie raised a crack pipe to his lips as often as he could and wound up as one of the lost lives of Lowell. In fact, he was one of the dubious stars of the HBO documentary filmed by his distant cousin, Rich Farrell, called *High on Crack Street: The Lost Lives of Lowell.*

In the film, Dickie is seen walking around wearing a pair of shorts and a backwards baseball cap. He is emaciated, gaunt. He looks far worse than he ever did at the end of one of his twenty-nine pro fights. While holding a lighted match about an inch away from a homemade crack pipe, he pauses and looks directly into the camera and says, "I fought Sugar Ray Leonard on HBO."

He is standing in the middle of a rundown crack house off Branch Street in the Lower Highlands of Lowell. Curtains cover the windows, but nothing covers the smell, a mix of burning plastic, severe body odor, and rotting food. Furniture is sparse. The couch serves the dual purpose of being about the only place to sit and the place where the matches, crack pipes, and assorted other drug paraphernalia are "hidden." A crack house is nothing but squalor. Even the crack addict wants to leave. The people who wander in and out are in and out of their minds. They are psychotic. Their faces are distorted. Paranoia strikes deep, and violence is always a distinct possibility. "It ruins everyone's life," says Brenda. She is one of the film's main characters. "Nobody can handle it. I do it because I love it more than anything, more than life itself. But yet I hate it worse than anything. I wish I could wipe it off the face of the earth. It's the devil."

Farrell, a former heroine addict himself says, "Crack cocaine is something you smoke, and it gives you this incredible high. In some cases when you've been doing it for a while, you get this incredible high for thirty seconds, and then you come right down, and you have to do it again."

For a mere thirty seconds of euphoria, the crack addict has to face the intense agony, hypersensitivity to pain, chronic nausea, and uncontrollable tremors of withdrawal.

Dickie would spend days inside a crack house, stepping out only long enough to rob someone of his or her money to pay for his next fix.

"I just knocked people out for their money," he says. "I had to be sober to beat somebody up, because when I was high I'd do anything you want. If you told me to go sit in the corner, I'd do it and be happy."

But when the money or the crack ran out, Dickie would get clean and return to the gym and pick up right where he had left off. By the time, *High on Crack Street* was being filmed, Dickie was thirty-two-years-old and had been retired for several years, but he could still throw punches incessantly, and he could still outlast anyone in a sparring session. He had a motor and could go all day. Then he would go all night.

"It's a battle for the rest of your life," Dickie tells the filmmakers. Then he calls his three-year-old son, Dickie Jr., over to him and says, "I love you."

"There's no danger out there for Dickie," Alice Ward says. "He can do anything he wants to do. Just say, 'I'm not doing it today.'"

But Dickie adds a truthful piece of personal reflection: "The biggest danger is the whole world out there."

Dickie, by the way, refers to *High on Crack Street* as "that scumbag movie." He claims that Richie Farrell gave him money knowing full well that he would run out and get crack, and that would make the film better.

"He'd stop by at midnight and give me fifty bucks," Dickie says. "Sometimes he'd just come by to say 'Hello,' and then when he'd leave, there'd be a fifty on the ground. He left it there, and he knew what I was going to do with it. They never paid me for the movie, though. They got Emmy Awards, and I got nothing. Richie's fucking blood, man. He's fucking blood, and he does that to me."

The bloodline was such that Dickie's maternal grandmother (Alice's mother) and Richie's paternal grandmother were sisters. Beyond that, Richie Farrell and Dickie Eklund simply grew up in the same town. They went to different schools. Richie's father taught at Lowell High School; to avoid any conflicts of interest and to get him out of Lowell as much as possible, Richie was sent to Austin Prep, the Catholic high school a few towns over in Reading. Dickie and Richie didn't know each other until they were teenagers, but everybody knew who Dickie was and what he was doing with his life. So, after six months of searching crack houses for the most articulate addicts, Richie settled on three candidates, Brenda, Boo Boo, and Dickie, and began shooting a documentary film in his troubled hometown for the next eighteen months. Dickie had actually lobbied for a part in the film. He was going to be a star.

For his part, Rich Farrell says Dickie was never given any money during the filming, but that ten thousand dollars was put away in a trust fund for Dickie Jr. He suspects that the boy's mother got her hands on the money and spent it.

"Dickie would come to us and threaten to tell the newspapers that we were giving him money to buy crack, but that never happened," Richie explains. "So, we told him to go ahead and do whatever he wanted."

Dickie never went to the newspaper. After all, he was a crack addict with a long arrest record and a bad history with the police. What could he say, and who would believe him? Instead, Dickie made suggestions on how to make the film better.

"He wanted us to film him robbing people," Farrell says. "We knew they were robbing prostitutes and Johns, and he wanted us to film that."

Dickie and a couple of his hooker friends had devised a creative scheme to victimize horny guys with money to spend. The girls took their positions on the street, and when cars driving by slowed down enough to indicate an interest, the girls would wag their tongues in a lewd pantomime. That would generally get a would-be John to stop. A girl would get in and direct him to a secluded place around the corner.

Once the hooker had confirmed the mark had plenty of money, she would light a cigarette. That was Dickie's cue to come screeching up in another car with his high beams pointed directly at the unsuspecting mark.

"I would never tell them I was a cop," Dickie says. "But everything I did made them think I was. I would yank them out of the car, pat them down, and I'd say something like, 'I'll bet you're married, too! You scumbag!' They almost always were. They were so scared that their wives would find out that by the time I sent them off, being robbed was the least of their worries."

Dickie never showed the victim a gun, but he always had one with him, just in case. For most of his robberies, he preferred a sawed-off shotgun. The rest of the time he carried a 9mm. Drugs and guns and hookers and jail. Dickie had ventured onto a road he'd never imagined.

Dickie's life of crime started small enough. There were a few early arrests for being disorderly or drunk in public when he was still a teenager. He took it to the next level with assault and battery and larceny charges in 1981, a month after his twenty-third birthday. He went the next five years without further arrests, which only means he wasn't caught, but it was in January 1986 that he popped a police officer in the mouth and ran. Two months later, a man tried to break up an argument Dickie was having with his sister Gail so Dickie broke his jaw and robbed him. He then fought with the police who came to arrest him. For those offenses, which he admitted to, he was sent to the Billerica House of Correction for three months. While he was awaiting sentencing, he was released and fought with another police officer who was arresting him for being drunk and disorderly. There wasn't much Micky could do to help his brother.

"I was drinking one night," Micky begins a story. "Just a couple of beers, but I hadn't seen Dickie in a couple of days, so I went after him. He was in a house on Branch Street. I knew where he was gonna be. I get up there, and they tell me he's not there. Somebody had told me he was in there. But at the door, they tell me he's not. But I just go right in and everyone's fucking scared of me, because they're messed up, and I guess I was looking pretty angry. But I just plowed right through and started looking all over the house. Finally I find him hiding behind the shower curtain. He was all dressed and everything, but he was so stunned and whacked out at the same time when I pulled that curtain back. I just yelled at him for a while. 'What are you doing? Where have you been?' Stuff like that. Then I just left him there. There was no talking to him. An addict doesn't want to hear you tell him what a fuckup he is. He gets enough of that. He's got to do it himself anyway. The next day he comes up and says he's never gonna do it again. I just stopped listening after a while. He never listened to me anyway. He'd just rebel and go back out there again anyway."

The next time Micky and Dickie saw each other after their encounter at the Branch Street crack house was at the gym. They didn't speak about the incident. They just began working out. Micky was training for his eleventh professional fight against Randy Mitchum, which would be held at the Lowell Memorial Auditorium. It would also be Micky's first fight on national television, and Dickie would be by his side.

A day before the fight, Mitchum broke his foot, so Micky wound up fighting Carlos Brandi instead. Micky handed Brandi his first loss by knocking him out in the second round. Micky and Dickie were interviewed after the fight, and Dickie spoke proudly of his brother's performance.

"Each and every fight he comes out with something better. The reason he didn't switch [to southpaw] was because we had gotten film of this other guy, and we found out the night before that we were fighting this guy. After we studied for him and trained for him, but Micky was ready for anybody tonight."

A few days later, the pride was gone from Dickie's voice and the cell door closed behind him. He was in the Billerica House of Correction, which is just a short ride from his home. In jail, Dickie started working out every night, even contemplating a comeback.

"There's no beer in jail," he says.

He was released on New Year's Eve, the biggest party night of the year. But he didn't go out partying. But he didn't continue his training either.

"He kept saying he was going to," Micky says. "But as the days went on and the weeks went on, it just wore off."

So Dickie returned to the streets, and five months after his release from Billerica, his evening at the Cosmo escalated into another arrest.

Police Chief Sheehan was quoted as saying:

> First and foremost, Dickie is very concerned and interested in Micky's career. Of course his heart is in the right place. But then you have to look at his lifestyle, his frame of mind, his approach to life. What are the proper influences for a young boxer like Micky? Is Dickie doing these things for himself? He has to do it for his brother. I've seen it generation after generation after generation. The similarities jump right out at you. All of these fighters have outstanding amateur careers. They win title after title and they have no trouble with the police. Then sometime between their amateur and professional careers, something happens. Every once in a while a kid comes along with the caliber of Micky Ward. In time, somebody's got to come along, take him under his wing and keep him on the straight and narrow.

That protective wing didn't come until much later, in the second half of Micky's career. In the early going, he had his mother managing him, and not particularly well, and he had Dickie training him.

"Dickie should be more smarter," Ouchie McManus said. "He's Micky's big brother, right? If Dickie handles him right, the kid's going to make it. But life is one big party."

The party ended when Dickie stood in Lowell Superior Court on the morning of March 20, 1995. The charges against him: ". . . breaking and entering in the nighttime with the intention of committing a felony, masked armed robbery, kidnapping, possession of a firearm without a license."

Judge Wendie Gerahengorn ordered Dickie to serve eight years at the state's maximum security prison, MCI-Cedar Junction in Walpole. His mother and three of his sisters were there for the sentencing. They cried. Dickie was led hurriedly away in cuffs.

Dickie was late for court that morning. He had spent his last night as a free man with Boo Boo smoking crack. Boo Boo was kind enough to offer, "Dickie, you want to go first since you're going up?"

Dickie accepted and said, "This stuff destroyed me. It destroys everybody." Then he flicked a lighter with his left hand, brought the pipe to his lips, and inhaled with inexplicable pleasure the very thing that had destroyed him. "We've had a lot of good times," Boo Boo said.

When Dickie finally did race up the court steps in his gray sweat suit, he was immediately admonished by the judge, but politely and apologetically, he explained his tardiness.

"It was so important for me just to tell my son that Daddy's going away. I'm sorry."

Dickie was going to jail because one of his victims finally went to the police with a story of Dickie's violent, abhorrent, criminal behavior. On most days, a John went into one of several Grand Street apartments looking for a prostitute. Once the mark was inside, preferably in a vulnerable position with his pants down, Dickie would jump out of a closet with a shotgun, frighten the man half to death, steal his money, and send him away crying, thankful that he was alive and swearing to himself that he would never go looking to buy sex again. The victim would be too embarrassed to tell the police his story, not wanting his complaint to become public record. But on one bad day, September 20, 1993, Dickie ran into an innocent man, or someone who was willing to lie about one important detail.

"Grand Street was wild back then," Dickie recounts. "I had all the Cambodians doing whatever I wanted them to do. My sister Gail was on one side, and this other girl was selling crack in her house. Now, this guy shows up, and he claims he needed to use a phone. But he comes into the house, and I've got a bag over my head, and this other guy's got a bag over his head."

Dickie never identified his accomplice, and he was never found.

"Anyway, I've got this musketlike thing. It's not even a real gun, but he thinks it is. I put the gun to his head, and by this time, the girl already had the money. So, I went in his car to see if he's got anything else. He's got golf clubs in the back, so I throw those out on the street. We got about seventeen hundred dollars and a set of golf clubs."

That's Dickie's story, and he's sticking to it. The victim, a Pepperell man, told police he had stopped to use a pay phone on Appleton Street, and that Dickie and his accomplice forced him back into his car and took him to Grand Street where they robbed him of 150 dollars.

"That's bullshit," Dickie says. "The girl stuck her tongue out, and he came into the house, just like all the rest of 'em. He was there to pick up a hooker."

In both accounts of the story, the Pepperell man was released unharmed and went straight to the police, directing them to the apartment where the robbery took place. The police knew right away who they were looking for.

"The next thing we hear is the cops are coming, so I run into my sister's house and hide in the closet," Dickie continues. "The cops come by and asked if she's seen me, and she says 'No.' But I seen her. I was looking out through the closet door, and I seen her. She kind of moved her head in my direction while she was saying 'No.' I mean, I know she tipped them off. That's all right."

To support his account, Dickie says he could have taken the matter to trial, and it would have been revealed that his fingerprints weren't inside the car.

"I never carjacked him, but I wanted it to go away."

He also claims that the police coerced the prostitutes into testifying against him by telling them that they wouldn't have anything to worry about, granting them immunity, and offering them a new place to live. The cards were stacked against him, so he gave in, but it's very important to him that people believe that he only jumped out of a closet with a fake shotgun, and that he didn't bring his victim to the Grand Street apartment.

"I did my time. Thanks buddy, you saved my life, but I hope he didn't go home and give his wife AIDS, because all those girls on that corner had it. They all died."

Meanwhile, Dickie survived. He survived while wearing a green jumpsuit with white socks and flip-flops. In prison, he had two beds, no cellmate, and he says he didn't sleep for the first year. He was unable to escape the truth that put him there, the guilt and remorse of what he had done, and the stench emanating from the toilet located just a few feet from where he slept. A man who had spent so much time in the stench and squalor of crack houses considered that toilet the ultimate indignity. "I fought Sugar Ray Leonard! Took him the whole ten rounds, too!" He thought to himself, and then he mumbled, "And now I have to shit in full view of anyone walking past those bars."

Dickie never even approached his full potential as a fighter or as a man, but the final bell had yet to ring. There was still time for both himself and his brother. As soon as he heard that awful clang of the cell door slamming hard behind him, Dickie started dreaming about training Micky again and, this time, turning him into a champion. That was also Micky's dream, but he would have to get started toward making it a reality on his own.

CHAPTER THREE

Micky Ward could have been the junior welterweight champion of the world, but he had failed to make his dream a reality. He came from Lowell, a home to users, abusers, and assorted other losers. He had seen so many around him fall and fail. He had had a run of bad luck, bad management, and lingering chronic pain in his hands. He had absolutely no idea what his potential for greatness was, because nobody around him had ever reached his potential. If he quit, who would notice? Lowell had a lot of quitters, but Lowell also had a lot of fighters. Dickie Eklund was both. Micky Ward was a fighter.

So, as he sat on top of a three-ton roller preparing to pave another street in his hometown, his body dripping with sweat as if he were once again training for a big fight, Micky began wondering why there were no more big fights. There hadn't been for nearly three years, and there was nothing on the horizon. Nothing hurt quite like the stomach punch of untapped potential. Micky Ward looked down the highway he had just made smooth. He was good at his job. Heck, he'd be doing it since he was fourteen years old when he went to work for his mother's brother, Gerry Greenhalge, at the Ideal Paving Company. He was paid by the day back then.

Fifty bucks was good money for a teenager in 1979. It was here that
he began to demonstrate that he liked a good challenge.

Fourteen is too early to be entrusted with a large piece of ma-
chinery, but when he showed up to help his uncle one day, he told
the foreman he had used a roller lots of times before.

"Climb on up then, son."

Micky was initially startled and confused, but he was in the
habit of doing as he was told, especially when he could make a buck
doing it. So he climbed up on the roller and got it moving in the
right direction. He was scared and repeatedly looked over the side
to see how high up he was.

"What are you doing up there, kid?" the foreman yelled.
"You've got to keep that thing in a straight line. You're screwing
it up!"

When Micky climbed down, he had more time to explain what
he meant when he said he had used a roller many times before.

"I used a hand roller," he said. "I've never been up on one of
those before. But I'd sure like to try it again."

And he did. Over time, Micky became adept at paving roads.
He liked it too. It was an honest day's work, and it helped bring
a level of peace to his otherwise turbulent life. These were troubled times in the city of Lowell.

Lowell was incorporated in 1826, but travelers had been visiting there and settling there since 1653. Some thirty miles
northeast of Boston, Lowell was named after Francis Cabot Lowell,
an innovative industrialist and inventor of weaving machines. At
the confluence of the Merrimack and Concord Rivers, Lowell was
a perfect setting for the cotton textile mills of the nineteenth century. Nearly six miles of power canals were built, braiding their
way through the city, and once the mills began lining the
Merrimack River and Pawtucket Falls, the city grew quickly. Some
forty mills, five and six stories high, dominated the Lowell land-
scape, and by the outbreak of the Civil War, Lowell was the second-
largest city in New England and the industrial center of the United
States. The city's cultural and ethnic diversity stemmed from the

vast number of people who came from central and southern Europe, eager to work in the mills.

An unknown Scottish visitor echoed the sentiments of many who considered Lowell one of the wonders of the world when he said, "Niagara and Lowell are the two objects I will longest remember in my American journey, the one the glory of American scenery, the other of American industry."

Leader of the "beat generation" and noted author Jack Kerouac wrote five books that were largely set in Lowell. It was his hometown, and he did a lot of his writing and drinking at Nicky's Bar on Gorham Street, just around the corner from the Highland Tap. Nicky's was owned by Kerouac's brother-in-law, Nicky Sampas.

In one of his novels, *The Town and the City*, he refers to Lowell as "Galloway":

> *The Merrimac River, broad and placid, flows down to it from the New Hampshire hills. The grownups of Galloway . . . work in factories, in shops and stores and offices and on the terms all around. The textile factories built in brick, primly towered, solid, are ranged along the river and the canals, and all night the industries hum and shuttle. This is Galloway, milltown in the middle of fields and forests.*

Lowell was a city that sprang up along the river and marched triumphantly toward the industrial revolution. It was a leader, strong, proud, and fearless in its heyday. But that was not the Lowell that Micky Ward grew up in.

Micky was born October 4, 1965, and by then Lowell had already begun a steady decline, one that eventually brought this spirited city to its knees. The Lowell that Micky experienced as a child was wild, violent, and lawless. The city's cultural diversity, which had always been one of its strengths, was becoming its greatest weakness—and potentially its fatal flaw. No longer were the immigrants merely bringing a cultural richness to the city, they were importing problems.

Joining the French Canadians in Little Canada along the Northern Canal and the Greeks in the Acre along Market Street and Poles, Portuguese, and Russian Jews in various little communities within the city were the Southeast Asian immigrants and the Cambodian refugees. Ed Davis, a police officer who was on the streets during the drug wars of the 1980s and later became the police superintendent, gave a speech in August 2000, saying:

> *Lowell's population may well be more heavily Cambodian than that of any other city in the country. Mostly hard-working people with a tremendous desire for education and a strong work ethic, some of their children have, unfortunately, gravitated toward gangs. This has resulted in turf battles that turned deadly. Young children were killed in drive-by shootings. With other groups, the drug problem surfaced and became intractable; prostitution and related violent crime became common throughout the city.*

That's the Lowell Micky knew, the one in which a twelve-year-old boy could ride his bicycle to the park and pass prostitutes and drug dealers along the way. Junkies were already gathering every morning on Lagrange Street, less than a mile from City Hall. Like some sort of new-wave, degenerate coffee klatch, the addicts packed into alleyways between public housing complexes and tenement buildings. They were there before the school buses rolled by, and they were still there as the police cars cruised by as well. Crack houses were opening up in what used to be respectable neighborhoods. Drugs, crime, and violence had infiltrated the city limits, and the children were exposed to it.

"The drugs were right there, in your face all the time," says Tony Underwood, who was one of Micky Ward's closest friends growing up. "It could have been avoided. Anything could have been avoided, but it was very easy where we grew up. It started with pot, and then it was the cocaine and the crack. Right through the eighties."

At fourteen, Micky had very little trouble getting into bars, and if he and his friends were turned away by the Cellblock or J.J.'s, there was always the Cosmo or the Highland Tap. And there was always the Townhouse. After all, Micky's parents were usually there. Alice and George Ward liked to go out and immerse themselves in the drinking, partying culture, and they didn't seem to mind if their underage children were with them as full participants.

So, at fifteen or sixteen, Micky would often stumble home at two or three in the morning after a night of drinking. And it wasn't uncommon for him to return home bloodied after having found himself in the middle of a violent, street-fighting brawl. Those were the nights when the police would show up, not with the sole intention of breaking up the fight as quickly as possible, but to inflict a little punishment of their own, and to send a message to the young punks who were disrupting another Lowell evening.

"I was arrested a few times," Micky's friend Underwood says. "No felony or drug charges, but I've been around. And the cops would always come up, grab us, and beat the shit out of us in the early eighties. Micky, too. They knocked Micky around quite a few times. Lots of times, we had to stand there and watch our buddies get beat up."

Sometimes the fights could have been circumvented with a little wisdom or diplomacy, but Micky never took a backward step in the ring, and he wouldn't do it in the street either. Micky's personality was dominated by his childlike playfulness and his desire to have fun and make people laugh, but he also had a bit of a mean side to him. If somebody thought that they could look at Micky and say, or even so much as think, "You ain't nothing," Micky would tear him apart. Although history usually blames Micky's ill-fated night at the Cosmo for his fragile hands during his boxing career, friends admit, "He was always busting up his hands in street fights."

Having garnered a certain amount of hometown fame as a Golden Gloves champion by the time he was fifteen, Micky was a target when he went out. Wannabe-tough guys would fixate on him, noting how small and young-looking he was, and figure knocking down the little boxing star was a way to build themselves up. Although Micky wasn't the guy looking for trouble, he didn't seem to mind when trouble found him.

"We've seen years and years of a lot of street fights with Micky," says Underwood. "Very rarely did Micky ever lose a street fight. He probably weighed like 130 pounds back then, and he took on some 200-pounders, but Micky would always win."

Sometimes the fights were quick and easy, such as the night when Micky was still only sixteen years old, and a big kid described as a "real monster" confronted him at a house party. Micky tried to walk away, but the monster was dead set on proving he could beat Micky Ward. He didn't.

"The other guy kept pushing and pushing and pushing," says Richie Bryan, another close friend of Micky's. "Finally, Micky had to do what he had to do. He knocked the kid out."

Sometimes street fighting can be a matter of life and death. For instance, there was a night when Micky and his friends were out on the house-party circuit, a small group of sixteen-year-old boys looking for a place to hang out, drink beer, and find willing girls. They made their way to a two-family house off Wilder Street. They were supposed to meet some girls on the second floor, but nobody was home yet. While Micky and his friends were waiting outside, some guys on the first floor gave them some lip—nothing explosive, but sparks were about to fly.

Tony Underwood entered the house alone. He had found an open door, and simply walked in. He didn't have time to look around because he was immediately met by another boy who slammed a gun in his chest. Tony's instinct wasn't to run or to shout out for help or even to piss himself. He did the first thing that came into his head: he punched the kid in the face. Maybe the gun wasn't loaded, or maybe the kid just wasn't in a killing mood, but he didn't shoot Tony. Instead, six vicious teenagers who were either drunk or high and were looking to beat the crap out of someone surrounded him.

Tony held them off for nearly ten minutes, wondering if his friends were going to help him, not knowing if they even knew he was in there fighting for his life. Finally, the cavalry arrived. Micky led the charge and started knocking people down. Bodies were flying. Blood was spewing. Bones were cracking. The violence was frightening. The damage to people and property was extensive. But Micky's gang won the fight decisively.

Again, their instincts were not to flee the scene, nor did they ever think to call the police or a rescue squad. Instead, by the time the fight was over, the girls on the second floor had arrived, so the combatants went upstairs to clean up. The boys talked and laughed and traded stories about what had just happened and reassured one another about how tough they had all been, and a few of them even wondered if there were any dead bodies downstairs. They knew that was as bad a scene as they had ever been a part of. With so much blood, so many punches thrown, kicks landing, and heads cracking on the floor, they all wondered if this time things had gone too far.

The first ambulance came within the hour. From their perch on the second floor the boys listened as two of the victims were loaded onto stretchers and taken to the hospital. The second ambulance came a few minutes later, and a third ambulance arrived while the second was still being filled with injured teenage boys. In all, five kids were taken to the hospital that night, none of them seriously hurt, all of them treated and released. But there would be more flashing lights arriving at the house off Wilder Street that night.

The police showed up and started asking questions. They were given the answers that they expected. "I don't know who did it." "We didn't see anything." "Whoever did it must have left already." The police, glancing past Tony Underwood's swollen cheek and beyond Dave Mendoza's fat lip and ignoring the abrasions on both of Micky Ward's hands, listened to the lies, turned, and walked back down the stairs. There would be no arrests made that night.

If they couldn't get these boys tonight, chances are they'd find them soon enough inside the Laconia or the Cosmo. No matter how much trouble these Lowell kids found or averted, no matter how many near-death experiences, or how many times they got hurt or arrested, they kept coming back for more.

How does a teenager walk through a war zone like that? Without fear, that's how. No backing down. Hit them before they can hit you. A child growing up in Lowell had better learn how to fight, or how to run. Micky started fighting when he was seven years old at the West End Gym.

When Art Ramalho wasn't working with Dickie, who by then was fifteen years old, he was showing Dickie's scrawny little brother a few things.

"I started Micky Ward out when he was seven years old," Ramalho says. "He was carrying Dickie's bag. I'll never forget it. It looked like he was dragging the bag. That's how small he was."

Small or not, his heart was already big enough for battle. So, with boxing gloves that climbed up to his elbows, little Micky Ward stepped into an undersized ring at the Lynn Harbor House and prepared to duke it out with a tough ten-year-old kid from Dedham, Massachusetts, named Joey Roach. Roach was also part of a boxing family. He and his brothers, Freddie and Pepper, would combine to fight more than six hundred amateur fights, each taking a turn at the professional circuit as well. Joey turned pro ten years after his fight with little Micky. Freddie became a top-ranked featherweight contender and a highly respected trainer. Pepper hung out for a few years with Dickie Eklund, developed a drug dependency, and ended his pro career after only ten fights.

On that Saturday afternoon at the Lynn Harbor House in 1972, a small crowd gathered to see two small boys go toe-to-toe. It was the last time Micky would ever step into a ring afraid. Micky's family was out in full force hoping to detect the start of something special. They watched as Micky connected with the first punch he ever threw in competition. He fought courageously, if not wildly, for two rounds. After six exhausting minutes of windmill punches, and off-balance haymakers, the scheduled three-rounder was called on account of rain. Micky and Joey both received medals for their bravery and sportsmanship.

While Micky was bouncing around Lowell, in and out of Milloy, Lincoln, Bartlett, Daly, and Washington elementary schools, he was also bouncing in and out of boxing gyms. He started at the West End where Ramalho focused him on the fundamentals: the jabs, right hands, hooks, and uppercuts. Micky was a quick study.

By the time he was twelve years old, he was training at the Billerica Boys Club. There he found a couple of friends in Leo Lydon and Ben Doherty. Back in 1949, Doherty was the first-ever Silver Mittens champion. He continued on to a brilliant amateur career, including a controversial battle with Larry Carney for the New England Championship of the Amateur Athletic Union. The fight was held at the Boston Garden, and Carney, who had already won the Golden Gloves and the Diamond Belt, was going for the triple crown of the Amateur Athletic Union (AAU). Doherty knocked Carney down three times, but still lost the fight. A newspaper account of the bout explained what happened:

> Ben punched his way into the finals with quick knock-outs in the trials and semi-finals. He knocked Carney down twice in the second round and again in the third before the referee stepped in and stopped the fight at 1:56 of the third round because of a cut over Ben's left eye.

The story went on to say that "Doherty's eye was cut but not bleeding at the time."

Meanwhile, Carney was taken to the hospital because his head was split wide open.

Doherty was surprised that he didn't win the fight by a knockout. He couldn't believe Carney was able to keep getting up.

"When you hit a man, you can feel it right up your arm," he says. "I hit Carney with a beautiful right hand and I says to myself, 'He'll never get up.' But he got up. He was a tough kid."

It was when he was coaching a team at the Billerica Boys Club that he first met Micky.

"Micky was a classic boxer," Doherty explains. "He had all the skills in the world."

Harnessing those skills was a combined effort from a multitude of tutors, trainers, and mentors. At different times Micky was trained by Ouchie McManus, Larry's brother Micky Carney, Ben Doherty, and even a cop, Mickey O'Keefe, as far back as the Silver Mittens. But the person Micky listened to most was Dickie. Dickie, who would never reach his own potential, had a knack for tapping into Micky's. He could get Micky to work harder, focus better, and stay in the gym longer.

O'Keefe, who, in his role as a police officer, could have arrested Dickie any number of times but chose to hurry him along instead, says, "No matter how fucked-up he got on crack, when he made his way back to the gym, he was fine. He had a gift. He had a capacity to come back. If Dickie had trained, he could have been a champion. He wasn't a great puncher, but he was quick."

Joe Lake, another local trainer and manager, remembers Dickie much the same way.

"When we were kids, Dickie used to go to the New Garden Gym across from the old Boston Garden," Lake explains. "He was the only kid who could go in there shit-faced. He'd be drunk on a Saturday afternoon and start sparring ten rounds, and you couldn't hit him with a bag of rice. He was that good. He had that much skill. If he lived the pure life like his brother, he'd have been a champion. Dickie had the great physique. Long, tall, lean. Micky was short for his weight division. He had short arms. He had a million things going against him, and he stepped over every hurdle. Whereas, with Dickie, his first hurdle was drugs and he never got over it."

And maybe Dickie was a natural. Despite his transgressions, Dickie sure knew a lot about boxing, training fighters, and getting in shape. He was able to pass a lot of that knowledge down to his younger brother. Micky was his own man, even as a boy, but he listened to Dickie, and often followed his lead.

For example, when Micky was fifteen years old, he was jumped and beaten up just a few blocks from where he lived on Stevens Street. There were five assailants, and even though Micky was already becoming an accomplished boxer, they beat him badly.

Dickie was livid when he learned what had happened. He took Micky to the home of each kid Micky had identified, and either by banging on the door or shouting from the street, he called each one out, alone. There would be no gangs to help this time. This would be a series of fair fights. It took about a week, but Dickie was able to persuade each boy to come outside. He then stood back and watched as Micky beat up each one of his attackers. The fights didn't last long, and Micky was never jumped again. The point was made.

Not long after that, Micky, in his junior year, dropped out of Lowell High School. Boxing tournaments, travel, and a general apathy and lack of supervision caused or enabled him to miss a lot of classes, and he was falling woefully behind. Besides, his future was laid out as smoothly as the roads he'd been paving. He would be a hot topper and a boxer. Neither profession required much formalized education. Sitting high atop a steamroller, Micky could go as far as the city limits. And with boxing, far beyond. He turned pro a few years later.

Micky had a promising pro career. He had title shots. He fought on national television, but he was always one or two fights away from making any real money. So after six and a half years of too many hits and a few near misses, Micky did what every other boxer from Lowell had done before him, he quit. By 1991, he was back to paving parking lots, side streets, and highways.

Micky sat on the roller and took a swig from a large water bottle, the kind his cornermen used to squirt into his mouth between rounds, and wondered if things would have been different if he had listened to the sage advice of his friend Skeets Scioli.

Scioli was the president of the New England AAU for more than forty years, even as the organization became USA Boxing. When Micky was making the decision to turn pro, Scioli pulled him aside.

Scioli recounts, "He's the only fighter I ever talked to to tell him what to do and what not to do, because in this area here, they had a real bad reputation, selling drugs and all that jazz. This town here was bad. So I says to Micky, I says, 'Look, get the hell out of Lowell. The town is getting buried with the drugs.' I says, 'If you want to be a decent fighter, get out. Get the hell out of Lowell.'

"I said to him, 'Look, you're winning titles. You look like a pretty good fighter. You're the only fighter I've ever seen, and I've seen an awful lot of them in my day, that throws that left hook to the body, and you paralyze people with it! And that's a very effective punch. Just make sure that you continue with that punch. And, 'Get the hell out of Lowell.'"

CHAPTER FOUR

Micky never did get out of Lowell. He stayed and fought. He won titles at the Silver Mittens and the Junior Olympics, as well as three New England Golden Gloves titles and two New England Amateur Boxing Federation titles. Still, his fights were not all relegated to the inside of a boxing ring.

"I don't know what it is," says Richie Bryan, one of Micky's closest friends. "Around here, everybody just likes to fight."

But one night in particular, Micky and Richie had been on their best behavior. Their double date at the VFW Hall was completely without incident. It was so uneventful that as they were leaving, Richie boasted to the girls, "See that? No fights."

Then he looked to his left in the parking lot and saw ten kids beating up one kid.

"Oh, look. There's one now," he said.

Upon further inspection, that one kid proved to be Tony Underwood. Richie rushed to his rescue, wondering why Micky wasn't there to help, too. He finally looked over to see Micky aiding their other buddy Mike Thyne. Mike had been losing a five-on-one battle until Micky arrived. Now, it was an all-out brawl, one that

Micky, Richie, Tony, and Mike would ultimately win, though Tony ended up getting arrested.

This time, when the cops arrived, the arresting officer was a fan of Micky's and a friend of the family. He was willing to cut Micky some slack, but he slapped the cuffs on Tony. Richie tells it this way:

"When the cops showed up, they grabbed Tony. And Micky was like, 'Let him go.' He knew the cop, and so he was pulling on Tony and the cop was like, 'You let go of him, or I'll have to arrest you, too.' The cop was a real nice guy, but he finally went to cuff Micky, and I pulled Micky away and got him in the car."

A few months after that, Micky turned pro, but despite his best efforts, the street fighting wasn't over. The unsolicited challenges continued, and his friends started stepping between him and potential problems before they could get too far out of hand.

"Once he turned pro, we had to keep Micky from hitting people," Richie says. "We jumped in a lot more because we realized he was going to have some kind of career."

Another night. Another party. Another guy spots Micky and wants to go a few rounds with the big-shot boxer. On this particular evening, Richie steps up and tells the guy, "We don't want any trouble." As was often the case, the guy explains that he doesn't have any problem with Richie, who is over 6 feet tall and about 200 pounds. For undisclosed reasons, his problem is with Micky, and he's "gonna kill him." Richie encourages the guy to go away, but the advice is unheeded.

"He kept persisting, about four or five times," Richie recounts. "He finally shoved Micky pretty good, and Micky had to defend himself."

The result?

"Micky kicked the shit out of him."

It was the same story inside the ring. Micky wasn't quite twenty years old when he dropped David Morin at the roller-skating rink in Lawrence on June 13, 1985.

"I remember being real nervous, not throw-up nervous, just nervous," Micky recalls. "But once you get in there, it all disappears and you go right to your training. I remember I hit him with a good body shot in the first round and tore the ligament in my left thumb. That bothered me ever since."

It was his first professional fight, and it almost didn't happen. Micky's originally scheduled opponent, Snooky Covey, dropped out on the day of the fight. Promoter Tom Marino, who had sold about a hundred tickets to the fight, drove all the way up to Gorham, Maine, to find a replacement. Morin was a glass cutter at Portland Plate Glass, and he couldn't get off work early. Marino waited around until Morin's shift was over at six o'clock. They raced to Lawrence for the eight o'clock fight, arriving just in time to dress, get taped up, and enter the ring. Two minutes later, it was time to go back to Maine. Micky had broken Morin's ribs with that body shot.

Dickie gets a lot of the credit for teaching Micky to throw to the body. He'd tell him, "Get in there, and hit him good. He'll drop his hands, and you can go up top, and then finish back downstairs."

It's the advice a lot of fighters are given, but Micky not only listened, he also threw the left hand to the body perfectly. Before he turned pro, Micky spent some time training with Sean Mannion from Dorchester, Massachusetts. Micky was only nineteen years old when Mannion was training to fight Mike McCallum for the World Boxing Association (WBA) light middleweight title. Mannion went to Lowell to get in a few rounds, and Micky kept hitting him with hard body shots. Mannion's trainer actually halted the sparring session in the middle of a round and shouted, "Sean, stop letting him hit you in the body!"

"Listen, you fucking asshole," Mannion said. "I'm not letting him hit me to the body. It hurts too much to let him do it."

Micky was younger, and about fifteen pounds lighter, but Mannion said before going on to lose to an unbeaten McCallum in fifteen rounds, "That kid hits to the body like nobody I've ever been in with."

Two months after Morin, Micky was back fighting in his own backyard, this time, with three thousand supporters cheering him on.

It was in August 1985 that Micky had his first pro fight in the Lowell Auditorium, the same place where he had fought and won so many times as an amateur. The Lowell Memorial Auditorium was built on East Merrimack Street in 1922 and renovated in 1984. It was an impressive structure erected in a once prosperous and proud city.

On fight nights, the ring was positioned in the center of the auditorium. The theater seats climbed gradually from the main floor and only went back ten and twelve rows, so everyone on the lower level had a good view of the action. The balcony extended nearly to the ring, making front-row balcony seats the best and most sought-after tickets. It was an outstanding venue for boxing, the occasional riot notwithstanding.

When Dave Ramalho, Arthur's boy, fought Jimmy Farrell of Rockland, Massachusetts, for the New England featherweight title in March 1978, the fight was ruled a draw. Lowell fans who thought the Lowell kid had won the closely contested bout expressed their displeasure by throwing chairs, beers, and whatever else they could get their hands on. A mini riot ensued. Freddie Roach was there, and says, "Lowell's a tough place. We usually got in trouble when we went there from the outside."

Welcome to Lowell, where anything can happen.

Rocky Marciano fought at the Auditorium in 1947. Mike Tyson fought there in his Golden Glove days. Sugar Ray Leonard won there, so did Marvin Hagler. Each of them prepared for his battle downstairs in the boiler room, just like thousands of other kids whose greatest feeling in life would forever remain the night they landed a few good shots on the chin of some other twelve-, thirteen-, or fourteen-year-old.

Fighters got dressed next to other fighters in the brightly lit makeup rooms for the theater productions. They had their hands taped and their gloves tied under the glow of domed lights that outlined the large mirrors. Warm-ups, shadowboxing, meditation, and stretching were all done wherever a fighter could find the space. But there wasn't any space. Each of the dozens of fighters brought a manager, a trainer, a family member, or all three. The bathrooms, makeup areas, and hallways filled up rather quickly.

In their amateur days, their matches on any given night were made when organizers put numbered pills into a bottle and picked out two pills at a time. If a fighter was number seven, he learned at six o'clock that he was fighting number five at seven o'clock. "Good luck, kid. You're on in an hour."

That's how it had been for Micky throughout his amateur career, but as a professional in 1985, he had known for several weeks that he'd be fighting Greg Young on August 27—not that it did him any good to know. He didn't have much information on the kid from Catskill, New York, other than that he'd only fought three times before, losing twice, and that he was coming in light, at 131 pounds. Micky fought most of his career at or around 140 pounds. He was a classic light welterweight, 5 feet, 8 inches tall, skinny legs, well-defined abs, and a strong upper body. And that's about all the kid from the Catskills knew about Micky when he arrived, that and the fact that Micky's nickname was "The Baby Faced Assassin."

"I didn't want any nickname," Micky says. "But I definitely didn't want that one. The promoters just gave me that without asking, just looking to promote the fight, I guess. I asked them to change it, and the next time I showed up for a fight, I was "Irish" Micky Ward. I didn't mind "Irish." They just put it on the card one day, and it stuck."

The Baby Faced Assassin definitely got his career off to a good start, and Irish Micky picked it up from there. After knocking Morin out in the first round two months earlier, Micky's battle with Young lasted until the fourth round, when referee Ed Fitzgerald mercifully stopped the fight at the 1:45 mark. Micky had inflicted enough damage. He had beaten Young up for a few rounds, then he threw a right hand, and a left hook to the body, and he finished him off when he came up and hit him with a good hook to the head. That knocked him out. Micky was 2–0 and looking for his next victim.

Just a few days after his TKO of Greg Young, Micky was added to a fight card in Atlantic City. New Jersey regulations stipulated at the time, however, that a boxer had to wait at least ten days between fights, even if he had won. When Micky was filling out his licensing form for the Atlantic City fight, he failed to mention that he had just fought.

He blamed his managers Bernie "Boss" Bergeron and Don DiRocco for failing to advise him more prudently, and for not knowing the New Jersey rules before accepting the fight. The commissioner at the time, Joe Walcott, suspended Micky indefinitely. Four months later, in December 1985, Larry Hazzard was sworn in as the new commissioner of boxing in the Garden State. He recalls:

"I started getting all these phone calls about Ward—from a priest, from a policeman, from his mother—all asking me to reinstate Micky Ward. I didn't even know who Micky Ward was, or what he'd done to get suspended, but there seemed to be a lot of interest, so I figured I'd better find out."

Within his first week in office, Hazzard reinstated Micky, permitting him to begin fighting in New Jersey, and more specifically, Atlantic City. In the first seven months of 1986, Micky fought there seven times.

"We were going to Atlantic City almost once a month," Tony Underwood remembers. "We'd drive eight hours down. He'd knock the guy out in the second round, and we'd drive all the way back. It got so we were asking him to hold the guy up a little while longer just so we could see more action. But Micky was too good."

He was fighting guys who either had losing records or less experience. They were easy fights, intended to build his confidence and his record. Micky was being managed rather well by his mother. And he had begun the prolonged difficult process of dropping Bergeron and DiRocco, his two original managers, who didn't let go easily. Alice Ward had managed Dickie's career for a few years, and with two daughters who had married professional fighters, she was certainly no stranger to the fight game. No longer a stay-at-home mom raising nine children, Alice was ready to throw her "baby" into the ring. She began as any mother would: very carefully.

In his first Atlantic City fight, he knocked out Chris Bajor in the third round. That was in January 1986. Fourteen days later, he beat Michael Peoples in a lopsided four-rounder that went the distance. That was the first time Richie Bryan made the long trip to Jersey. He and Mike Thyne arrived late and discovered that the fight was sold out. They had made the trip for nothing, or so they thought. They were then surprised by the generosity of a stranger.

"We're standing outside, and some cowboy from Texas says 'How you doing, boys? You want a ticket? You want to see the fight?' We said, 'Yeah, you got extra tickets? How much?' He says, 'They're on the house. Take 'em. Have a good time.'"

Richie and Mike got inside the Resorts International Hotel's ballroom just in time to see Micky walking down the aisle on his way to the ring. Richie had an even better seat for his next trip to Atlantic City, but he also had added responsibilities.

Working the corner with Dickie was supposed to be one of Micky's friends, Lance Taylor. When Lance didn't show up, Micky grabbed Richie and said, "C'mon, you can do it." And that was the first of some twenty-five fights during which Richie worked the corner for Micky. Richie had no experience, but the primary tasks for the second man in the corner are mostly just making sure that the water bottle is full and that the spit bucket is nearby. Richie could handle those tasks.

Richie and Micky met for the first time when they were ten years old, but they traveled in different childhood circles until they started hanging out in high school. Richie had to ignore the advice of many who told him, "The Wards are crazy! What the hell are you hanging around with one of them for?"

By the time Micky turned pro, Richie started going to the Bullseye Boxing Gym with him every day. Since he had never boxed before, Micky, Dickie, and old-timer Ouchie McManus started teaching Richie a few things. Richie gained enough confidence and got in good enough shape that he started talking trash. He'd pound the heavy bag for eight to ten rounds, appraising his performance and announcing a fictional fight much the same way every day, "Oh, he's got Ward on the ropes! Oh, and Ward's down again!"

Micky listened to this good-naturedly for about two weeks before he invited Richie into the ring with him for a sparring session.

"He kicked the shit out me for two rounds," says Richie, who at that time outweighed Micky by about forty pounds. "I was so tired. I couldn't believe it. It was a whole different level."

Micky took his fighting, his training, his profession very seriously. The rest of the time was spent searching for fun. After winning his sixth fight in a row at the start of his career, Micky was back in Atlantic City getting ready to fight Luis Pizzarro. Richie, Tony, and Micky drove down together the day before the fight, but another close friend, Dave Mendoza, had to work. He finished his shift, left at midnight, and arrived at Micky's hotel room at eight o'clock in the morning, just as the guys were heading down to breakfast. Dave decided he'd crash in the room for a while and meet up with the group later. That was Micky's opportunity.

When the three friends got down to the lobby of the Trump Casino Hotel, Micky stopped to talk to a security guard and complained that there was a strange man in his room.

"I don't know who he is or how he got there," Micky told the guard, "But I want him out."

Micky turned to his other friends and said, "Now, let's go get something to eat." A few minutes later, hotel security had awakened Dave Mendoza and was forcibly escorting him from the room. Fortunately for him, Boss Bergeron, still Micky's manager, was staying in a nearby room. He heard the commotion and came out to see what it was all about. He was able to vouch for Dave, and the whole matter was quickly dropped.

Twelve hours later, Micky was in the ring with Pizzarro. Mendoza was there cheering wildly for his good friend who had pulled the prank that nearly got him arrested.

This was a wonderful time in Micky's life. He was enjoying success as a boxer, hanging out in Atlantic City with his friends, and gaining national acclaim. His first fight on ESPN was just his third pro fight, against Chris Bajor. This bout with Pizzarro would also be telecast on ESPN in front of a national audience. Here was a chance to increase his fan base outside of Lowell and also a chance to impress promoters, matchmakers, and potential opponents. Every win came with the promise of bigger paychecks down the road.

Micky entered the ring wearing blue trunks. He was sweating only slightly from his pre-fight warm-up. He looked confident and loose. Dickie climbed between the ropes right after him wearing tight white slacks with a red T-shirt that read BULLSEYE BOXING on the back. Pizzarro, a young fighter from Rio Grande, Puerto Rico, was fighting for the first time in the United States, and for the first time in three years. He came in with a professional record of 9–1 with seven knockouts.

By the third round, Micky forced Pizzarro against the ropes but was unable to seize the advantage. Pizzarro counterpunched effectively. Micky assumed a southpaw stance, and while Pizzarro bobbed his head and threw with both hands, he stood stone still, absorbed the punishment, and waited.

"Since he turned lefty, this has been a disaster for Micky Ward," ESPN announcer Al Bernstein said.

Finally, a left hook hurt Pizzarro. From the same motionless, almost lethargic position in which he was taking Pizzarro's best shots, Micky's shoulder rotated smoothly and efficiently, and with a short, circular, chopping motion, he snapped a left hook, and the punch landed cleanly on Pizzarro's jaw. Micky followed that with an explosive straight right hand. Pizzarro was in trouble.

There was about a minute to go in the round, and both fighters starting wailing away in the corner. Pizzarro threw wildly and continually out of desperation. Micky threw measured, accurate punches, sensing that he could put his opponent away with one more clean shot.

"He nails Pizzarro and sends him down," Bernstein announced. "A big uppercut and a straight right. Luis Pizzarro wobbles to his feet. That's it. Ted Pick has seen enough, and Luis Pizzarro is a knockout victim here in the third round."

Seven pro fights, seven wins, six knockouts. This was an impressive start to any boxing career. Regardless of the quality of his opponents, Micky was dominating, and he was entertaining. ESPN, Top Rank promotions, and others were taking notice. They would not only pay close attention to the young star on the rise, they would also try to cultivate his career and his confidence.

Micky fought a staggering nine times in 1986, improving his record to 11–0 with eight knockouts. But Micky knew the journey to a title fight would take years. He would have to be patient, trust his handlers, and continue to be successful. He took any fight that was offered, showed up in shape, and gave everyone reason to believe that finally a kid from Lowell might one day be wearing a championship belt. Life had been hard for Micky Ward. But right now, life was good.

The last of his string of Atlantic City fights was against the lightly regarded Rafael Terrero on the Fourth of July 1986. Micky had had a chance to see him when they both fought on the same card three weeks earlier. On June 15, Micky had outpointed Ken Willis in a six-rounder, while Terrero lost the fourth of his five pro fights to then undefeated Henry Hughes.

Although Terrero was from Jersey—Union City—out-of-state Micky was the crowd favorite. Cleo Surprenant did his part, as always, selling tickets out of the Highland Tap. Bus trips were organized, and about 450 people made the trip down from Lowell to see if Micky could knock out another one. He had already won six of his first eight pro fights by knockout.

The referee for the bout was Steve Smoger. He came out in a bow tie, blue shirt, tight pants, slicked-back hair, and a mustache. "I expect you both to obey my instructions," he told the fighters at the center of the ring. Both men nodded and returned to their corners.

Dickie was there in tight white slacks and a black T-shirt, this time bearing the words MICKEY WARD BULLSEYE BOXING,

LOWELL, MASS. on the back. Micky had been training for the past year at Bullseye Boxing and "Mickey" was the way his name was mistakenly spelled for the first several years of his career. Once the error was made, posters were printed, newspaper articles were written, and even Dickie's clothing confirmed it. Micky's name was unofficially and unintentionally changed. He didn't mind, at least not enough to speak up at the time. That would come later.

Micky was wearing blue shorts with white trim, looking every bit of his youthful twenty years. Dickie inserted Micky's mouthpiece. The bell sounded. And the warrior went back to work.

Micky began with a few jabs and some active footwork. He had a light bounce in his step, but he was only throwing one jab at a time, no combinations. This was the feeling-out process. Finally, two minutes into the round, Terrero, who hadn't landed a punch yet, learned that he was in a fight. Micky connected on a straight right and then snapped off a stirring combination of left and right hooks to the head and body.

"Doing good, doing good," Dickie said to him between rounds. "When you go in there, throw the jab, keep your hands up. Throw the left hook, double left hook."

Dickie pantomimed what he wanted and concluded by asking Micky how he was feeling. "Good," was all Micky said.

The second round was sloppy and concluded prematurely. Without any noticeably hard punches thrown or landed, midway through the round, Terrero was done.

"Something's wrong," ESPN boxing broadcaster Al Bernstein said. "He's quitting. He may have been hurt."

Micky and Terrero had gone into a clinch along the ropes, and Smoger separated them. At that time, Terrero pointed to his right cheek, waved his right hand, indicating he could not or would not continue, and walked slowly toward his corner. Smoger hadn't called the fight, and Micky would have been well within his rights to clock Terrero, but in a show of good sportsmanship and confusion, Micky just dropped his hands and watched Terrero go by.

Smoger jumped in, pointed Micky to a neutral corner, and got right up in Terrero's face.

"Do you want to keep fighting or not?"

Terrero shook his head "No." And the fight was over.

Micky recognized what had just happened and walked calmly over to his corner where Johnny Dunn and Boss Bergeron each took a hand and began cutting the tape off Micky's gloves. Micky's mother was quickly up on the apron of the ring, taking pictures.

Ring announcer Michael Buffer grabbed the microphone and announced: "Here's the official end of this bout. It ended at 1:12 of the second round. Referee Steve Smoger stops the bout. What happened is there's a possible fractured jaw on Rafael Terrero. The winner and still undefeated, Micky Ward!"

Terrero was unable to close his mouth and was taken to the hospital. Micky tried to explain what happened.

"I threw two left hooks in the first round. The first one caught him, and the second one caught him. Then I went downstairs to the body, and we clinched up and blood started dripping from his nose. I came in leading with the right hand. When I caught him the first time, he dropped his hands and I caught him again. I didn't want to go too quickly because he didn't look all that hurt. So, I just took my time."

Apparently, one of those two left hooks in the first round fractured Terrero's jaw. He tried to continue, but it would have been futile to go any further. He couldn't win the fight, and his face hurt.

Dickie offered this assessment of his brother's performance, and of his own past performance, "He's calming down. He ain't doing no showboating. He does everything that I didn't do. He trains hard. He does all the right things. He's gonna go all the way."

Five weeks later, Dickie was arrested for assault and battery on a police officer and disorderly conduct. It was his tenth arrest and the third that year, for when he wasn't helping Micky train, even sparring with him regularly, Dickie was still finding trouble on a regular basis. He was also arrested for assault on January 16, 1986, six days after Micky knocked out Chris Bajor in Atlantic City, and eight days before Micky won a four-round decision against Michael Peoples, also in Atlantic City. In March 1986, Dickie was arrested for larceny and given a suspended sentence. In April, Micky knocked out Darrell Curtis at the Trump Casino Hotel in Atlantic City. Dickie was always in Micky's corner on fight night. In between, he had his own life to live, or rather, his own life to destroy.

"I was fine," Micky says. "But that was the drugs. When you're doing that, nothing else matters. Dickie thinks he helped me early in my career, but he didn't. He held me back."

Micky explains, "I didn't know if he was coming or not. It's weird. You want to have everything working for you as a boxer, best training conditions, best diet, best people, no distractions, and I never really had that. I would have fired Dickie if he wasn't my brother. I kept him with me, because my mom kept telling me, 'Oh c'mon, he's your brother.' But I never knew if he was going to show up for a fight, or worse if he was going to show up drunk or high or something."

Dickie never did show up stoned for a fight, but he arrived a few times after having been up for three-straight nights, and Micky couldn't understand what he was saying in the corner between rounds. Those nights, Micky might have been better served to send Dickie home, but he never did.

"He'd come into the gym after getting wrecked for a week, and he'd be like new," Micky says. "Once he stepped in the ring, he still had it. He was tough. We'd go at it 100 percent when he sparred with me. I knew he was trying to hit me hard, so I had to go right after him. I even knocked him down a few times later on. Sure I was pissed at him for a lot of stuff, but that didn't really matter in the ring. There, we were just fighting. Somebody hits you, you want to hit them back harder. Dickie knew that."

Dickie also knew firsthand the dangers of excessive drinking and drug use. It had ruined his career and killed his dreams. He truly believes he could have been a champion if he had stayed clean. There was no denying his work ethic. He could out-train just about anybody, but when he wasn't training, he was jumping off track.

Still, he never lectured Micky or told him to stay away from the drug scene.

"He couldn't tell me anything," Micky says. "I stayed away from that scene growing up because I saw what it was doing to people around me. I mean I tried a little pot, and I would have a few beers, but that other stuff was real bad. No, Dickie never told me to stay away from it."

Micky stayed straight. He was on an upward path. It was impossible, however, to tell how far Micky could go based on his abridged battle with Terrero or any of the other fighters that he had dominated in the first fourteen months of his career. Once the tomato cans were out of the way, Micky was presented with his first significant test. He fought Johnny Rafuse at the Lowell Auditorium on August 29, 1986. Even though Dickie had been arrested for assault and battery on a police officer and disorderly conduct only eighteen days earlier, he would accompany Micky into the ring that night; however, Richie Bryan would not.

Gerry Callahan, writing for the *Lowell Sun*, told the story under the headline MICKY DELIVERS ON HIS PROMISE:

> It was concentration time. Micky Ward was sitting in his dressing room, trunks on, gloves on, robe on, jabbing at himself in the mirror, rolling his head around, his neck muscles were loose. His manager and trainer, brother Dick Eklund was going over some last minute instructions. Richie Bryan, one of Eklund's helpers, and Ward's buddy, asked him if he needed anything. Ward wasn't really listening to anyone. It was concentration time. There was a knock on the door. It wasn't time to go just yet. Someone wanted to talk to Richie. It was bad news. The most important thing to this trio in the past month didn't seem important anymore. Richie's father was dead.
>
> "I was really down," Ward said. "I had trouble getting up again. But I told Richie before he left, 'This one's for your father.' I was dedicating this fight to his father."

Richie was the youngest of seven children. His mother was a Lowell rarity. She didn't drink, smoke, or swear. His father was different. Richie fondly refers to his dad as a "screwball," but is quick to point out that his dad stopped drinking right before he was born and stayed sober for about sixteen years before starting back up again. He'd been sick for quite some time, and his death at the age of sixty-seven didn't come as a big surprise. Still, the locker room turned somber. A close friend was hurting, but the fight had to go on.

The Rafuse encounter would be Micky's eighth fight that year, but this time he'd be coming home to face a kid he knew well, a kid from Malden, a few towns over, a kid who was 12–2. Finally, after nine pro fights, Micky would be challenged by a fighter who shared the same dream of one day getting a shot at the light welterweight title. Johnny Rafuse was a good fighter and a capable threat to Micky's unblemished record.

The fight was on Labor Day weekend, and it was the first boxing show ever promoted by Al Valenti, who was determined to follow in his grandfather's footsteps. Anthony "Rip" Valenti fell into the sport of boxing, literally. Back in 1920, Rip was nineteen years old when he tripped over a boy sleeping outside his home in the North End of Boston. The boy, Sammy Fuller, had been thrown out of his own house by his stepfather. Rip unofficially adopted him, gave him a home for the next nine years, and then helped manage his boxing career. Fuller, already a fairly polished fighter when he was thirteen and homeless, went on to claim the world junior welterweight title in 1932, beating Jackie "Kid" Berg in a split decision at Madison Square Garden.

Rip Valenti lost money on most of the fights he promoted, especially through the Great Depression, but he finally struck it big in 1985 when he was given twenty-two closed-circuit locations throughout New England for the Marvin Hagler–Thomas Hearns fight in Las Vegas. Rip grossed 1.8 million dollars that night. He was eighty-four years old and died eight months later.

Eight months after his grandfather's death, Al Valenti was ready to pick up the torch. It made him feel good to walk around the córner from the Boston Garden, turn down Canal Street, and look up to see Valenti Way. The street was named in memory of his grandfather, a man who left a legacy in Boston and in boxing. Canal Street is where the Valenti Ticket Agency stood for decades. It's where Rip had once promoted the only heavyweight championship fight ever held in Boston, when Joe Louis knocked out Al McCoy of Waterville, Maine, in 1940. Nearly five decades later, Al Valenti was determined to keep the family legacy alive. He knew he'd never regret getting involved with Micky Ward. After all, Rip had always told him to find a white Irish kid who could fight.

Valenti received his indoctrination into boxing when he chased the footsteps of his grandfather to the Garden Gym to see Tony DeMarco, Joe DeNucci, and "Irish" Tommy Collins. He loved being around the boxers, and he loved the adrenaline rush that surrounded the sport.

He got into it, first when he helped his grandfather with the closed-circuit portion of the Hagler–Hearns fight, and then when Bob Arum handed him five thousand dollars to promote the Ward–Rafuse fight in Lowell. Arum owned and operated Top Rank, Inc., and he needed someone with local connections to fill up the auditorium. It was the first time in two years that ESPN broadcast a fight in Massachusetts, and what the network wanted was a sold-out show. They didn't quite get it. Although having Micky involved certainly helped, Valenti was only able to sell about two thousand of the three thousand available tickets. Still, it was an exciting night.

"That was the first televised event out of the Lowell Auditorium," Valenti says. "And the Lowell Auditorium, in boxing circles, is probably the Caesars Palace of New England. It's a great old building. It's a circular building with no obstructions, no bad seats. And everyone in the building is literally on top of the ring. Plus, because it's Lowell, you've got that history. The Golden Gloves started there in the thirties."

And there were three local guys in the ring that night. Ward, Rafuse, and the referee, Tommy Collins, another fighter that Rip

Valenti had taken in off the streets. He started out as a popular street kid and club fighter and went on to win the New England featherweight title in 1951. Collins retired after seventy-two professional fights in 1954 and became a court officer at the Middlesex County Courthouse in Lowell.

Collins appeared to revert to his club-fighting days during the third round when he failed to separate the fighters during a clinch. In apparent frustration, he bear-hugged Rafuse from behind and threw him forcefully back against the ropes.

"What was that all about?" ESPN announcer Al Bernstein wondered during the broadcast. "I have never seen a referee manhandle a fighter like that before, and I'll tell you what, I hope I never see it again. That was bizarre!"

Rafuse barely noticed. He bounced off the ropes and started after Micky again, but Collins stopped him mid-stride, poked him in the chest, and scolded him for holding too much. In truth, the first three rounds involved a lot of clutching and grabbing, but it was hard to tell which of the fighters was the guiltier party.

As the third round ended, Bernstein said, "This fight's getting out of control, and I'm not sure if the referee isn't out of control right now."

But it was just getting good. Rafuse, who looked like a nervous street fighter in the first three rounds began fighting like the warrior he had always been. And Micky moved forward as if defense were a dirty word. The punches he took to get inside weren't even distractions. This battle with Rafuse was the first of Micky's best fights.

In the fourth, Rafuse went to the body well, and Micky landed several straight rights and good lefts to the body. His seamless switches from an orthodox to a southpaw stance bothered Rafuse, so naturally, Micky kept doing it.

In the fifth round, Micky's jab came out of hibernation. He slid from side to side with his back along the ropes and repeatedly threw his left hand into Rafuse's face. Rafuse did a good job of cutting off the ring, and he was at his most aggressive in this round, but Micky responded in the final minute with a hard right hand and several pinpoint-accurate lefts.

"Rafuse is in some trouble," Bernstein bellowed. "He's being worked over by Micky Ward."

The bell sounded. Rafuse recovered. And there was more of the same in the sixth. Fans were getting a glimpse of the exciting fighter Micky could be and would be later in his career. He was an excellent boxer who moved well, possessed a solid jab, and threw a variety of hard punches with both hands, but much more than that, he was a boxer who was ready and able to brawl. He was willing to put his will up against anybody's. "You take my best, and I'll take your best, and we'll see who's still standing when it's over." That was the bold philosophy Micky would employ many times over many years, and it was on display for the first time against Johnny Rafuse, a willing participant in this exercise of brutality.

"They are waging a brutal war on the inside," Bernstein observed. "Rafuse just took a hard right hook without blinking."

The fighters rested their heads on each other's shoulders and threw punches from hunched-over positions. Uppercuts would land, and heads would pop up from the force of the blow and then return to the opponent's shoulder. Their hands stayed in front of their faces, except for the momentary flash when a left or a right would snap to the outside and land a hard hook to an ear or a cheek or a chin. Once separated in the seventh round, Micky landed three consecutive straight left hands out of the southpaw position. Rafuse nailed him right back with a big right hand of his own. Ward was landing more power punches, but Rafuse landed enough damaging blows of his own to make Micky's corner anxious.

"This is the eighth round now. Last round, Micky," Johnny Dunn told him after the seventh. Dickie squeezed Micky's rib cage and added, "You're looking good. Deep breath. C'mon, Mick. Don't get careless now. When you're doing that banging, you're looking good. Keep your hands up. Don't give him this shit no more." (This "shit" referred to the occasions when Micky was dropping his hands and taking unnecessary punishment.)

Micky had never been eight rounds before, but he still looked fresh coming out. Rafuse did, too. At twenty-five, Rafuse had said before the fight that his encounter with Micky would let him know if he should keep fighting.

"If I win, I'll know I should continue," he said. "Otherwise, you know, I'm a Teamster, and maybe I'll have to find other ways to make a living."

Well, Rafuse had done himself proud. He continued to throw and land hard punches right up until the final bell. He must have realized that he was behind on points, and he went after Micky with reckless abandon. Micky, who must have known that he was ahead in the fight, refused to play it safe. The result was a thoroughly entertaining and violent final round.

"They are both going for the home-run ball," Bernstein remarked. "They say Micky Ward is quite a prospect in the junior welterweight division, and if he is, he will look back on this one."

The crowd rose to its feet and offered a resounding ovation. The majority of the fans didn't go to the auditorium that night to root for Rafuse, but by the time they left, Rafuse had earned their respect.

Dickie ran up to Micky after the final bell, toweled him off, and said, "You won, Mick. You won!"

A few moments later, ring announcer Michael Buffer pulled the microphone down from the ceiling, "Here's the official scoring. Judge John Costello scores the bout 80–76. Judge Don O'Neill has it 80–76. And Judge Tommy Collins has it 79–75 for the winner by unanimous decision, Irish Micky Ward!"

Micky made good on his promise to Richie Bryan and earned the unofficial title of best young junior welterweight in the Boston area by winning the eight-round slugfest with Rafuse on points.

Meanwhile Valenti was learning quickly just how messy the financial part of a fight can get. Starting with only four thousand dollars, he made checks out to Micky, Micky's mom, and a lawyer from Lowell who showed up that night with a writ. The writ was intended to keep Micky from fighting unless his original managers were paid. Even though Alice was managing Micky's career, the original managers were hanging around to make either a little trouble or a lot of money.

"When we first started off, it worked out all right," Micky says. "But they don't know the game. When I got suspended in New Jersey, they said they got it dropped, but they didn't get it dropped."

He added further complaints about Bergeron and DiRocco.

"They would never ask who I was fighting. What's his record? Is he righty or lefty? I've got Dickie training me, and if it hadn't been for him, I wouldn't know anything about who I was fighting."

And when it came to money, Micky says, Bergeron and DiRocco wanted more than their fair share.

"One day, they say it's over. Next day, the old man's there saying they want to bring me to court for five hundred thousand dollars, and they want to sue my mother for two hundred thousand dollars. They said they had me when I was nobody. Now, that I'm someone, I want to go with Top Rank. That's not true, though."

What was true, however, is that Top Rank wanted Micky, and that was very good for his career. Just ten fights, all wins, into his new profession, and Micky was already fighting on ESPN for a second time. Two months after fighting Rafuse, Micky was back in the ring in the Lowell Auditorium. Teddy Brenner, Arum's main matchmaker on the East Coast, made the Ward–Carlos Brandi fight. He loved Micky for the same reason any matchmaker or promoter would love Micky, he was white, Irish, and could fight. That sells tickets, even if the fight is a mismatch.

Brandi was an Argentinean fighting out of Miami, Florida, and making his United States debut. It didn't matter. Top Rank wasn't looking for a great fight. This was just supposed to be an easy fight for Micky, something to put another three thousand dollars or so into his pocket, something to build his name recognition and create a fan following, and something to further strengthen his relationship with Top Rank and ESPN. It worked on every count.

Ring announcer Michael Buffer, who hadn't yet adopted the catch phrase, "Let's get ready to *r-r-r-r-r-umble!*" began the evening with: "Man your battle stations. This is the first of our featured ten-round bouts. This is in the junior welterweight division."

Brandi shifted his weight from one foot to another as Buffer announced his name. He didn't appear surprised by the resounding chorus of boos emanating from the crowd or the raucous applause when Micky was introduced. Brandi was about to go toe-to-toe with a hometown hero. Micky hadn't done much to deserve hero status at this point in his life, other than to give the citizens of Lowell something to hope for, to brag about, and to feel good about. Micky kept his head down during the pre-fight instructions, not looking at Brandi. He wasn't interested in having any kind of macho stare-down. Brandi stared at Micky's scalp instead. Dickie stood right behind Micky, giving him a shoulder and neck rub, and then the fighters touched gloves and returned for a moment to their corners. Johnny Dunn was in Micky's corner that night as well.

Midway through the first round, Brandi launched a wild assault. He landed a solid right before Micky slipped the next one and moved quickly around him. In a flash, Micky was standing behind Brandi. No damage was done, but what Brandi's flurry seemed to do was give him confidence. He had swung wildly and paid no price. Micky never countered. He simply avoided. So, with ten seconds to go in the round, Brandi began another attack. This time, Micky countered.

"Left hook sends Brandi to the canvas," ESPN announcer Al Bernstein exclaimed. "From nowhere the left hook by Micky Ward. Wow! That's a surprise. Brandi having a very good first round, but the left hand puts him down."

The bell rang seconds later, and Brandi rose to his feet and made his way back to his corner. Micky didn't have a noticeable reaction to what had just happened. He merely slumped his shoulders, put his head down, and waited a moment as Dickie readied the stool for him to sit down on. Dickie slid gracefully through the ropes and patted down Micky's chest, sides, and stomach. He spoke hurriedly. Micky listened attentively. Finally Micky nodded and rose for the second round.

Brandi, who didn't appear to have been hurt by the left hook that ended round one, stood momentarily in his corner with blood running down from his nose. He came out flailing wildly. Micky stood right up to the aggression, and when Brandi charged, Micky nailed him with a stinging right hand.

To his credit, Brandi walked through it and kept coming forward, but it was clear that this fight wouldn't last long. Brandi wasn't in the same class as Micky.

As the fighters moved toward the corner, Brandi was hit with another hard right hand and began to fall on one knee. He rose quickly, only to be hit again by another punishing right. Brandi dropped into a catcher's position this time, and the referee, Nick Previti, stepped in and separated the fighters. Previti ruled it a knockdown because Brandi had grabbed onto the rope to maintain his balance. While Brandi was given a standing eight-count, he tried to remove the cobwebs by shaking his head repeatedly. He indicated that he could continue. Moments later Micky fired a left hook that landed flush on Brandi's right cheek. Brandi crumpled to the canvas as Micky walked to a neutral corner with his hands raised. He knew no one could get up from a power shot that clean. Micky had jumped into that left hook. He delivered it with bad intentions and had a great result.

Bernstein observed, "Micky Ward has sent this crowd into a frenzy with as powerful a performance as we've seen from him. Anything he does here, they're going to like, and I'll tell you, they've got to like what they saw here tonight."

In just under six minutes of work, Micky's night was done. He was still undefeated, still the pride of Lowell, Irish Micky Ward.

He told ESPN after the fight, "I didn't know his style or nothing. . . . He hasn't fought in the United States. So, in the first round I was just taking my time, keeping my hands up because I didn't want to get caught with that style he's got. He was wailing at me, and I knew he was pretty strong. He was just missing and I thought, 'Wow, he's got a pretty good punch.' So, I waited and caught him in the first round. Once I put him down, I knew I could do it again. I didn't have any plan coming in. . . . I knew he was a righty and that's it. So, I had to watch what he did and counterpunch off of that."

While Micky returned to the basement of the auditorium to change into his street clothes in a bathroom stall, Freddie Roach went on for the night's co-main event and fought David Rivello. Roach lost a ten-round majority decision. It would be the last fight of his career, closing with a record of 39–13. Roach was once the local kid with promise and potential. Now that distinction belonged to Micky.

After another quick trip to Atlantic City to beat unheralded Hilario Mercedes, Micky was heading out west, still undefeated. For the first time in his short career, he'd be fighting in Las Vegas at the famed Caesars Palace. As Dickie had done many times, Micky would be fighting on the undercard of a Marvin Hagler fight. This time, though, Micky would be receiving incredible exposure, because he was fighting on the same card as Hagler and Sugar Ray Leonard, and the fight would be part of the international closed-circuit *Super Fight* broadcast. This would be Micky's first taste of the big time, and it would serve as a reminder that Dickie once had had that taste as well.

This was Micky's first trip to Las Vegas, and he arrived four days early along with Dickie, his good friend Richie Bryan, and his eighty-year-old trainer, Johnny Dunn. Micky duly noted the expansive Vegas strip and spent just enough time inside the casinos to play a few slot machines. Then it was time to get to work. The work always made boxing much less of a gamble.

Micky had been scheduled to battle a Venezuelan southpaw by the name of Alfredo "Scarface" Rojas. Micky trained for the fight in Florida where he could spar with as many left-handers as possible. For some reason, lefties were easier to round up in Florida than they were in Lowell. And Micky even studied film of Rojas. Usually, Dickie looked at the tapes and then provided Micky with a fight plan.

But Micky's time spent sparring southpaws was wasted. Rojas withdrew shortly before the fight. Micky would fight Kelly Koble, a right-hander who had just been destroyed a month earlier in the California light welterweight title fight against Andrew Nance.

It was a historic night for boxing. Thousands of people were there to witness Hagler and Leonard. Millions more would watch in their homes or local bars. But only a handful arrived early enough to witness the up-and-coming twenty-one-year-old from Lowell take on a twenty-seven-year-old from San Jose, California. Micky's fight was nearly four hours before Hagler and Leonard slipped through the ropes. He and Koble went at it outdoors in the desert heat around five o'clock in the afternoon.

Dickie helped Micky peel out of his white robe, revealing his white trunks and white boxing shoes. Oddly, Micky's robe spelled his name correctly, "Micky Ward," while Dickie's blue T-shirt spelled his brother's name "Mickey Ward." No one noticed, or no one cared.

Koble, though three pounds heavier at 142 pounds, looked skinnier than Micky. He was wearing blue trunks, and perhaps because he was the more experienced fighter, he came out more aggressively.

"You talk about young kids getting nervous . . .," said long-time trainer Gil Clancy working in the broadcast booth for the fight, "I've seen Ward fight before. He's normally a walk-in puncher, very, very active. Tonight, he seems very tentative and very stiff."

He was right. Micky usually moved in only one direction, forward. On this night, he was bouncing around the ring, going side to side, and throwing an occasional solitary jab. It lost him each of the first three rounds.

"Micky Ward's . . . the young Irish kid on the way up," Clancy, the proud Irishman, said. "He's got a lot of snap on his punches when he lets them go, which he's not doing enough of so far this evening."

This was the biggest night of Micky's career. He was on the biggest stage of his life, and he was blowing it. Micky was struggling through the first three rounds. The fight was only scheduled to go eight, so Micky had to turn things around in a hurry.

"He ain't hurting ya!" Dickie yelled in the corner. "But you're standing there and he's getting points on you!"

As the fourth round opened, play-by-play man Tim Ryan said, "The unbeaten Micky Ward, so far has been unimpressive. You can see he has some natural skills and sharp punches, but he has not used them to any real effect so far."

Moments later, Micky pounced. He seemed to spring forward from his haunches and landed a hard right hand that knocked Koble to the canvas. The punch was a beautiful right-hand counter over a jab, and the result was a flash knockdown. Micky backed away immediately, and Koble shot right back up to his feet. Referee Richard Steele directed Micky to one corner and brought Koble to another. Koble indicated that he was fine, and the fight continued.

"Koble wasn't hurt by it," Clancy said. "But it sure got his attention. It built Ward's confidence and changes things around a little bit. He's much more alive, and throwing combinations now."

That one punch changed everything. Micky went on the offensive. He landed a straight right hand and two left hooks that stirred the small crowd up. He was initiating all the action. A big right hand found its mark. Two big lefts to the body were followed by two more shots to the body. By this time, Koble was bleeding badly from his right eye. Blood had smeared all over Micky's chest, and shoulders, and even his back. As the fourth round came to a close, Dr. Donald Romeo went over to Koble's corner to take a look at the gash over his right eye. It was deep. Too deep.

"That's all," Romeo said. And the fight was over. Micky was awarded a fourth-round technical knockout. He had walked through the first three rounds without a hint of urgency. His record went to 13–0. His right hand was raised by Richard Steele. He spit his mouthpiece into Dickie's hands, and the brothers walked out of the ring together, Dickie's arm around Micky's shoulder. A decade ago, Micky had sat in the audience and watched Dickie fight Sugar Ray Leonard. Tonight, Dickie sat and watched Micky fight on the same card as Leonard. And that night the two Massachusetts brothers watched Leonard make millions fighting another Massachusetts kid named Marvin Hagler.

Leonard won a controversial split decision over Hagler. It was the last time Hagler ever fought. He and Leonard split just over twenty-three million dollars that night. Micky and Kelly Koble left with just a few thousand dollars each. But the seeds had been planted. This was the world of big-time boxing, and Micky proved he belonged in it. He walked the streets of Vegas as comfortably as he walked the streets of Lowell. He was not impressed with the glittering lights. Vegas offered him nothing more than a place to ply his trade.

When the Leonard–Hagler fight was over, the night was over, at least for Micky. He celebrated quietly in his room. Dickie's night didn't end until morning. Vegas did lure him; it suited him better than Lowell.

The next day, Dickie spotted Sugar Ray getting out of a limousine at the Las Vegas airport. He yelled to Leonard and started walking over to him, but a bodyguard intervened. When Leonard acknowledged Dickie, the bodyguard stepped aside and the two men shook hands. Nine years earlier they had touched gloves. For that moment in time, they were equals. Ten rounds later, three judges determined that Leonard was the better man. On this day, no one would dispute that. Dickie stood there still smelling of alcohol. Leonard stood there smelling of the finest bath products. They spoke casually for a few moments, Dickie congratulating Leonard on his big victory the night before, Leonard wishing Dickie and his brother the best of luck. Then they parted ways and flew as they had always traveled, in different directions.

Three weeks later, Dickie was in the middle of the fight at the Cosmo.

As part of his probation Dickie was ordered to enroll in an alcohol rehabilitation program, and he told friends that he was thinking about making a comeback. The rehab never happened. The comeback never happened, either. What did happen is that Dickie continued going to the local pubs, but was a little more careful about getting into fights. Some progress was made. Dickie was only arrested three times in the next three years, once for possession of cocaine, once for drunk driving, and once for being disorderly in public.

Two months after the Cosmo incident, Micky and Dickie spent another night drinking inside the Cosmo. This time they met Ian

Thompsen, a writer for the *Boston Globe*, outside at two o'clock in the morning to show him where the violence had taken place.

"The fight began here," Dickie told the newspaper man.

"Then it came around the corner over here," Micky said. His words were slurred. "They threw Dickie on the ground, *boom!* Then I came over and they started hitting me—*crack, crack, crack!* There was blood right here."

"There was a lot of blood," Dickie added.

A few months after the Cosmo incident, in August 1987, Micky's hands had healed enough so that he felt confident about getting back into the ring. Returning to Atlantic City, he needed just four rounds to dispose of Derrick McGuire.

Micky was now 14–0 with ten knockouts. Teddy Brenner, the chief matchmaker for ESPN on the East Coast, was crazy about him and was looking to make a Micky Ward–Vinny Pazienza match at the Boston Garden. Pazienza was a white Italian kid. Another New Englander, from Cranston, Rhode Island, he was skyrocketing up the ranks with a 27–1 record. Two months before Micky maintained his unblemished record with his win over McGuire, Pazienza won the IBF (International Boxing Federation) lightweight title with a unanimous fifteen-round decision over Greg Haugen. It was a perfect time to get Ward and Pazienza into the ring together, perfect for Micky. For Pazienza, Ward was a bit of a step backward. Pazienza was three years older, and had already fought for and won a title. There was tremendous risk in fighting Micky and very little to gain, other than New England bragging rights. So Pazienza headed to a rematch with Haugen. Pazienza spent the final thirteen years of his career fighting between 154 and 171 pounds. He went from being figuratively "too big" for Micky to being literally too big for Micky. Micky would have to wait to get his chance to duke it out with a white Italian kid who could fight. It would be fourteen years later, and well worth the wait.

CHAPTER FIVE

Micky continued to enjoy success inside the ring. He'd been a professional fighter for twenty-six months and won all fourteen of his fights, most of them by early knockout. But the knockout he was most interested in was Laurie Ann Carroll. Laurie was only twelve when she started dating the fourteen-year-old boxer with a wild streak. It was an on-again off-again childhood romance that ended after three years. By then, Micky was seventeen, out of high school, and heartbroken. He moved in with his friend Tony Underwood, who says Micky could have had any girl he wanted, except for the one girl he wanted most.

"He loved Laurie, and could never get over her," Tony says. "We had girls over all the time, two single guys, but he couldn't get another relationship started without having Laurie in the back of his mind."

So, after a four-year breakup, Micky and Laurie started dating again and eventually moved into an apartment together. Micky had his personal life right where he wanted it and there were no bumps in the road regarding his career path—until he squared off against Edwin Curet.

"I knew Micky loved going to the body," Curet would say years later. "I just kept bringing that hand down, blocking that body shot. He might have hit me in the head, but he wasn't getting me with that."

He was right. Micky was never able to land enough effective body punches on Curet. His left hand was swollen so much and so often, it had become more difficult to train and even more difficult to land his left with authority. Micky landed a few hurtful, stinging blows to the body and the head, but not nearly enough of them. He couldn't knock Curet out, and he wasn't nearly busy enough to win on points. Micky wasn't beaten up, but he lost a ten-round decision.

He returned to his hotel room with Richie Bryan, who had worked the corner that night in Atlantic City. The room was quiet for several minutes. Richie wasn't sure what to say, and Micky was staring at the carpet. Finally, Micky looked up and said, "What do I do now?"

Richie welcomed the opportunity to lighten the mood and responded, "Call your Uncle Gerald and see if you still have a job paving. Looks like you're gonna need a job."

Micky laughed, "I can't believe you just said that to me." But he knew that's what friends were for, and he kept laughing. "Everything was going to be all right," he thought. "Yes, this was a setback, but only a minor one."

Having suffered his first defeat to a non-title contender, it was important for Micky to have an impressive win, and soon. He got it against a Philadelphia welterweight named Joey "Bugsy" Ferrell. Ferrell had only won half of his fourteen fights, but one of them was against the previously undefeated Mike Mungin. He also went the distance against such ranked opponents as John Meekins, Buddy McGirt, and Tony Martin, and he had beaten Johnny Rafuse. This was a fight that Micky should win, but it wouldn't be easy even under the best of circumstances. Considering that Ferrell had never been stopped, Micky could expect it to go the distance, which was never a good idea because of the shape his hands were in.

Micky stepped through the ropes wearing a white robe and weighing just over 138 pounds. Ferrell was 7 pounds heavier. Micky, who felt he blew the Curet fight because he wasn't busy enough in the early rounds, came out firing several hard overhand rights, each one missing. But after one miss in particular, Micky found himself on the inside. *Boom*, a left hand to the body! That one hurt Ferrell. It was classic Ward. He tapped Ferrell on the head with a short left and then went downstairs with a vengeance. Ferrell should have dropped to a knee. Instead, he crouched and backed away toward the corner with Micky trying to tee him up.

Micky reached him and started to land several lefts to the body and rights to the head. The referee, Vinny Rainone, stepped in, and Ferrell, grateful for the reprieve, took a moment to rest on both his knees, then rose and paced around the ring. He grimaced in obvious pain. Rainone gave him a standing eight-count and rubbed Ferrell's gloves on his shirt.

"Can you continue?" Rainone asked, receiving a head nod in return.

With forty-seven seconds to go in the first round, Rainone signaled for the fighters to meet back in the center of the ring. Micky wasted no time. He knew his opponent was hurt, so he started throwing left hands to Ferrell's aching right side. Ferrell had no choice but to block those shots by dropping his right elbow down to his side. That opened him up for the head shots. And Micky delivered. Ferrell's hands went back up, and Micky went back down to the body. One more shot to those ribs was all it took. Ferrell dropped to his knee again. Rainone jumped in and Micky had his first first-round knockout since David Morin got this ride started two-and-a-half years earlier.

Ferrell returned to his corner, holding his side in agony. The fight doctor entered the ring and poked Ferrell in the side, causing him even more agony. The ringside diagnosis was that at least one rib was broken.

"The hand didn't hurt at all," Micky said after the fight. "I went to the body because I knew he was coming in heavy. I didn't want to go to his head right away. I thought I could wait for a later round. I tapped with the hook to the head, and then *Boom!* I put all my power downstairs. It gives me a lot of confidence to know I can stop a guy who's never been stopped before."

Dickie added, "I'm happy. He listens good. He came in at 139. Last time he fought Curet at 133. He was too light. Now he feels great. He's going all the way this time."

Micky did have his sights set on a rematch with Curet. He wanted to avenge the only blemish on his record. He readily admitted he lost that fight, but he believed that he gave it away in the first five rounds and was certain he could remedy that mistake if given another opportunity. The fight was made and scheduled for ESPN on March 30. But before he got there, he had to get through the Pasadena Kid, Joey Olivera. Olivera had proven five months earlier that he could stand in there with one of the best fighters in the junior welterweight division. Olivera had gone ten rounds with former USBA (United States Boxing Association) junior welterweight champion Terrence Alli, ultimately losing a unanimous decision. Alli was ranked in the top ten, a place where Micky could find himself with another impressive win. Olivera stood in the way, and he was confident that he could beat the rising star.

"Micky's only loss is to Curet, and that's the only real class fighter he's been in with," Olivera said. "I've been in with a lot of them."

True enough, but he had also lost to each and every one of them. Micky squared off with Olivera on February 19. It was Micky's first time back in Las Vegas since the Koble fight, but this time he was at Bally's Casino Resort. Despite undergoing back surgery just nine days prior to the fight, Dickie was in Micky's corner. He was wearing a button-down dress shirt, dress slacks, and dress shoes. He never looked better. Also in Micky's corner was Freddie Roach. He was an important addition to Team Ward because he had fought and lost to Olivera three years earlier. It was Roach who devised the fight plan, and it was Micky who executed it perfectly.

There was nothing subtle about the plan. It was obvious from the opening bell that Micky intended to outbox Olivera. Micky was light on his toes, sliding quickly around the ring. He was a moving target that Olivera couldn't catch. Micky used his jab effectively and kept his opponent at arm's length as much as possible.

"This is as much movement as we've seen from Ward in any of his fights," Al Bernstein commented. "This is more like the style of Dickie. We've seen Micky slug it out more, but they must have decided this is the way to beat Olivera. Micky goes inside a few times, lands some shots, and then backs away. For an aggressive fighter like Micky, that is tremendous discipline and a willingness to listen to advice. Micky lands combinations and then gets out quickly."

Micky was sticking and moving, darting in, landing a few substantial body shots, and backing out quickly. He showed tremendous foot speed and boxing skills. He was putting on a clinic, and Olivera could see the fight slipping away from him. "All right, Mick," Freddie spoke in the corner this time. "Let's go with the hook upstairs and the double hook down. Double down is there for you. You're hurting this guy to the body. Okay? Good combinations and quick out, okay?"

Micky listened again. He held his street-fighting instincts in check and spent the entire ten rounds moving gracefully and scoring with quick bursts and flurries. This was not the kind of fight that made him a favorite of the ESPN audiences, because there just wasn't enough blood or confrontation. Both fighters escaped without any real evidence of having been in a ten-round fight. But Micky was back on track. He won the unanimous decision by scores of 98–93, 98–92, and 97–94, and he improved his record to 16 and 1. He also showed everyone that he was capable of doing whatever was needed to get the job done. On this night, that meant working from the outside.

"This has been the most disciplined effort Micky Ward has had as a pro, by far," Bernstein said. "All he has to do is keep fighting better fighters. At twenty-two, he's developing the skills he needs."

Micky returned to Lowell to prepare for his rematch with Curet, but the fight never came off. Micky hurt his right hand against Olivera, and he just didn't have enough time to let it heal. Micky pulled out, and Curet fought Livingstone Bramble on March 30 instead. Bramble knocked him out in the eighth round, and Curet's career spiraled downhill from there.

After canceling the bout with Curet, Micky grabbed a fight with a New York kid named David Silva in May 1988. It was nothing more than a chance to keep busy and make a quick buck. Silva had never won a professional fight, and he never would. Fourteen tries, fourteen losses. He did manage to take Micky the full ten rounds, but Micky, who was still bothered by two bad hands, was simply another class of fighter.

Two months later, Micky needed only two rounds to knock out Philadelphia's Marvin "Machine Gun" Garris. That was in July. In August, Dickie was arrested back in Lowell for cocaine possession and fined 375 dollars. It didn't slow him down, though. He continued doing drugs and training Micky. In September, one month after Dickie's arrest, Micky fought another boxer from Philly with the nickname "Machine Gun." Machine Gun Mungin altered the course of Micky's career and offered him an important life lesson, specifically: "Nobody else is looking out for you. So, you better look out for yourself."

Micky had returned to Atlantic City to fight Saoul Mamby on September 9, 1988. "Sweet Saoul" Mamby was a black Jew who turned pro after serving in Vietnam. He began fighting in 1965 and won the WBA junior welterweight title from South Korea's Sang-Hyun Kim in 1979. Three years earlier, he had lost to the great Roberto Duran on points in a non-title fight. By 1988, he was forty-one years old, had fought in eight title fights, had just upset Glenwood "The Real Beast" Brown, and was ranked eleventh among junior welterweights. He was still a well-respected fighter, and a pretty big name to put on Micky's resume. He also was known for his willingness to fight anyone anywhere, if permitted.

Unfortunately Mamby was too sick too fight. Despite his protestations that included prolonged shouting and creative cursing, the fight doctor would not permit him to enter the ring with a fever. Either the fight would have to be canceled or a substitute fighter would have to be found on extremely short notice. No one involved wanted to cancel the fight. There was too much money to be made. Ron Katz, the matchmaker for this bout, frantically went about the business of making a new match. Dozens of phone calls were made to various managers, promoters, and boxing gyms within a radius of ninety square miles. There had to be someone available, someone respectable, someone with a credible record. Even a criminal record would do.

Enter Mike "Machine Gun" Mungin. Mungin hadn't fought much in the past three years, and that's because he had been in prison. Upon his release, he fought on the undercard of Micky's fight with David Silva four months earlier. Once upon a time, he was considered a potential title contender, and his record now stood at 17–2. Katz thought that he had found his match, but he had to run it by Micky, Dickie, and their mom.

"We've got a guy from Philadelphia," Katz said as he rushed into the locker room of the Resorts International Hotel.

"Who is it?" Dickie asked.

"Mike Mungin."

"Didn't he just get out of jail?" Alice asked.

"Yeah, but you remember him. He fought on the card right here back in May. He lost to John Meekins. Really, Micky, this should be an easy win. You take him out, and we'll move into position for a title fight later this year."

In an effort to increase his foot speed and durability, Micky had begun training more with Nautilus equipment and came into this fight a little lighter than usual at 136 pounds, not a concern if he were to fight another junior welterweight. And since Mungin had been approved by Katz and the boxing commission, Micky had every right to assume that Mungin would come in at an appropriate weight.

But just a few hours before the fight, Mungin arrived weighing 154 pounds. Micky and his advisors, such as they were, were in quite a bind. Micky was the main event. If he backed out, the entire fight card would be canceled. Nobody would be paid. Micky had the option to turn down the fight, and who could blame him if he did? Weight divisions were established in boxing for a reason. Someone weighing eighteen pounds more than his opponent had a distinct advantage. The difference in size and strength could actually be dangerous for Micky, but as a former street fighter who routinely took on kids sixty pounds heavier than himself, Micky didn't seem too concerned.

"I'll fight him," Micky said.

A more astute manager might have attempted to talk Micky out of the fight. Even he concurs several years later.

"I shouldn't have fought Mungin," Micky says now. "I wish I had somebody around to tell me not to. I just told my mom and Dickie that I was gonna fight. What could they do?"

Matchmakers, managers, and promoters are in control of a boxer's career. Without them, boxers would spend an awful lot of time shadowboxing and perfecting their work on the speed bag. Alice could have stood up and said, "There's not going to be a fight unless you get somebody in here who qualifies as a junior welterweight."

Instead she renegotiated for more money, upping Micky's purse from fifteen thousand to seventeen thousand five hundred, and the fight was on.

Katz, Dickie, and Alice, all in good conscience, probably had every reason to believe that Micky would beat Mungin. That was a reasonable belief, and they probably held on to it right up until the time they saw Mungin with his shirt off.

He was huge—a tank, only stronger.

"Mungin's the strongest guy I ever fought, just because of the size," Micky recalls. "He could really punch hard. He was a strong kid. That was the first time I ever got knocked down."

With Mamby watching from ringside along with heavyweight champion Larry Holmes, Mungin stepped into the ring, and it was announced that he weighed in at 145 pounds. Micky and his family knew better. Micky weighed in at 136 pounds.

Mungin appeared to be in outstanding physical condition. He was cut. Bulging biceps, big shoulders, and abs of steel. Clearly, he'd been working out in jail, and training since his release. He was two inches shorter than Micky, but loomed much larger.

The plan was to stay away from Mungin for as long as it took for him to get tired, and then try to take him out. Dickie believed that Mungin, despite the physical appearances, would be out of shape and would get tired sooner. It was a sound strategy. But it didn't work.

There were too many times when Micky didn't jab enough, and Mungin was able to get on the inside where he could use his strength to his advantage. In those instances, Micky wasn't just getting hit. He was getting hurt.

"I think Micky is making a tremendous mistake by not trying to use the jab," Al Bernstein said during the ESPN broadcast. "Micky Ward's a good inside fighter, but he's facing a man who weighs a lot more than him. One forty-five is what he's listed at. Mungin could be at 150, and he's much stronger on the inside."

As Micky stood for the start of the fifth, Dickie started to leave the ring, but turned back for one final instruction, "Mick, the first thirty seconds, run! All right!"

They were still waiting for Mungin to show fatigue, but it only happened in spurts, then Mungin would appear revitalized and would begin to take control of the fight.

"Micky Ward is making this a really tough fight," Bernstein observed. "He's standing there taking those shots from Mungin. I'm not sure why. He's shown the ability to move. He's going to look back at this fight and realize the reason it was so difficult is because he didn't use his jab."

Micky's nose was bleeding intermittently throughout the fight. His cutman, Ed Aliano, known as "The Clot," was doing a good job keeping it under control between rounds, but each time Mungin connected, the blood would begin flowing. In the sixth round, a cut opened over

Micky's left eye. Micky was trading punches too often. In one exchange against the ropes, Mungin popped Micky's chin with a couple of uppercuts, snapping Micky's head upward like a Pez dispenser.

Late in the sixth, Micky made a crucial mistake. He pushed Mungin against the ropes preparing to trade blows on the inside, but then he thought better of it. He stepped away to regroup, dropping his hands just a bit, and Mungin sprang off the ropes and landed a fully extended straight right that sent Micky sprawling across the ring. Micky took three off-balance steps backward before falling to the canvas on his backside. It was the first time he'd been knocked down in his professional career. He popped up quickly, but he was clearly hurt.

As the round neared its conclusion, Micky tried to tie Mungin up, but Mungin broke free of the clinch and tossed Micky across the ring like a rag doll. Micky flew across the ring, landing face-first into the turnbuckle.

There wasn't much said in Micky's corner, nor was there much time to say it. Aliano had to tend to Micky's bloody nose and the cut above his eye. Dickie had to explain to the ring doctor that Micky was fine, and Micky had to confirm that by nodding his head and saying, "Yes, I can continue."

Despite Aliano's best efforts, Micky appeared for the seventh round still bleeding from his nose and eye.

"This would be an upset of major proportions if Mike Mungin could win this bout," Bernstein said. "Micky is taking a real beating at this stage."

Micky made it to the final bell. He made it through a fight in which he was knocked down for the first time. But Micky had never been so beaten up, not on the streets, and not in the ring. In the last round, another cut opened up. It was a nasty, deep gash high up on his left cheekbone just under his eye. It was swollen and wide open. In the end, Micky's face was bleeding from three different places. He looked awful, and Mungin didn't have a mark on him.

Waiting for the decision was a formality. Micky knew he had lost. Mungin knew he had won. The three judges were less certain. All of them scored the fight for Mungin, but two of them had it 95–94, and the third scored it 96–93. They were the only three people who witnessed the fight who thought it was that close.

Back in the locker room after the fight, Micky received a surprise visit from Carmen Graziano, a well-known trainer from New Jersey. Graziano offered Micky his business card right in front of Dickie and offered to train him.

"Give me a call if you ever want some help," Graziano said. "And by the way, that was bullshit. You should never have fought that kid. You should have just took your money and went home."

But not taking the fight was never an option for Micky.

Micky's second loss in the last twelve months wasn't much of a setback. Promoter Bob Arum saw it for what it was—a mismatch. Micky was a junior welterweight, and he had lost to a middleweight.

"They shouldn't have fought," Arum was quoted as saying in the *Boston Globe*. "Losing in this case is no big deal."

Then he confirmed that Micky would be headlining at the Boston Garden in November against a highly ranked perennial contender named Harold Brazier for the North American Boxing Federation (NABF) junior welterweight championship.

"That's an important fight," Arum said.

But that fight didn't happen. The problem with Micky's right hand had been exacerbated during the Mungin fight and got worse during training. He couldn't hit the heavy bag two consecutive days without his hand swelling up. There was no way he could be ready on November 15. He was, however, ready for a quick tune-up a month later.

It was a mere three months after his loss to Mungin that Micky was back inside the same ring at Resorts International taking on the Brazilian junior welterweight champion, Francisco Tomas Da Cruz.

Micky entered the ring with his white robe and trunks, the robe still reading MICKEY WARD with the incorrect *e* in his first name. Mickey O'Keefe, whose name *is* spelled with the *e*, and who had trained Micky a dozen years ago in the Silver Mittens, joined Dickie in the corner for this fight. O'Keefe had been assisting Micky and Dickie at the gym for the past couple of months, and Dickie was impressed with his contributions in such a short time.

The referee, Ted Pick, brought the fighters to the center of the ring, voiced the customary instructions and said, "Give me a nice clean fight. Good luck to both of you."

Da Cruz came out and landed beautiful body shots, but they weren't punishing like Micky's could be, and Micky was starting to land a few.

"Micky taps you here," O'Keefe explains pointing to his head, and then to his ribs. "Then he taps you there, and then he steps. Then it's harder. Then it's faster. And that's how it wears you down."

Sometimes the wearing-down process took a little longer. They call it chopping down a tree. Usually that takes a lot of swings with an axe, but that tree eventually falls. Tonight, Da Cruz fell in the third round.

The crowd was quiet until Micky switched to his southpaw stance and tapped Da Cruz with a soft shot to the head. Micky immediately followed it up with a left hook that he slipped below Da Cruz's right elbow, nailing him in the ribs. The fans knew right away that that shot did some damage.

Da Cruz bounced away from Micky and fell back into the ropes, but the ropes propelled him back toward Micky, who had now returned to his orthodox, righty stance. Unable to strike the flailing target, Micky returned to the body. Da Cruz dropped to both knees. He was able to rise quickly, but while Pick began counting, Da Cruz indicated that he was in too much pain to continue. With fifteen seconds to go in the third round, the fight was stopped, and Micky was back. He was a winner again.

"Micky's got a gift," O'Keefe says. "God gave him a gift. He's got little hands. It's like he's got a woman's fingers. I shit on him about it all the time. But when he puts that glove on, it becomes a part of him. . . . And when he hits with that hook to the body, it's like being shot. It feels like it comes out the other side. And when you see guys with that delayed reaction, and then they fall. That's what it is."

O'Keefe knows firsthand what he's talking about. Micky cracked O'Keefe's ribs during a sparring session once.

A month later, Micky faced the biggest fight of his career—a title fight—for the USBA's junior welterweight champion. All he had to do was beat Frankie Warren, a task far easier said than done.

At thirty years old, Warren was considered a seasoned veteran whose age had yet to significantly slow him down. He was hard to hit, and he hit hard. With that style Warren had won his first twenty-five fights before dropping a lopsided decision to Buddy McGirt in a battle for the vacant IBF title. Warren won his next two fights and the USBA title along with it. Now he was putting it on the line against an up-and-coming Irish kid from Massachusetts.

Granted the USBA title wasn't as prestigious as the WBC (World Boxing Council), the IBF, or the WBA, but it was a title, and it could lead to another one. This was the shot that could give Micky a series of bigger and better shots.

Micky was only twenty-three, preparing for a championship fight, and soon to be a father. Laurie was pregnant. It was joyous news for both of them. Though they weren't married, they were living together, and they were happy. As one of nine children, Micky was excited to be starting a family of his own, and he was confident that boxing would provide his child with a good home and a sense of security. Things were happening very quickly now.

It was a *CBS Sports Sunday* telecast when Micky Ward met Frankie Warren at Caesars in Atlantic City on January 15, 1989. By this time, Micky was ranked number ten by the USBA. Warren was the champion. He was also ranked fourth in the IBF and number nine in the WBA. Micky was stepping up to the big time.

More than a hundred people from Lowell came to New Jersey to see Micky's championship bout. Among them were his mother, father, and seven sisters. They were all ringside. Dickie was in the corner along with O'Keefe. The fight took place three days after Dickie had been arrested for drunk driving.

O'Keefe had been there off and on since Micky's days in the Silver Mittens, and it was O'Keefe who kept Micky training long after Dickie would say, "That's enough." O'Keefe had watched several tapes of Warren's fights, and he told Micky:

"Right now, Frankie Warren is in the gym. He's in there right now, and he's on that heavy bag going *bop, bop, bop, bop.* . . . He's gonna come after you, and he's not gonna stop throwing punches."

So, Micky and Mickey continued their long days of training. If Micky was going to lose this fight, it wasn't going to be because he was unprepared or not in good enough shape.

Warren was tiny, and he was huge at the same time. He stood only 5-foot-3, and possessed squatty little legs. But he had broad shoulders, a thick chest, and rock-solid arms. He stayed low and lunged forward with his jab, and that's how he got himself within range to land his vicious body blows. He threw with everything he had and was relentless in his pursuit of Micky.

Early on, Micky was taking a beating. It was as if he knew Warren couldn't hurt him, so he didn't worry about the punches that were landing. Most of them were landing on his arms anyway, but he wasn't even trying to avoid them. He didn't move his feet much, and he didn't make Warren worry about return blows.

Micky finally landed a good body shot with his left hand in the fourth round. He followed that up with a solid right and a big left-hand uppercut. Another body shot, and a left hook to the head that rocked Warren. The fight was turning in Micky's favor.

"He does have a beautiful left hook to the body," CBS analyst Gil Clancy said. "I hope he utilizes it."

But Warren was able to retreat and jab his way out of trouble. Soon, Warren was back on the attack, once again throwing nonstop punches. The fight resumed its original pattern. Warren was perpetual motion, by far the busier fighter, and Micky tried to be economical and efficient. It wasn't working.

Alice Ward left her seat after the sixth round and went over to speak with Micky. She told him what Dickie and Mickey O'Keefe had been telling him all night long.

"You have to fight back, Micky," she said. "This is for the title, honey. Look at him. He just keeps punching. You do that, and you'll win."

Her words of encouragement went unheeded. The next six rounds were identical to the previous six. Micky was pounded to the body with wide, looping punches. When he engaged and fired punches in combinations, he got the better of Warren. When he stood there and let Warren beat him like a heavy bag, he lost the rounds.

"Frankie Warren does leave himself open," Clancy said. "But Micky just doesn't punch at all. With Warren, the shoulders are coming at you, the head is coming at you. The punches keep coming, and he always gets off first."

Before the decision was announced, Clancy concluded, "Even if Micky Ward loses this fight, he's going to learn what it takes to be a top-ten contender."

Micky lost on the scorecards of all three judges. Lynne Carter scored it 117–111. Al Morris had it 116–112. And Joseph Pasquale saw a slightly more even contest, but gave it to Warren, 115–113.

Micky had lost his first title shot. In order to reposition himself in the junior welterweight division, he had to take a small step backwards. The opponent chosen for him was twenty-five-year-old Clarence Coleman. It was Coleman whom Frankie Warren had beaten for the USBA light welterweight title in July 1988, only six months before Warren defended that title against Ward. That made Coleman a perfect match. He was eminently beatable, but he still represented a quality opponent. Beating him would put Micky right back on track, and losing to him wouldn't completely derail Micky's career. So, with Laurie eight months pregnant, Micky returned to Atlantic City to fight "Classy" Clarence Coleman at the Showboat Hotel on May 23, 1989.

Micky jogged to the ring in his white silk robe. Dickie led the way. Richie Bryan was right behind them. Micky's robe had his name, MICKY WARD, on the back. Dickie's shirt still read MICKEY WARD.

Micky needed a win. He entered the ring as a hungry fighter, and he was met by a man equally starved for a victory. Coleman had followed up his loss to Warren with a loss to Tony Martin, so he needed to win to be considered a contender.

In the fifth, it looked to be over.

"A big right hand again by Ward drives Coleman back into the ropes," play-by-play announcer Barry Tomkins exclaimed. "That hurt Coleman. An uppercut! And another right hand. And Coleman's in trouble. A left hand drives him back into the ropes, and down goes Coleman."

It had as much to do with the pressure as the punishment. Micky's punches were coming from all directions, and all Coleman could do was dodge and duck and flail with his back against the ropes. The assault was so fast and furious that Coleman wasn't able to throw anything back. He finally collapsed to the canvas. Perez jumped in to protect him, and Coleman bounced right back up.

Tomkins reported, "There is still a ways to go here in round number five for Clarence Coleman, and Micky Ward will try to get him out of there right now. An uppercut again!"

Coleman's head snapped back from the force of a right-hand uppercut. Coleman was wobbling as he backed up. Micky had finally found his distance. He was landing the uppercut repeatedly and forcefully. Micky got Coleman with a good body shot and another uppercut, leaving him slumped against the ropes. That was it. Perez waved off Micky and stopped the fight.

Ron Katz, who eventually took over the East Coast promotions for Top Rank when Teddy Brenner grew ill, said, "The objective with Micky was to put him in solid fights, show him different styles, and then maneuver him into a world championship, and then go from there."

But when all the maneuvering was done, Micky wasn't ready. His hands consistently held him back, either because he couldn't train sufficiently or because he couldn't fight effectively. There remained plenty of faith in a healthy Micky Ward, but an injured Micky Ward was attracting some doubters.

In one way, however, the injuries to his hands turned out to be a blessing in disguise. Four weeks after his victory over Coleman, Micky became a father. Kasie, a beautiful baby girl, was born on June 20, 1989. Micky put his boxing career on hold and became a stay-at-home dad, although he continued paving to bring in some much-needed cash. After the Coleman fight, Micky wouldn't fight again for nine months. It was a long, unwanted, and unplanned vacation made a little easier by the birth of his daughter. Micky needed to provide for his growing family. He needed to get out of the house and into a six-thousand-seat arena and make some money punching someone in the ribs.

That was the plan for August 8, 1989, when Micky was scheduled to fight Harold Brazier for the NABF super lightweight title, but Micky hurt his knuckles just a few days before that fight and had to withdraw. The knuckles couldn't have hurt as much as watching Livingstone Bramble knock out Brazier in the second round. It was Micky's replacement winning the title that night, not Micky. Fragile hands are the bane of many fighters' existences, but each time Micky's hands let him down, he had to wonder if they would have betrayed him so early and so often in his career if he had stayed out of the fray at the Cosmo that night. How much was that night going to cost him?

When Micky finally stepped back into the ring in February 1990, he was still celebrating his daughter's birth, but he was also mourning his good friend's death. John D. Donarumo (Johnny Dunn's real name) died of heart failure at his home in Chelsea on December 8, 1989. He was eighty-three years old. A month before his death, he was at the gym training local fighters.

"This fight is for Johnny," Ward was quoted at the time. "He always told me to do the right thing. He said to always be in shape. And when you make money, don't be stupid with it."

Dunn had worked with world champions Terry Downes and Bob Foster, and he had worked with Dickie Eklund and Micky Ward. He had promised to make Dickie a champion, but he had no way of knowing the directions that Dickie would travel. So, over time, he transferred that promise to Micky. He told Micky, "Before I die,

Mick, I'm gonna help you get that championship belt." Indeed, Micky had fought for a championship against Frankie Warren, but he didn't win. He still had the promise. But the man in the big glasses, with the thick cigar and shoe-polished hair who walked with Dickie up the aisle and between the ropes the night he fought Sugar Ray Leonard was gone.

The Leonard–Eklund fight was held at the Hynes Convention Center in Boston back in 1978. Now, almost twelve years later, Dickie was back at the Convention Center, watching Micky saunter out to the middle of the ring to trade blows. Standing across from Micky on a frigid February night was another Bay State banger from Attleboro, David Rivello. Four years earlier, Rivello had won a majority decision over Freddie Roach at the Lowell Auditorium, a result that had convinced Roach that it was time to retire.

The Rivello fight would be Micky's first without Johnny Dunn in his corner, but Dunn's spirit was somewhere in that smoke-filled room. And Micky made good on his dedication to his longtime mentor. He completely dominated the fight. Micky hadn't sparred in more than six weeks because of a fractured thumb, and he had a little trouble getting down to the 138-pound weight limit, so he wasn't as strong as he would have liked, which is probably why the fight ended up going the distance.

By the time it was over, Rivello was badly cut over his right eye. He was bleeding from his nose and from a cut on his mouth, and he had a badly swollen left eye.

"I learned that it's a different world from regional fights to world-class fights," Rivello said. "Those guys play for keeps. I fought my heart out. I did the best I could, but the things you can do to the guys around here you can't do with a world-class fighter like Micky."

Soon after, Micky was back in Atlantic City with a chance to win the IBF Inter-Continental junior welterweight title. It was another one of the underwhelming titles offered primarily to give a fight a little extra cache.

The importance of the fight must have been lost on Dickie, because he prepared to enter the ring with his brother by throwing a huge party in his hotel room the night before.

Micky didn't go to the party, but his room was right next to Dickie's, so it was impossible for him to get a good night's sleep.

The next day, Micky entered the ring with a black robe with a green shamrock on the back. Dozens of loyal fans held up signs reading WE LOVE MICKY! Harold Brazier came down the aisle a few minutes later wearing a red robe with black trim. He was three pounds heavier than Micky and three times more experienced. Brazier's record was 67–10–1, a total of seventy-eight professional fights. Micky had fought only twenty-four pro fights, losing only three, so far. Brazier had twice as many knockouts, fifty, than Micky had fights. He was ten years older, that much wiser, and had a reputation for being a harder puncher.

Micky took his robe off and revealed black trunks with white lettering and a lean, muscular frame. Dickie gave him a gentle shoulder rub during the pre-fight instructions from referee Rudy Battle, and then the battle was on.

Brazier, recognizing that Micky had come in a little light, went immediately to the body. In each of the first two rounds, Micky bounced around the ring, content to stay on the outside in the early going. Brazier worked to cut off the ring, but Micky easily slid along the ropes, switching seamlessly from his traditional stance to southpaw. Late in the second round, Micky threw his head-tap-and-body-blow combination, and Brazier responded with an effective flurry to close out the round.

"Listen," Dickie said to Micky in the corner. "When you're throwing those punches, hook, jab, hook, move around again. Don't let him get off four or five straight punches. That's how he wants to beat you. Hook to the head, hook to the body. Move around, side to side. Feint him. All right? When you're just standing there in the corner, he's adding up points, and that's what he wants."

Late in the fourth round, Brazier accidentally delivered a shot right to Micky's cup. Protected and relatively unfazed, Micky relaxed momentarily, anticipating that Battle would step in and call the low blow. Battle wasn't as quick as Brazier. When Micky relaxed, he let his hands drop, and Brazier stung him with a hard right hand. That was the best punch of the night. Battle did step in, belatedly, sending Brazier to a neutral corner, and that gave Micky time to recover from both the low blow and the head shot. But there was no point deduction for the low blow, and the fight continued.

"Fight back, man!" Dickie screamed in the corner, barely noticing the egglike swelling that had formed under Micky's right eye. "Fight back!"

Micky tried, but something wasn't right. He was tiring quickly. Twice in the fifth round, he stepped away from an even exchange of punches and took a deep breath. He was winded and needed a moment to inhale deeply.

By now the fight was slipping away from Micky. It didn't appear that he had won even one of the first seven rounds. Brazier had landed 218 punches to Micky's 76. His attack was relentless.

"Harold Brazier has a look in his eye that is different than what I've ever seen from him before," ESPN analyst Al Bernstein said during the broadcast. "He is so intent on winning this fight. It just looks in his eye that nothing is going to stop him."

Play-by-play announcer Barry Tomkins added after the eighth round, "Brazier, who has spent some time as an auto-body mechanic, is putting a dent in Micky Ward tonight. Another workmanlike round by a workmanlike fighter, by Harold Brazier who is piling up the points."

Micky only landed four punches in the eighth. He was bleeding from cuts on the bridge of his nose, on the outside of his left nostril, and under his right eye. He looked beaten and worn out as he returned to his corner before the final round.

"You have to knock him out, Micky!" Dickie shouted and repeated what was obvious to everyone. "You have to knock him out!"

The knockout never came. Micky never responded with the necessary desperation. The last round looked a lot like the first, except that Micky's face showed the ill effects of being beaten for an additional half hour.

"I may be rhapsodizing over Harold Brazier tonight, but this is a special performance," Bernstein summarized. "For Harold to be doing this a year after a rotator cuff injury, this man willed his way back. A virtuoso performance."

The body blows and the sleepless night conspired against Micky in his attempt for the twelfth-round knockout. He fired wildly in the final minute of the round, but took as good as he gave until the final bell sounded.

All three judges scored the fight 118–110 for Brazier. It was the right decision, just as the party the night before had been the wrong decision.

Micky hung his head in disappointment. He had just lost the third of his last six fights. He had failed in his attempt to win the USBA light welterweight title against Frankie Warren, and he had failed to win the IBF Inter-Continental light welterweight title from Harold Brazier. His hands hurt, and his future looked bleak. He turned and looked at Dickie, who wrapped his arm around Micky's shoulder and led him away from the ring. Back in the locker room, the mood was sullen. Few words were spoken. Micky stepped into the shower and let the warm water run over him. He thought about the twelve rounds he had just fought and the things he wished he'd done differently. He thought about the pain in his hands and the number of days it would take for the swelling to go down enough for him to lift his ten-month-old daughter without grimacing. And he thought about Dickie.

Dickie had always tried to look out for his little brother. He had been bringing him to the gym since he was old enough to lug around an equipment bag. He was the reason Micky became a boxer in the first place. He was a big part of the reason why Micky was there that night at the Resorts International in Atlantic City fighting for a title. Dickie was an excellent trainer—when he was around. He was a terrific sparring partner—when he showed up. He was a trusted ally—when there weren't doubts about how he prioritized boxing, parties, and drugs. Micky knew that Dickie was doing the best he could for him, but he had to wonder if Dickie's best was good enough.

Micky stayed under the showerhead long enough for the water to run cold, but still he didn't move. His mind was filled with more pressing concerns.

"I'm alone in the ring anyway," he thought. "So, what should it matter if Dickie's partying all night? I wasn't tired in there. Yes, it's a pain in the ass to have to waste time tracking him down and dragging him out of crack houses, but if I'm distracted, that's on me. That's my fault. I've got no one to blame but myself. I need a champion's focus. I have to throw more punches. I have to forget about my hands hurting. If I ever get another chance at a title, I'm going to win it or lose it on my own."

He was right, and he knew it, but he also knew that a fighter is at his best when the conditions around him are at their optimum. No disagreements with the manager. No tension with the trainer. The less stress the better. Micky didn't have that. He had Dickie.

"He's your brother, Micky," his mom would say. "And you're good for him. Who knows what would happen to him if he didn't have you and the boxing to keep him busy?"

Working as a trainer was the only thing Dickie was qualified to do, so training his brother, who just happened to be a world-class boxer, made sense. Furthermore, the better Micky performed, the more money there would be to go around, the more fame and recognition there would be for everyone involved.

For Dickie, it had to be difficult. His love for Micky seemed genuine and deep, but every step Micky took toward the top of the mountain was a reminder to Dickie of what he himself could have been.

By now, the water in the shower was freezing, and Micky suddenly became aware of it. He jumped back, and with a skilled boxer's lateral movement, sidestepped the water streams, and threw a straight left toward the faucet to turn the water off. Micky dressed slowly, still thinking about his future. He was determined to keep fighting, to work toward another title shot, and to get to the top with his brother, Dickie, by his side.

When he was ready to go, Micky left with Mickey O'Keefe, who had always been in his corner, either literally or figuratively, the man who had never been a distraction, who had never been anything but kind. Three months later, Dickie was arrested again for disorderly conduct. It was his fourteenth arrest, and he had served only a matter of days in prison.

CHAPTER SIX

It didn't take long for Micky to get yet another chance at the now-vacant USBA light welterweight title. At one time, Micky was the hot prospect who was put in the ring against fighters with better reputations than punches. Now, after losing a couple of big fights, Micky was the veteran who could serve as the launching pad for a young up-and-comer. That was Charles "The Natural" Murray, undefeated at 17–0, but with no experience against a guy with Micky's pedigree, talent, or experience. This could be a fight that could make Murray or break Micky.

It took place at the War Memorial in Rochester, New York, Murray's hometown. Murray had an abundance of supporters, and so did Micky. In his corner were Dickie, his father, George Ward, and perhaps the man he trusted most, Mickey O'Keefe.

But Micky didn't seem to have the fire on this night. He looked like a fighter without confidence and no apparent plan.

As Micky approached the corner following the fifth round, Dickie jumped between the ropes, put both hands on Micky's shoulders, and pushed him toward the stool imploring him, "Micky, you gotta punch! You've gotta fight! They know they've got to stop you in the next couple of rounds, because you're gonna tear him apart, but don't get hit in the process. Just fight. Don't let it go that long!"

Micky didn't seem especially hurt, nor did he seem especially inspired. Through six rounds, Murray had landed ninety more punches, 163–73. ESPN's Al Bernstein was starting to wonder if this fight might not go the distance.

"It would be an unbelievable feather in Charles Murray's cap if he could knock Micky Ward out," Bernstein said.

Round seven may have been the worst of Micky's career. Murray picked his spots and landed his shots with power and precision. Micky whiffed on each of his counters. Micky was being outclassed by a twenty-two-year-old kid.

"Micky is just not the same fighter he once was," Bernstein said. "He might be much closer to the end of his career than to the beginning or the middle."

It was an observation that was both sad and accurate. Micky was going down without a fight, but his corner wasn't.

"Now you look like Micky Ward," O'Keefe exaggerated after Micky's moderately effective flurry ended the tenth round. "Now you're doing it!"

"Are you gonna do it?" Dickie asked.

O'Keefe continued, "If you want this fight, you gotta go get it! You're fighting nobody over there! Two rounds. Give it every fucking thing you've got!"

"Don't go out there and give it away," Dickie ordered. "You're giving away the entire round. Don't just come alive in the last thirty seconds. You're losing! You've got to knock him out! You've got to knock him out! And you can do it!"

And finally, from O'Keefe, "He's setting you up. He's waiting for that big right hand. Now beat him to it, Micky!"

Spurred on by his corner and acknowledging some sense of urgency, Micky's best rounds were the eleventh and twelfth, but it was too little and too late. At the end of the night Murray had landed 398 punches to Micky's 171.

Micky walked back to his corner. Dickie patted Micky's shoulder, and O'Keefe rubbed him down with a towel, and they all waited for the decision to be announced. It was unanimous. All three judges gave Micky the first round and awarded Murray the next eleven.

"I went twelve," Murray said. "He looked like he was there to survive. He wasn't opening up, so I went out and did what I was supposed to."

Micky was surviving, but no longer thriving inside the ring or outside of it. His job paving streets barely managed to cover the bills. He added various construction jobs to his workload to earn extra money, and he knew he had to be ready whenever another fight came his way, so he kept training as much as he could. As a result, he was seldom home, and when he was, he was moody. A rift began to form between him and Laurie. She had signed on to be with Micky Ward, the local celebrity, the boxer with the promise to make serious cash. She liked the limelight, even if it was only concentrated in a small community. She wasn't sure she wanted to spend her life with a road paver. Micky took another seven months off before getting back into the ring. It would have been a good idea for him to grab a couple of easy tune-up fights in order to build his confidence back up, but his handlers at Top Rank kept matching him with tough opponents. And Micky's mom, Alice, approved the matches because she believed that Micky could win, and that would position him for title shots and paydays.

Micky says, "My mother did a good enough job as a manager. I don't know, there were a bunch of fights there in a row where every one of them was a tough fight. I lost my confidence. I just think Ron Katz and Top Rank threw me to the wolves, putting me in there with guys who were trying to kill me. It would have been better to get a couple of easy fights, build up my confidence. Without confidence you're hesitant. I was nervous before those fights. You start having thoughts about losing, or what if I didn't train hard enough. Will I be able to handle everything? I kept going in there against contenders, and it wasn't good."

Micky did have an offer for new management from Ben Doherty, who had trained Micky at the Billerica Boys Club nearly
fourteen years earlier. Doherty, who was on his way to becoming the
Massachusetts boxing commissioner, tells the story that he and a
couple of friends were looking for a fighter to back. Their plan was
to invest money in a fighter, pay him a weekly salary, and cover the
training costs—that sort of thing. They hoped to see a return on their
investment when the fighter started making big money. Doherty
offered to form a corporation called the Micky Ward Association.

Doherty talked with Micky, first on the phone, and later at a
dinner meeting, and explained the terms of the deal. Micky would
earn five hundred dollars a week, and he'd do all of his training in
Providence, Rhode Island.

"It was critical that we get him out of Lowell," Doherty says,
echoing the sentiments of Skeets Scioli who had long ago told Micky
to "Get the hell out of Lowell."

Micky agreed to the deal, and the wheels were put in motion,
but everything fell apart about a week later.

"I called to talk to Micky to set up another meeting," Doherty
explains. "And his mother answered the phone. She was wild! She
started blasting away and said we weren't going to take over. 'I'm
going to manage him,' she says. 'He's my son.'"

Doherty believed that Alice Ward "single-handedly destroyed
the careers of Beau Jaynes, Larry Carney, and Dickie Eklund," so he
asked her, "Why are you going to destroy Micky's career, too?"
Micky was forced to back out of the deal.

Years later, after he became boxing commissioner, Doherty frequently barred Alice from entering the ring.

"She wanted to get up there in her high heels, and that was dangerous," Doherty says. "She was really bullshit at me for that, even
threatened to punch me out."

Doherty's biggest criticism of Alice was that she, along with Top
Rank, overmatched Micky, giving him too many tough fights, and
giving them to him consecutively. His point was made when the next
wolf to come knocking on Micky's door was a twenty-eight-year-old

from Philadelphia named Tony "Pound for Pound" Martin, another legitimate contender. Like Micky, Martin had already beaten Joey Ferrell and Johnny Rafuse. Martin also had dominated Livingstone Bramble, the former WBA lightweight champion who had beaten Edwin Curet twice, and who had scored a second-round knockout of Harold Brazier. Essentially, Micky was fighting a guy who had beaten a guy who had beaten a couple of guys who had beaten him. This would not be easy.

While preparing for the Martin fight, Alice Ward persuaded Micky to accept the help of another trainer, Carmen Graziano, the man who had approached Micky after the Mungin fight. Graziano knew boxing, and he also thought he knew what Micky's biggest problem was. He thought Micky was running on empty at the end of his fights, and he thought the cause of the empty tank was a dearth of electrolytes. Micky tended to lose as many as five pounds during a sparring session, so Graziano started pouring orange-flavored Gatorade into him. It wasn't a bad idea, but Micky had bigger problems than electrolytes.

The two fighters met at the Trump Taj Mahal in Atlantic City. Micky had been losing with regularity while Martin had won each of his last seven fights and entered the ring with a record of 22–3. Sugar Ray Leonard, who was calling the fight for ESPN along with Al Bernstein, summed things up for Micky as the fight began.

"Micky has been very tentative in his last two fights. He has to be a lot more aggressive. He can't lay back. He has to take the initiative."

Leonard also ran into his former opponent Dickie Eklund, who told him, "My brother's going to rush out and be aggressive."

But it didn't happen. Micky landed all of six punches in the first round. He was covering up, and putting his back against the ropes.

"C'mon, Micky!" Dickie shouted from the corner. "Head, body! Pick it up. Head, body."

Micky didn't listen, so Dickie tried again in between rounds.

"You've got to get to him," Dickie urged. "Don't stay like that. I want you to get him this round. No more waiting. No more waiting! This is it. Do or die! No more waiting. He realizes, Micky, that he can't really get to you, so he's blocking. Now, you've got to show him. *Punch!*"

Dickie screamed the last word, but he could tell it hadn't sunk in. So he continued.

"You must earn his respect, Micky. You haven't got it. Are you going to fire this round?"

Micky responded, "Yeah."

"Are you gonna loosen up?"

Again the response, "Yeah."

"Go at him! Go, Micky!"

Just two rounds into the fight, and there was already a desperate cry coming from Dickie. He had seen this from his brother before. It wasn't easy to watch, and it was guaranteed to spell defeat.

"It becomes a mental thing," Leonard explained. "After a fighter suffers a couple of losses, a fighter can get a mental block."

Micky had nothing all night. After the bell, Martin raised his arms in victory. Micky hugged him and congratulated him and then ambled over to his corner. He put on a blue baseball cap and smiled while the scores were announced. Micky lost another lopsided unanimous decision: 98–92, 98–92, and 97–93.

He was no longer a young, promising fighter. He wasn't a contender or an up-and-comer maneuvering for a shot at a title. He wasn't even a cagey old veteran. The lasting images he was leaving in the eyes and minds of promoters and fight fans was that Micky Ward was an inactive fighter, a boring fighter, and a loser. Being a white Irish kid who could fight had been his meal ticket. Now, all he had was his ethnicity, his bad hands, and no confidence.

After his loss to Martin, Micky went back to paving roads and waited for the phone to ring. When the call finally came in, it wasn't exactly what he was looking for. Boston radio celebrity Eddie Andelman was attempting to put together an all–New England fight card in August 1991. Andelman planned to have as the main event a rematch between Micky Ward and Johnny Rafuse. Their first fight had taken place five years earlier, and fans immediately began clamoring for a rematch. But Micky and his family weren't satisfied with the five-thousand-dollar offer for the fight and began haggling over money. Rafuse wasn't happy about the money either and demanded at least twice the proposed purse.

Neither fighter was in much of a position to demand anything. Micky had lost three straight fights, and nobody was knocking down his doors offering him more than five grand to fight anybody. For his part, Rafuse had lost ten fights since he had last faced Micky, including fights with common opponents such as Edwin Curet, Tony Martin, Harold Brazier, and Joey Ferrell.

The Andelman promotion, with Andelman receiving a lot of help from Al Valenti, was scheduled for mid-August at Boston University's Nickerson Field. Micky had just fought in May and said he wanted a couple of tune-up fights before he fought Rafuse, but there wasn't going to be time for that. Ultimately, Andelman and Valenti tired of dealing with Micky's demands and delays and matched Rafuse with Miguel Santana, who had briefly been the IBF lightweight champion a few years earlier. That fight, not surprisingly, never came off either, and Rafuse ended up beating Jose Hiram Torres of Hartford, Connecticut. It was not the fight New Englanders were hoping to see. Torres was 6–8 when he fought Rafuse, and wound up losing forty-eight of his sixty-three professional fights.

Micky found another opportunity. He was given one more shot at either proving himself or proving to be a stepping-stone for another fighter. On October 15, 1991, Micky returned to Atlantic City to fight a young prospect named Ricky Meyers. The fight would be broadcast on the USA Network, and Micky more than doubled the five grand he had been offered to fight Rafuse. It was a good move on his part. More money, more exposure, more to gain, and less risk.

"Micky is tough, and rugged," Meyers said respectfully before the fight. "His fights have come against quality opponents. This is a chance for me to prove that I belong. I'm going to be coming forward and aggressive. I'm going to be moving my head, and just coming in and making him miss, and pressing him, working the body and wearing him down."

Micky said he'd be ready. "He thinks he's gonna be getting the same guy that was in there running and stopping and letting the guy punch," Micky said, referring to his bout with Charles Murray. "That ain't gonna be the case. I'm gonna fight, throw more punches. That's the bottom line, gotta throw punches. If I keep throwing punches, there's no way he can beat me."

Micky walked into the ring at the Broadway by the Bay Theater at Harrah's Hotel and Casino in Atlantic City wearing black trunks with multicolored trim, weighing 142 pounds. Ricky "The Rock" Meyers met Micky in the ring weighing 141.5 pounds and wearing red trunks with gold trim.

The two men stared each other down with white-hot intensity as legendary referee Arthur Mercante gave them the pre-fight instructions. Mercante had already worked ninety-five world championships, so Micky and Ricky were in good hands.

After the first round, a round in which Micky did not live up to his promise to keep throwing punches, Meyers returned to his corner and was told by his trainer, Kevin Rooney, "He's got nothing. Go right at him."

Two minutes into the second round, Micky tried to connect with a big left hand, but failed. The miss threw him off balance, and he finished in a low crouch. He was vulnerable and Meyers countered by clubbing him with a hard right to the top of Micky's head. Micky rose and felt a left hand sting him with tremendous power. Micky went down in a heap.

It was only the second time in his career that he'd been down. He was more embarrassed than hurt, and he sprang back to his feet. Mercante wiped Micky's gloves on his shirt and signaled for the fighters to resume action. Micky aggressively fired another hard left. He missed and slipped to one knee. It was not ruled a knockdown, and the fight continued uninterrupted. It must have appeared to Meyers that Micky was hurt and working on wobbly legs, because he went after Micky with ferocity. Micky took several big shots and was unable to respond in kind.

Former lightweight champion Sean O'Grady, who was calling the fight for USA Network, said that he had been with Micky before the fight and noticed that his right hand was badly swollen. The doctor must have seen it as well, because on the morning of a fight, a doctor gives each fighter a physical. During the examination, the doctor routinely squeezes the fighter's hands and asks if there's any pain. Certainly Micky had pain, but he had learned not to grimace.

In the fifth, Meyers just pummeled Micky in the midsection. After witnessing another three minutes of his brother being beaten, Dickie asked in the corner, "Do you feel like fighting? Are you okay? If you want to fight, get out there and throw punches."

But it was clear that Micky was just going through the motions. O'Grady noticed it, too, and said, "At the age of twenty-six, he could be a shot fighter. You know when fighters see the punches, and they can't get out of the way, or they stand around and they do nothing, and they wait for their opponents to score, they may be nearing the end of their career."

O'Grady was saying what no one in Micky's camp had wanted to say up to that point. O'Grady continued, "Micky's worrying about taking a year off and letting his hands heal. If I were him, I would take the year off now . . . get my hands fixed, and then decide a year from today if I'm gonna box anymore."

By the end of the sixth, Dickie was beside himself with anger and frustration. As bad as Micky had looked in other fights, he had never looked this bad. He was still going out there round after round, but he looked like a quitter.

"Punch!" Dickie yelled two inches away from Micky's face. "As soon as you get in there, bang, bang! If he moves like this, hit him in the back of the head. What are you, stupid? He's doing it to you."

Micky gave no response, no acknowledgment that he had heard a word of Dickie's tongue-lashing. His focus, along with any chance of winning the fight on points, was gone.

"You've got to knock him out," fellow cornerman Carmen Graziano said. Then Dickie added the necessary punctuation, "You're a fighter. What are you, a jerk? *Punch!*"

Micky went back out for more abuse. When they got to the tenth round, Micky was as listless as he had been in the prior nine rounds. The best anyone could say about Micky's performance that night was said by O'Grady, a former boxer who had great respect for all boxers. O'Grady said, "A lot of guts from Micky Ward. He's put up a good little match, even though it's been one-sided. He could have easily checked out of this fight. Nobody would have said a word. He's taken some big shots."

All three judges scored the fight 99–90 in favor of Ricky Meyers, and the *Boston Globe*'s Ron Borges wrote a few days later, "Lowell's Micky Ward got hurt early and pounded around by Ricky Meyers last Tuesday in Atlantic City, losing a lopsided decision. In case his mother, who manages him, hasn't noticed, it's time to stop."

Micky did stop. He retired from boxing just like 99 percent of all boxers—a hard-luck loser. As always, boxing had been honest. It told a fighter exactly what he was. Micky had tried, and he had failed. That seemed to be the inescapable destiny for tough kids from Lowell. Micky returned to Lowell unfulfilled, unsatisfied, still hungry, and disappointed. He had been unable to bring a championship home. Knocked down and bloodied, he got back up on a street roller in Lowell and tried to make an honest living.

CHAPTER SEVEN

The decision to retire did not come easy, and it did not come without consultation. When a person is faced with a life-altering decision, that person tends to seek the counsel of a trusted advisor. Micky chose Richie Bryan, a friend who had been with him through the good times and bad, and who never asked him for anything but friendship.

"I'm thinking about retiring," Micky said on the phone one night.

"Go ahead," Richie responded without hesitation. Micky was surprised by how quickly Richie had agreed to the possibility. Richie's response did not come across as a dare. It was more like encouragement.

"You know, they want me to fight," Micky said. He didn't specify who "they" were. His parents, Dickie, even Top Rank wanted him to keep going, because Micky still had a recognizable name and a decent record. They could keep setting him up as the fall guy for younger, more promising talents. Micky knew they were using him. He knew that any blood spilled would be his. He also knew that there had been too many days that he trained without the enthusiasm he once had and there were too many nights when he went inside the ring uninspired. Richie knew all this, too.

"Nothing for nothing, Mick," Richie said. "But you gotta do what you want to do. It's not what this one wants or that one. You had a decent career. You have nothing to be ashamed of. You're not into it. You're not fightin'. Your head's not into it. Your hands are bad. You've got plenty of reasons to quit."

"But everybody wants me to fight."

"Fuck everybody! Sure they want you to fight, but they're not in there getting hit. You are. The fire's not there. You're getting beat by these guys who shouldn't beat you. You're going in there, and you're a punching bag. You're not into it. You've got nothing to be ashamed of. Retire. If you're asking the question, you know what the answer is."

With the same determination and conviction that carried him into the ring for twenty-eight professional fights, he called his parents and informed them of his decision. He left it up to them to tell Top Rank and Dickie.

Micky's decision to retire came at the beginning of 1992. Within a year, Dickie was arrested three times. Micky's boxing career ran from 1986 to 1991, and Dickie was arrested at least once in each of those years. But the nature of those arrests tended to be along the lines of drunk and disorderly conduct. Then, in the early nineties, Dickie's criminal activities escalated to armed robbery and kidnapping.

"In 1993, I got arrested for robbing a guy, and they put me in jail in Cambridge," Dickie recalls. "I looked at myself with my shirt off. I was 118 pounds. I started crying. And I thought, 'Who is this guy?'"

It was frightening for Dickie to see himself aging and emaciated. He may have been something once, but now he was nothing more than the strung-out crack addicts he saw on the streets.

He spent nearly four months in jail before his mother finally bailed him out. She'd done the same thing for him many times

before. In fact, when Dickie was jailed for punching a police officer in 1987, Alice held a fund-raiser to scrape together the five
thousand dollars required to get Dickie out of jail. The event was
held in the VFW Hall in Lowell and featured a video of Dickie's
fight against Sugar Ray Leonard. Only about thirty people showed
up and paid the five-dollar admission fee. Not surprisingly, a fight
broke out. With Micky's help, the skirmish was quickly settled,
but Alice and her daughters didn't come anywhere close to raising
enough money to get Dickie out of jail. So, Micky pitched in with
the balance due.

The memory of his skeletal frame, wrinkled face, and ghostly
complexion haunted Dickie as he left the Cambridge jail. He walked
with a determination to turn his life around, to find a job, to support his son, and to become the father he'd never really had. A few
weeks later, he was caught with another gun attempting to commit
another robbery. He was back in jail where he saw the same picture
of himself. He was a mess. He acknowledged it and told himself
repeatedly that he was screwing up his life.

"I have to get straight," he said over and over again. "I have to
get straight, and I will. This time, I'm gonna get the help I need.
This is a fight I'm not gonna lose, God damn it!"

He was bailed out again, but returned a few weeks later when
he was caught attempting to rob a drug house.

It took twenty-seven arrests and a rap sheet five pages long
before Dickie was finally sent away for a long time. He was sentenced to eight years, of which he served a little more than half. He
was facing a life sentence but accepted a plea bargain on charges of
carjacking, kidnapping, and armed robbery with a sawed-off shotgun. He also pleaded guilty to carrying a firearm without a license,
breaking and entering at night with the intent to commit a felony,
larceny under 250 dollars, unlawful possession of ammunition, and
possession of burglary tools.

His court appearance was originally scheduled for a Friday, St.
Patrick's Day 1995, but Dickie was late for court and quite obviously drunk, so the judge postponed the hearing until after the

weekend. The following Monday, Dickie heard the news that his freedom now belonged to the state, and said, "I just want to get this over with and get on with my life."

In a temporary holding area, Dickie was allowed a visit from his son, Dickie Jr. In their most tender father and son moment, Dickie laughed and said, "C'mon, hit me in the nose. Real hard! C'mon, give me a knuckle sandwich right now, right in the nose."

Dickie Jr. didn't comply, opting instead to wait until his father gave him a little kiss and said good-bye. The boy left with the grandmother who would raise him. Alice had raised nine children of her own, and she willingly accepted the responsibility of a tenth child to nurture—and an eleventh. Dickie's other son, Tommy, now just over a year old, would also need someone to be responsible for him. Alice could only hope that these boys would turn out better than the son who appeared before her in a green jumpsuit and an unashamed smile on his face.

"Good-bye, Dickie," Alice said. "Maybe this is for the best. You'll come out stronger and healthier. I know you will, honey. You're a good boy."

Dickie listened to his mother's words, and he believed them. He was a good boy. But he had failed to become a good man. He was thirty-seven years old, and he was destined to hear the clanging of a jail door closing behind him several times a day for the next several years. What had happened?

"Drinking was what screwed me up," Dickie told the *Boston Globe*. "When I'm standing on the street with a beer in my hand and people walk by, I feel like two cents. I think, what happened to me? The only time I'd get arrested was when I was drinking. . . . You leave a bar and something happens. It hurts, how I screwed up. I screwed up my life. That's how people talk. Everybody sees me, they say, 'Dickie, how are you doing?' Then they walk past and they're saying that you're doing too much drugs or doing too much drinking. If you box here, you're a bum, really."

Dickie blamed the booze and the drugs for his plight, and he never gave up the dreams or the fantasy about himself, or about

Micky. He never stopped believing that he had what it took to be a boxing champion, never admitted that part of what it takes is the discipline to stay away from the booze and the drugs.

Alone in his jail cell, staring at the corroded toilet and the sink that never seemed to have hot water, Dickie remembered the words he'd told *Boston Globe* reporter Ian Thompsen following the Cosmo incident some seven years ago.

"Micky won't leave me," Dickie said. "We're going to stick together. I'm going to make him champ. I'm positive. I know what he's going to do. I know we're going to make it. He ain't going to be drinking booze or doing any drugs. He ain't, and I'm going to stop myself from doing it. I'll be in the gym with him every day if he needs me. I know all the bad things that can happen now. You can't get a better guy to teach you than that. I've got to be more on the ball now. It's not just myself now. Look, name one trainer that does everything I do for him. I run with him. I go down and spar with him. I taught him everything he knows, and everybody blames me. Everybody thinks it's me, that if I'm out partying, Micky's going to be out. Everybody talks about me hurting Micky Ward. Micky Ward is what I made him. At least I sure helped him. I'm dead serious. Micky could be a millionaire. He can't miss being champion. He's going to be back."

But as Dickie sat in jail, he couldn't deny that so far he'd been wrong on nearly every count. And it was right then and there that Dicky started dreaming about getting out of jail, and making Micky a champion. It wouldn't be too late. With good behavior, Dickie could be out in less than five years. Micky would only be thirty-four years old then. That's old, but not too old. "It could happen," he thought. That was the dream that he fixated on while enduring the muscle tremors.

The withdrawal symptoms had begun soon after his lockup, and for the first two weeks he felt like he was going to die. Intermittently, he even wished that he would. The pain he felt was worse than anything he had ever experienced in the ring. If he could keep his hands in front of his face when fatigue demanded that he lower them, if he could withstand a brutal shot to the jaw and simply smile and continue to stalk his assailant, then he was certain he could handle depriving his body of crack. But what he didn't know was that part of the "crash" was a hypersensitivity to pain. So the bad back, the aching legs, and sore hands that were part of his life as a boxer were rising from chronic and tolerable to acute and torturous. And the Walpole prison he was transferred to wasn't exactly a posh rehab clinic. Dickie wasn't about to receive any sympathy from the prison guards. There would be no trips to the sick ward, no extra food to quell his cravings, no substitute drugs to help ease his landing.

"Those guards just listened to me scream night after night," he said.

Like any crack addict deprived of his addiction, Dickie experienced insufferable nausea, headaches, and vomiting. He was disoriented, paranoid, and depressed. And those were on the good days. Every day he yearned for a piece of the rock. He knew it would alleviate his anguish. But he also knew it was a dead end. He says, "I used crack once. The rest of the time it used me." The echo of the cell door slamming shut seemed to go on forever.

His cell was a little less than half the size of a boxing ring. When Dickie was feeling better, he found he had room to stick and move in there. He could shadowbox. He could do push-ups and sit-ups on the cold, cement floor. He could do dips on the edge of the bed, which was bolted to the floor.

As Dickie's health returned, so did his passion for boxing and keeping in shape. He started heading down to the prison's gym on a daily basis. There he found a few fifty-year-old heavy bags and speed bags that had been put there so that the inmates would hit the bags instead of each other. Once Dickie started going to the gym, he began training some of the inmates. He tells the story this way:

"I trained everybody. They all knew me. So, I'm training guys who weigh like 275 pounds. In three days, these big guys are hitting the bag like *boom, boom, boom!* It was beautiful. Then one of the guards comes up to me and explains why they weren't going to let me do that anymore. He says, 'Look at it our way. If a fight breaks out, they'll kill us. Look at the way you're training these guys.' So, they got rid of all the stuff, and I couldn't train anybody no more."

Meanwhile, Micky was also spending a lot of his time in jail. He had studied for and passed the high school equivalency exam and became a prison guard at the Billerica House of Correction. Richie Bryan, who had been working there for several years, helped get him the job.

"I didn't really like it," Micky says. "It's just that I wasn't used to being inside all the time. It was a tough job to have.

"I went to school with a lot of those guys," he continues. "A lot of them were from Lowell. It was a little weird, because I used to hang out with these guys. But they were all pretty respectful. I think it helped that when you're around boxing, you're around rougher people. Plus, I was a regular guy in there, not a celebrity. I only had to break up one fight the whole time I was in there."

But Micky didn't like the job, and soon after his boxing career ended, Laurie left him and took Kasie with her. There was no big blowup, no last fight. Laurie just tired of living with a prison guard barely making minimum wage. So, she drove north and took up with a man thirty years her senior. At first, Micky was depressed. Then he was determined. He quit his job at the prison and started making plans to return to the ring.

Nearly two years into his retirement, Micky started nosing around the Lowell gyms again.

"I'm just looking to stay in shape," he'd tell anyone who cornered him. "I don't like carrying around this beer belly."

In truth, however, he was at the gyms to test his hands and his stamina, and to find out if he still loved boxing. He needed to know if his body, now almost thirty years old, would fail him if he tried to return. So he worked out and renewed some old acquaintances. He knew that if he were seen around the gyms enough, someone would make him an offer he couldn't refuse.

With no offers forthcoming, Micky continued working the three-ton rollers throughout the streets and parking lots of Lowell. His days were long, beginning at five in the morning. Instead of hitting the hills of Shedd Park, Micky was showing up to work as part of a road crew. He wasn't a boxer anymore. There were no more questions about his last fight or his next fight. There was still plenty of respect for what Micky had done, and for the kind of hard worker and friend that he still was, but the awe was gone. Micky could feel it.

After putting in his ten to twelve hours during the cold days of New England winters and hot, humid days of New England summers, Micky would make his way over to the gym and spend a few hours either working out or hanging out. He was in no hurry to make it home to an empty house. So he stayed at the gyms past dinnertime and then frequently made his way out to the bars.

Micky was most comfortable inside the Highland Tap. It felt a little strange walking into a place where your picture is on the wall, but owner and proprietor Cleo Surprenant had always been a big fan. He loved boxing, and Micky was special because, according to Cleo, he was such a good kid, and he kept himself clean.

"There was a lot of temptation for him out there," Cleo says about Micky. "But the only habit he had was after a fight, he'd drink all night. That's normal. He's a kid. He worked hard for what he got. He might have gone further though."

Cleo had always looked forward to Micky's arrival at the bar, so one day when he didn't show, Cleo figured, "Maybe he's getting more serious about his training again. I'd sure like to see that kid get another chance."

But Micky wasn't training. He was in the hospital fighting for his life. There had been an accident at work.

Micky's crew was paving a Cosco parking lot, and Micky was working with the heavy roller, as he'd done thousands of times before. Nearing the completion of the job, Micky threw the tamper off the back of the roller. The tamper was a thirty-pound metal pole attached to a flat, rectangular bottom that was used to compress the new tar in the few areas that the roller had missed. It was time for the touch-up work, and as usual, Micky was hustling.

He tossed the tamper, expecting it to fall flat on the ground, and then he quickly jumped down off the roller. It was a maneuver he'd done so many times, he didn't even think about it. It certainly didn't seem dangerous, yet based on Micky's own calculations, what occurred actually had a 10 percent chance of happening.

"You know, nine times out of ten that tamp's gonna fall to the ground and lay there on its side," Micky says. "But this time, as I jumped off, it stayed standing straight up in the air."

Micky landed ass first on the top of the metal pole. "It didn't go up my ass or anything, but just to the side of my butt," Micky says. The downward force of Micky's body weight caused the pole to rip a one-inch gash in his rear end and travel four inches into his rectum. The pole toppled over with Micky attached to it. He laid there, scared and in more pain than he had ever felt before. He couldn't remove the pole, and the pole was impeding his movement. He couldn't get up. He couldn't roll over. He couldn't even inspect the wound. All he could do was lie there crying out in pain and waiting for help to arrive. His coworkers reacted quickly, and an ambulance appeared on the scene in a matter of minutes.

The paramedics first made sure that Micky wasn't paralyzed; then they removed the pole. Micky's rectum was ruptured, and the large gash began bleeding profusely. They packed the wound and then rushed Micky to the hospital, where doctors performed emergency reconstructive surgery on his bowels.

"I really could have been killed," Micky says matter-of-factly. "As it was, I was about an inch away from spending the rest of my life with a colostomy bag. Sometimes I think about people threatening to 'Rip you a new one.' I guess that's what happened to me. The damn thing ripped its own hole, and I had a new one."

Micky had only just recently stepped up his training regimen, and had grown much more serious about a comeback to boxing.

"I couldn't do anything," he recalls. "I had a visiting nurse come every day and pack my butt with peroxide and saline and water. . . .

For a long time I wasn't thinking about a comeback. I was thinking about my ass. What a pain in the ass!" He laughs. "Finally, I started to walk again, but I couldn't do any real training because of the pressure. I couldn't cough or laugh or anything. You know all the power comes from your ass when you throw a punch, and I couldn't do it."

The year was 1993. Micky was laid up in his bed for the next four months. Dickie was in jail. And Micky's father, George Ward, was on his way to prison. Ward had been charged and convicted with defrauding an eighty-year-old woman with Alzheimer's disease out of her entire life savings, more than ninety thousand dollars, and in a separate charge, an eighty-nine-year-old woman claimed that Ward took her for more than twenty thousand dollars.

Ward was a fifty-four-year-old roofing contractor who ran a business called Boston Slate and Coppersmith. Massachusetts State Police conducted a year-long probe into the company and determined that Ward routinely promised to do roofing work for elderly clients and then took their money without doing the job. The group of contractors used a "point man" who identified vulnerable targets, and then each of them charged for work that was never done. Ward pleaded guilty to larceny charges stemming from one case and was sentenced to two to four years in Middlesex County Jail. While there, he was awaiting trial on additional charges in Massachusetts.

In that particular case, eighty-nine-year-old homeowner Edith Lowney told the *Lowell Sun* in October 1993, "He put me in the truck with another man and took me to the bank. He was always demanding money. And he didn't really repair anything."

Ward was charged with two counts of larceny, indicating that he took twenty grand from Lowney and did what amounted to one-thousand-dollars worth of work.

"That was my savings," Lowney said.

Ward was caught when he brought Lowney to the bank and demanded ten thousand dollars in cash. The teller was suspicious and persuaded Ward to accept a check. Then the teller spoke to a social worker who cared for Lowney, learned what was going on, and stopped payment on the check.

During the time he was laid up and wiping his ass with cotton balls, Micky had a lot of time to think. Mostly what he found himself thinking about was returning to the ring. On the surface, he was a street paver out on workman's comp. But underneath, somewhere in his heart and his gut, he was still a boxer. Micky didn't lie in bed dreaming about winning titles or making millions. He didn't long for the days when he was recognized on the streets or the nights when strangers bought beers for him in the pubs. He would close his eyes and see the dingy locker rooms where he had sat on rickety wooden stools while his brother or Richie or Mickey O'Keefe wrapped his hands. He could feel the fine silk of his robes brushing against his chest and his back as he strode out to the ring. He could smell the smoke wafting above the crowds, could see the lights, could remember every opponent and nearly every punch. He dreamed about punching and getting punched, defending and attacking. As his body healed, his mind focused. He was ready.

With his father and brother in jail, Micky once again turned to Mickey O'Keefe. O'Keefe was working a detail in front of a firehouse on the same day that Micky was paving out front.

"How's the gym going?" Micky asked O'Keefe, referring to the gym he'd opened up in one of Lowell's toughest neighborhoods. It was a fourth-floor walk-up on Mount Vernon Street simply called the Lowell Boxing Club.

"Good," O'Keefe responded, not mentioning the fact that none of the kids who trained there were ever charged a dime. "How are you doing? How's the ass?"

Micky laughed, acknowledged that it was still a little sore, and said, "I was thinking of maybe coming down to your gym. You know, just to work out a little bit."

"Great. We'd love to have you."

O'Keefe didn't know whether Micky would make it down to his gym or not. He was merely happy that his friend had recovered from the accident and that if he did come to the gym, he'd be able to show some of the young kids there a few moves in the ring.

Those kids looked up to Micky Ward more than they looked up to a cop anyway.

But it wasn't long after their chance meeting that O'Keefe was in the storeroom of the gym and overheard one of Micky's cousins telling another fighter that Micky was putting the word out that he'd be interested in a fight if something came up. O'Keefe stepped out of the storage area and volunteered, "Hey, if Micky ever needs me, tell him to give me a call."

Micky called, and the partnership was created.

"Look, you want to work out, the place is yours," O'Keefe said. "I'll give you a key, so you can come and go as you please. Give it three weeks, and we'll see where we're at."

Micky took the key and was at O'Keefe's gym every day for the next twenty-one days. The first twenty-four hours were spent with O'Keefe's recommended approach of, "Let's see where we're at." The next twenty days were serious training sessions. Micky's workouts intensified. The time he spent on the heavy bag increased. The distance he ran grew longer, and the time he ran got earlier. The pop and the snap in his punches returned. He was in training. But training for what? There were no fights to prepare for. There weren't even plans to get a match made. And training with whom? O'Keefe was there from the beginning, but he wasn't a professional trainer. He worked with kids. The only professional experience he had was the few times he worked Micky's corner as Dickie's assistant. Still O'Keefe was prepared to help Micky come back.

"Micky, if you want to do this, if you want to work for me, we'll do it right," O'Keefe told him. "You'll make some money down the road. In the meantime, we'll just work. But you have to do it my way. I don't want any interference from your family."

Micky agreed. He and O'Keefe were both tough, hard-working, hard-drinking Irish guys who had managed to stare into the bowels of Lowell and step away from the precipice with good, clean hearts. O'Keefe, finally realizing that he was in fact a full-fledged alcoholic, stopped drinking in 1993, right around the time he started working with Micky.

Clean and sober, he began to sculpt Micky's body and mold his mind. Neither task was especially difficult. Micky's head was straight. His determination had returned.

There were reasons, he believed, for falling short the first time around. His hands were a big part of it. Confidence was another. The distractions introduced by his brother couldn't be denied. And poor management had been an issue.

Now, he believed, everything was different. His hands were better and that gave him confidence. He was developing an undeniable faith in O'Keefe's nurturing ways. What O'Keefe may have lacked in experience and overall knowledge of the professional fight game, he made up for in resoluteness and loyalty. It was strange and sad to acknowledge, but Micky knew that this time he had someone looking out for *his* best interests.

"I took control of the second half of my career," Micky says. "I came back because I wanted to do it, not because of the pressure from Dickie fighting, or my family wanting me to fight. I didn't have pressure from people saying I could or couldn't do it. The second time, I didn't care who wanted me to fight. I did it because I wanted to."

So Micky and Mickey went to work. For more than six months they worked, with no prospects on the horizon. But neither man grew discouraged. They were making good use of time. Finally, one day while O'Keefe was holding up the pads and Micky was pounding out combinations, O'Keefe shouted above the thunderous punches echoing through an empty gym:

"Are you ready for a fight?"

"Damn straight, I'm ready!"

The question had been asked and answered many times before, but this time Micky sounded more convincing, and O'Keefe noticed. He dropped the pads and said:

"So am I."

O'Keefe put his arm around Micky and walked him out of the ring. He was beaming like a proud father. And in truth, that's what he had become. While George Ward was in prison, Micky and Mickey trained together every day, and on most days they ate the late dinners that O'Keefe's wife, Donna, prepared. Theirs was a wonderful partnership, and though they weren't blood, it sure felt like they were born to it.

As they got to the door to leave that night, O'Keefe stopped and looked back. Micky stopped, too, and waited. The gym was dark now, but the shadows of the heavy bags were silhouetted by the moonlight coming through the windows. O'Keefe spotted a couple of dumbbells slightly out of place along the far wall. He thought it might be time to get a new speed bag or two. And he looked upon the two boxing rings standing side by side and thought about the kids who had dared to enter. He was proud of this gym and the kids he'd helped along the way.

O'Keefe knew he had a lot of work to do now, too. He had to find Micky a fight, a good fight. Micky needed a fight that would prove he was back and better than ever. There were a million things running through O'Keefe's mind—the gym, his job on the police force, his family, and now Micky's comeback.

O'Keefe smiled, turned to Micky, and said, "Do you remember all those lonely days in this gym? Do you remember, in the heat of the summer, when it gets to be about 120 degrees inside this gym? It's been just you and me. But we haven't been alone. I know somewhere God's been watching you. He knows. And he'll take care of you."

Now Micky smiled. After all, he had God and Mickey O'Keefe on his side. That and his devastating left hook to the body might be enough to get him to the top of the mountain this time.

CHAPTER EIGHT

Getting back into the ring proved to be as difficult a venture as O'Keefe had anticipated. His first move was to contact Al Valenti, but Valenti was reluctant to get involved with Micky and his family again. Valenti had promoted the Ward–Rafuse fight at the Lowell Auditorium back in 1986 and had navigated his way through a financial battle between Alice Ward and Micky's original managers, Bernie Bergeron and Don DiRocco. And then in 1991, Valenti had tried to put a card together with Eddie Andelman featuring a Ward–Rafuse rematch, from which Micky ultimately backed out, retiring a few months later. Valenti needed to be convinced that working with Micky and Mickey would not only be worthwhile, but also trouble free.

O'Keefe enlisted the help of his longtime friend Danny Gilday. Gilday had grown up around the boxing gyms and had known O'Keefe from the days when Micky was still in the Golden Gloves. They were strange bedfellows: O'Keefe was a cop, and Gilday was the nephew of William "Lefty" Gilday, who was convicted of killing Boston police officer Walter Schroeder in 1970. Lefty had been part of a gang of anti–Vietnam War activists who had rationalized that robbing banks could fund their efforts to end the war. While taking twenty-six thousand dollars from a Boston bank, Lefty had tripped a silent alarm. Schroeder, first to arrive on the scene, had exited his cruiser when Lefty opened fire from across the street, shooting him in the back several times with a Thompson submachine gun. Fourteen years later, Lefty Gilday was convicted of running a credit card fraud operation from prison.

Meanwhile, Danny Gilday was a member of the Teamsters Union and was friends with a fellow Teamster from Charlestown, John "Mick" Murray. Murray had spent time in prison after FBI agents and local police found him inside the Coolidge Bank and Trust Company in Cambridge well after business hours on December 23, 1989. Murray and his associate James McCormack claimed that they were fixing the bank's roof when they accidentally fell inside. The two men were convicted of attempted bank robbery.

Murray had served his time and was out now. A friend of Valenti, Murray offered to introduce O'Keefe, and the meeting took place on March 15, 1994, at Dominic's Pizza on Tremont Street in Boston. Dominic's was right next door to the Roxy nightclub, and on this night the Roxy was hosting a live boxing show. So Valenti, O'Keefe, Gilday, Murray, and Micky Ward shared a couple of pizzas at Dominic's and then went over to see the fights.

"Who are you?" Valenti asked O'Keefe after the two men had been introduced.

"I'm nobody," O'Keefe answered. "I'm just a guy looking out for Micky. All I can tell you is he'll be in shape. We're not looking for a lot of money. We just want to get back."

Valenti had arrived without much interest, and now, seeing that Micky was involved with another inexperienced outsider, wondered why this time around with Micky would be any different.

"I don't know, Micky," he said. "You know I like you, but I don't want to put up with any of your family's bullshit again. It's just not worth it."

"Look," O'Keefe interrupted. "I've been training every day with him, and the family's not involved. Micky's making a comeback.

He's gonna be great, and you can really help us out. It has nothing to do with the family. I'm gonna be training him. I'm gonna be taking over."

Valenti was summarily unimpressed by the stranger's declaration that he'd be in charge. Then Micky added, "Al, here it is. I'm back in the gym. If anything comes up, I'd like a shot."

Valenti offered nothing and made no promises. So, Micky and Mickey moved in another direction. Murray, it turned out, was also good friends with John Gagliardi, also known as "Johnny Gags." Gags had been a longtime promoter, but as far back as 1980 he had sworn to get out of the business when he lost nearly sixteen thousand dollars on a fight at the Hynes Auditorium between Vinnie Curto and Bennie Briscoe.

"I've had it. This is the last show I put on," Gags said after the fight.

But Gags never did get out completely, and now here was Micky Ward standing in front of him and looking to make a comeback. Ward was as close to a sure thing as Gags had ever seen. Certainly, there would be enough local interest to sell tickets to Ward's first comeback fight. Boxing fans would definitely want to see that. Gags was going to make sure he didn't lose money this time. He offered Micky only four hundred bucks.

"The last thing on my mind was the money," Micky says.

Micky found success immediately. In his first two fights, both in Lowell, he knocked out Luis Castillo and Genaro Andujar. Both fights were scheduled to go ten rounds. Neither made it past the fifth.

Castillo was a New York kid with a losing record who was knocked out in the second round the only other time he had stepped into the ring with a quality opponent. That defeat was suffered at the hands of Keith Holmes who would go on to win the WBC middleweight title. Still Castillo was an experienced fighter.

The fight took place at the Lowell Sheraton, not exactly world renowned as a boxing venue. Basically, folks checking in or waiting for beds to be turned down could step into a side ballroom and watch a less-than-spectacular fight card. But anyone who chose to do so on June 17, 1994, can say they saw Micky Ward's first fight in more than two and a half years, and they saw him knock out Castillo in the fifth round. It took a while for Micky to shake off some rust, and punches that were missing early started landing late. He depended on his old reliable—the left hook to the body. After a few of those brought the crowd to its feet, Micky dropped Castillo with a short right uppercut to the solar plexus. Castillo went down, and he didn't get up.

"That's the hardest I ever got hit to the body," Castillo said later.

Referee Mike Ryan grabbed Micky's right hand and raised it over his head. It was the first time in more than three years that Micky's hand was raised in victory.

Thinking back to his retirement Micky says, "When I left, I never thought I'd come back. I was so bad that night against Meyers. That's the reason I stopped. But it was still inside me. If I didn't do this now, it would have built up and built up and I'd have done it at thirty-five and probably got killed. I just want to see what's there. I just want to give this one last shot. It may be only this one time, but I want to know what I got left. This time, if my mind ain't a hundred percent, that's it. After the fight, if I don't feel good, I got the keys to the roller. I'll just jump back on and roll away and I'll know. I don't want to leave no doubts."

Clearly, Micky could still land hard punches.

Just three months after his comeback fight, Micky was contracted to fight a cagey veteran from Puerto Rico, Miguel Santana. Seven years earlier, Santana thought he had won a share of the lightweight title by defeating Greg Haugen, but the outcome of the fight was reversed the next morning on a technicality. Santana hadn't won, but he had battled Haugen evenly. He had also given stern tests to the likes of Pernell Whittaker, Terrance Alli, Buddy McGirt, and Sharmba Mitchell—all of whom won at least one title during their careers. True, by the time Micky came along, Santana had lost twelve of his last fourteen fights, but he had been facing some of the best fighters in his division. Plus, Santana was routinely fighting at about 150 pounds and would likely come in much bigger than Micky.

Micky's management team was wiser and more protective this time around. When Santana showed up at the Lowell Auditorium on fight night at 151 pounds, he was told that he couldn't fight. Santana was 7 pounds over the limit established in the fight contract. Johnny Gagliardi and Mickey O'Keefe took the decision out of Micky's hands, simply notifying him that a replacement fighter would be provided, one that weighed the right amount. That turned out to be a transplanted New Yorker now living in Maine, who had fought and lost three weeks earlier, Genaro Andujar.

Andujar wasn't in the same class as Santana, nor was he anything close to being Micky's equal. Micky knocked him down three times in the second round with a series of lefts to the body. Then, fifty-one seconds into the third round, Micky landed another vicious body shot, and as Andujar began to crumple, Micky knocked out his mouthpiece with a short right hand. Ten seconds later, the fight was over. Referee Jimmy Kasilowski counted out Andujar and then sprinted from the ring. Kasilowski's wife, Linda, had just given birth to a baby boy thirty minutes earlier up the street at Lowell General Hospital. Two months later, Micky's promoter and primary matchmaker, Johnny Gags, was one of eight men indicted in connection with a drug ring based at the Lawrence Municipal Airport. Gags pleaded guilty to five separate counts related to possession and intent to distribute more than one thousand pounds of marijuana. He was convicted and sentenced in U.S. District Court to eight years and one month in prison and four years supervised release. Three years later, Gagliardi's son Joseph was found dead of an overdose in the men's room of a Cambridge public library. And six years after that, his other son, John Jr., died in the Boston Public Garden at noontime after shooting up heroin with two other men.

Once again, Micky was managing to stay clean in a dirty world. He admits to using a little marijuana as a kid. And some of his closest friends have suggested that he may have been a functioning alcoholic at times, but Micky was able to dodge serious trouble and keep his nose clean. He didn't inherit his father's propensity to steal the life savings away from little old ladies or his brother's aptitude for robbing people at gunpoint. Somehow, he walked through the middle of the underworld of Lowell and rose above it.

In addition to his own family, Micky mingled and dined with the likes of Mick Murray, Johnny Gags, and even O'Keefe's friend Danny Gilday. Unbeknownst to Micky and Mickey at the time, Gilday's involvement in racketeering and extortion was growing. By the mid-nineties, the FBI was keeping a close eye on Gilday, Murray, and two of their known cohorts, South Boston gang members James "Whitey" Bulger and Kevin Weeks. They suspected that Murray was orchestrating a computer theft ring in which computer parts were stolen by Teamsters from hijacked UPS trucks. The FBI's break in the case came in 1997 when Gilday stole a package with an FBI tracking device.

"Micky was in the middle of all this," Gilday says. "But he didn't know any of it. I went to prison for hijacking the trucks, but I made a lot of money doing it. A lot of money! I was the steward, and I used my power to take the computer parts. I got caught, pled guilty, and did my time. I was in Pennsylvania and did about fifteen months. I could have walked out, but I didn't cooperate with the investigation."

But it was the Johnny Gags incarceration that handcuffed Micky. His career was on hold because he had signed a deal with Gags giving him exclusive rights to promote his fights. And Gags wasn't about to give up those rights just because he was in jail and completely incapable of promoting any fights. After several months of haggling, Murray contacted someone on the inside to convince Gagliardi to release Micky from the contract. The frustrating process took more than a year. Micky had knocked out Andujar on September 10, 1994, and didn't fight again until December 30, 1995. It was almost like a second retirement. "That's just the way things went," Micky recalls. "I got away from it again. There wasn't that much going on. I wasn't really discouraged, maybe a little. But the time just flew by. I didn't have a steady job. I was doing side jobs and under-the-table jobs. I was working here and there."

Between here and there, Micky could have been anywhere, but he was at the gym. He could have succumbed to the temptations of the street. He could have gotten flabby on beer and pretzels. He could have made any number of mistakes, but he had O'Keefe to guide him now. O'Keefe was committed to helping Micky, and Micky, in turn, was committed to not letting O'Keefe down.

"He was giving me everything he had. So, I had to give him back everything I had," Micky says. "It's pretty simple, really."

So, Micky showed up at the gym every afternoon at 4:30 and met O'Keefe's son, Brian. The two of them would run four miles and return to the gym at 5:00 to find O'Keefe waiting for them. O'Keefe would put Micky through a tough workout that included several sets of sit-ups, push-ups, curls, and dips. It was an old-fashioned, tried-and-true boxing workout. No Pilates. No aerobics. Just a lot of sweat, plenty of laughs, and several rounds inside the ring with Micky *bap, bap, bapping* on O'Keefe's hand pads.

Despite the inactivity and the lack of anything on the career horizon, O'Keefe managed to keep Micky motivated. Sometimes he'd tell Micky what he couldn't do and then sit back and watch him do it. Other times, he'd tell Micky he could do anything, as long as he kept his mind right and his body in shape. Micky listened. And he remembered that his return to boxing wasn't as much about the money as it was about being something, being someone. And simply by showing up at the gym every day and working his ass off, Micky knew that he was something much more than a part-time, unemployed laborer. He was a boxer. And that made him feel good.

Still, Micky didn't have a lot of opportunities to spar, so it was difficult to gauge just how skilled a boxer he was or how far back he'd come. He looked like the same old Micky when he pounded his left into the heavy bag, but he needed to shake off some ring rust. In February 1995, partway through his ordeal with Gags, Micky got a chance to test himself against another talented boxer.

There was a hot young prospect from Worcester named Jose Antonio Rivera who, like Micky several years before, had won his first fourteen professional fights. Rivera was on the rise, and two weeks before his fifteenth pro fight, he traveled to Lowell to get in a few rounds with Micky. He never seemed to fight more than a few rounds anyway. Among his fourteen wins were twelve knockouts before the end of the third round. In fact, three months after Micky had knocked out Genaro Andujar in the third round, Rivera knocked Andujar out in the second.

"I'm not gonna hold him back," Rivera's trainer, Carlos Garcia, told O'Keefe. "I'm gonna let him go all out and see what he can do, if that's all right with you."

"Sure, that's all right," O'Keefe said. "If you're sure that's what you want."

Garcia looked over at Rivera and smiled, "Jose, he sounds like he wants to know if you can handle Micky Ward. Can you handle Micky Ward, Jose?"

Rivera nodded. His nickname was "El Gallo" which is Spanish for "The Rooster," and even if he wasn't cocksure he could handle Micky Ward, he wasn't about to show that to anyone in the gym.

"There you go," Garcia turned and said to O'Keefe. "I'm gonna have him come after your guy."

Now, it was O'Keefe's turn to smile. "I'll tell my guy the same thing." Then O'Keefe clapped his hands together with authority and shouted over to Micky, "Bring it on, Mick. This is for real."

O'Keefe took a position next to Garcia. Both trainers were leaning against the canvas looking up through the ropes. Garcia looked at O'Keefe and then at Rivera as if to say, "Wait 'til you see what my boy can do." O'Keefe responded with a wink. He already knew what Micky could do, and soon, so would everybody else.

"I'm just gonna say this so there are no surprises," O'Keefe said to Garcia. "Micky's a seasoned veteran. He's gonna pop your guy once, and then he's gonna hit him a little harder, and then a little harder. If Jose drops his elbow to avoid the body shot, Micky's gonna drop him."

"Don't you worry," Garcia said. "He'll be fine."

The bell rang and thirty seconds later it was over. Brian Meade, a childhood friend of Micky's who'd been boxing at the gym to stay in shape, was there that day.

"It was a head shot," he says. "Micky just dropped him. Rivera's eyes were in the back of his head somewhere. He was out for quite a bit of time. They didn't have to call any medical people, but it was a while before he got his senses back. People who were there realized that Micky's hands were good again, and that he could still hit."

Two weeks later, Rivera won the Massachusetts State welterweight title. Four months after that, he knocked out Clarence Coleman in the third round. And eight years after that, he won the WBA welterweight championship, but he didn't last thirty seconds with Micky Ward that day in a dusty old gym in Lowell.

Unfortunately, that was Micky's last "real" fight for a while. His protracted negotiations with Johnny Gags took several months, and it was a few months more before Micky and Mickey met with Al Valenti again. This time Valenti was interested. In November 1995, Valenti sat down with Micky and Mickey at Joe Tecce's Ristorante, a short walk from his Canal Street office, and explained how things could work.

"Look, Micky," Valenti said. "They're doing these fights over at Wonderland Racetrack now, and these fights are a great thing. They'll let you get back into the game. I can make matches that are the right matches for you. I won't put you in there with a killer. We'll build up your confidence and get you back into the game."

Wonderland Greyhound Park in Revere, Massachusetts, is a racetrack that regularly doubles as a low-scale boxing venue. The ring is set up in the middle of the room opposite several betting windows. Gamblers filter in and out to place their bets, and while waiting in line, they can be distracted for a few moments by live boxing going on behind them. The racetrack also offers a 1-percent promotional fee for every dollar bet on the boxing matches. Valenti knew that when he promoted fights at Wonderland, the track would help him market the event, and the promotional fee would be just enough money to make sure that he had a cushion. These fights weren't going to be moneymakers for anyone involved, but they could be an investment with a big payoff for anyone on board from the beginning.

"As a local promoter, you know you're not going to make a lot of money on these local fights," Valenti said. "But you're looking for someone you can grow with. In the meantime, you don't want to lose money. You're really looking to break even. So, I found a nice middle ground there. I knew a couple of hundred people from Lowell would show up, and I'd be fine. I'm looking at this as an opportunity. I've got the momentum, and now I can look at a guy like Micky, and I say, 'Look, I can get you two or three wins and you're back in the game plan.' I'm looking at Micky further down the road."

Micky and Mickey also enlisted the help of Joe Lake, a trainer working out of the World Gym in Somerville, Massachusetts. Lake had trained or managed a lot of fighters such as Jon Mercogliano, Johnny Rafuse, and Dana Rosenblatt and frequently set up fights with Al Valenti.

"All I'm looking for is a chance," Micky told Lake. "I was thinking maybe you could get me on some of Dana's cards. You know, if you can help get me a fight, and then get me on the card, I'll fight anybody. I'm ready to go anytime."

Lake was impressed by Micky's willingness to humble himself. Micky had been the diamond in the rough, the TV star fighting on ESPN all the time, and now he was willing to deprecate himself by letting someone else be the main event. Lake wanted to help, but he knew that getting involved with Micky meant getting involved with everyone in his family. That was something he couldn't stomach.

"I'll tell you this, Mick," Lake said. "I can't do this if your mother's going to be telling me what to do all the time. I'm not gonna get involved if this whole thing is gonna be a fuck!"

Micky and Mickey knew what Lake meant, and they wanted what he wanted.

"What I will do is let everybody know I'm making the decisions," Lake continued. "If that can't be abided by, then I'm out. I'll step back."

"That's not going to be a problem," O'Keefe said. "We're doing this together. I get him in shape. He works his ass off. And you get him the fights. Nobody else will be in the middle of this. That's what Micky wants. And that's the way it's gonna be."

Lake was pleased, but unconvinced. He called Alice Ward directly and waited to hear her give the same assurances. Alice stepped up and volunteered to stay out of it.

"This is Micky's turn," Alice said. "He wants one more go-round. He's watching those kids out there, and he knows he can beat them. He can, you know. He can still beat them."

"I know that, Alice," Lake said. "And now that I know everyone's going to be on the same page, we'll see where this thing goes."

A month after lunch at Tecce's with Valenti, Lake and Valenti were able to put Micky on a fight card at Wonderland Greyhound Park. In fact, Micky was scheduled to fight even before he had an opponent. Only days before December 30, 1995, Micky learned he'd be fighting Edgardo Rosario from Springfield, Massachusetts. Rosario was making his professional debut. It was a match. But it was a severe mismatch.

Micky bounded out of his corner and knocked Rosario down with the first punch he threw. Rosario got up only to be knocked down two more times and the fight was over. The audience may or may not have gotten its money's worth, but according to Lake, Micky never got his money at all.

"In that first comeback fight we were supposed to get four hundred dollars," Lake says. "But Valenti, who promoted the damn thing, says he doesn't have enough cash on him. So, he hands me a hundred and fifty bucks in cash, and then writes a check for two hundred and fifty dollars. The check bounced, and we never got another dollar back."

There were two more fights at Wonderland, two more knockouts, and two more four-hundred-dollar paydays. The fights were coming quickly now, but the money was not. Micky fought Rosario in December, Alberto Alicea in January, and Alex Ortiz in March, knocking them all out by the third round. Alicea wasn't much more than a masochist who must have enjoyed pain and losing. He had lost thirty-one of thirty-seven fights when he faced Micky. Ortiz never won a professional boxing match, despite seventeen attempts. It had been nearly two years since Micky began his comeback, and he had only fought five times and made a grand total of two thousand dollars. Things were as Valenti had promised. Micky was being put in front of guys he could beat. There was a plan in place. He was essentially starting his career over again. As a twenty-year-old, Micky came out of the gate fighting inexperienced kids, and he knocked them all out. Now, as a thirty-year-old, he was doing the same thing. The difference, however, was that this time, Micky wouldn't have to wait as long to catch a big break.

CHAPTER NINE

Micky's big break went by the name of Louis "The Viper" Veader. He was a real up-and-comer from Providence, Rhode Island. Veader was unbeaten in his first thirty-one professional fights. It was the kind of a record reserved for only the best in the game. Nonetheless, Veader had only fought unknowns. "I was in a position where I had to take it," Micky says. "C'mon, if I didn't take it, I wasn't going to get any other shots at a title. It was my shot to get back on ESPN and get up there in the rankings, into the top twenty. . . . I look at it like this, it's pressure, but it's opportunity. I controlled my own destiny. It was all up to me. Boxing is in your control. A fighter can do that."

That's true inside the ring. Outside the ring, Micky's life had been frequently out of control. The same was true for Veader. Just another tough kid growing up in a housing project in Providence, Veader wasn't introduced to boxing until he was sixteen years old. That introduction was made by Carl Prout, the stepfather of one of Veader's friends. Prout did most of his boxing in prison, but his brother, Don Prout, was a heavyweight in the 1960s who had two memorable fights with Tom McNeeley. In 1962, a month after

McNeeley lost a heavyweight championship fight against Floyd Patterson, he also lost to Prout at the auditorium in Providence. McNeeley won the rematch two months later at the Boston Garden.

Carl Prout was training fighters at Grundy's Gym in Central Falls, Rhode Island. He recognized potential in Veader, who had shown some talent as a football player. After several tries, he finally convinced Veader to give boxing a try. Veader didn't expect anything from boxing other than a good workout. He ended up with much more.

"I never wanted to be a boxer," Veader says. "I loved football. I fell into boxing and got good at it pretty quick. When that happened, I just wanted to take it as far as I could take it."

Most of the kids Prout picked off the streets to come into his gym left when the work or the punches got too hard. Veader stayed, and Prout stayed with him. Three years after he had thrown his first punch, Veader just missed making the 1988 United States Olympic team. He won three Golden Gloves championships and then turned pro in 1990. His career didn't follow the same path as Micky's had. Micky became a regular on ESPN and fought most of his fights in Atlantic City. Veader never got a sniff of the big time and spent most of his ring time in places like the Windjammer Inn in Westerly, Rhode Island, or New Bedford High School and the Teachers Union Hall in Dorchester, Massachusetts. He was a victim of bad management.

"*Ring* magazine called me the most protected guy," Veader says. "That just pissed me off. I'll fight anybody. But my management guys wouldn't make any fights. And when they did, it would fall through, or it wouldn't be the guy I was training for. I don't think they had the connections."

Veader's first manager was Vito DeLuca, and two years into Veader's career when he was still fighting six- and eight-rounders against guys who could barely stand up on their own, DeLuca was preoccupied with his own legal problems. DeLuca was a reputed soldier in the Patriarca crime family. His criminal record included gambling and extortion convictions, and he was charged with the gangland-style slaying of Anthony Mirabella in May 1982. DeLuca, it was said, controlled the docks in Providence. He also dabbled in the fight game, and wound up with control of Veader's career. In February 1992, however, he was arrested by federal agents, convicted of insurance fraud and weapons charges, and sentenced to more than three years in prison. Just as with Micky and Gagliardi, that conviction put Veader's career on hold.

"I had a lot of fights with Vito," Veader recalls. "He had me locked up in a contract. He had legal issues. I wanted out. He was trying to manage my career while he was in jail. I wanted to break free from it. It was a contract issue. I couldn't fight. Nobody would touch me. Nobody would work with me."

For that reason, Veader didn't fight from May 1993 to June 1994. When he did start fighting again with the help of Rhode Island lawyers Mark Pass and Richard Dion, nothing much had changed. Veader was still fighting stiffs in back rooms, racetracks, and bars. It went on that way for eight more fights and two more years until Al Valenti got a phone call from Mark Pass. The two men had spoken a few times when Veader had fought on Valenti's card at Wonderland two months earlier. Micky had been on that card as well. Pass and Valenti met at a small deli not far from Valenti's office on Canal Street in Boston.

"Are you still handling Micky Ward?" Pass asked.

"Yeah, for what it's worth," Valenti answered. He was immediately intrigued. The guy managing Veader was asking about Ward. It was obvious where this conversation was headed. And Valenti liked the idea right away. Veader was a terrific boxer, but not a big puncher. He was a rising star, and Micky was either rising or fading. Either way, two New England kids with a solid fan base could sell tickets.

"There's not a lot out there for Micky right now," Valenti continued coyly. "He's kind of in limbo right now. He's not a contender. So the ranked guys don't want to fight him. And the young guys are looking for sure things, and they don't know what to make of Micky. It's just been tough to find a good match for him."

"What about my guy?" Pass said, getting right to the point. "Look, we're ready to move him. He's been lingering at the bottom of the division for too long. A fight with Micky should be worth something, both in terms of money and credibility. We want the fight. Can you get it for us?"

Valenti wasn't certain. He'd had several conversations about Micky Ward with Ron Katz and ESPN's Top Rank promotions, but there was no interest. Now, he had both Ward and Veader. That just might pass muster. He called Katz.

"Ron, I want to talk to you about making a Micky Ward fight."

Click.

Katz hung up. So, Valenti dialed again.

"Ron."

Click.

Katz had done it again. Valenti wasn't angry. He knew Katz was legitimately uninterested in promoting any more Micky Ward fights. Micky was old news to him. Micky had no future, and he had no money-making potential. It wasn't worth his time to discuss Micky Ward. Valenti persisted.

"Ron, don't hang up. Just hear me out. If you don't listen to me, shame on you."

"What is it?" Katz said impatiently.

"Look, I've got a great match. We're gonna make Louis Veader–Micky Ward."

There was dead silence on the phone for several seconds. Katz hadn't hung up. Valenti knew he had a chance.

"Here's the bottom line, Ron. The kid, Veader, is 31 and 0. It's a great local fight. One kid's from Providence. The other kid's from Lowell. I'm telling you it will work."

Katz was listening.

"Plus, we've got the show at the FleetCenter the weekend of the Boston Marathon. We've already got Dana Rosenblatt going up against Howard Davis. This gives us another local fight. Can't you just see those seats filling up?"

Katz paused and said, "Let me think about it."

Katz thought about it long enough to improve the idea. He called Valenti back and said, "Let's make it the co-feature with Rosenblatt. And we'll make it a twelve-round fight for the WBU Intercontinental light welterweight title."

That was little more than a fictional title to give the fight some prestige. The negotiations were quick and easy. After expenses, and cuts going to promoters, managers, and trainers, Micky and Veader would both walk away with a little less than ten thousand dollars. O'Keefe would be receiving his first check of any kind since he began working with Micky. The money was right for everyone involved, and Micky's team was brimming with confidence.

"I went down to Foxwoods with Cleo Surprenant to see Veader fight once," O'Keefe remembers. "Micky was with us. To me, that was good, because Micky never liked to watch tape on any of the fighters he faced. So, at least we knew he'd already seen Veader. And we knew that Micky was confident he could beat him."

Confidence was crucial, because it was a lack of it that had contributed to the end of Micky's first career. Now, even more than ever before, Micky was in the fight of his life.

"I have to win, or that's it," Micky told Ron Borges of the *Boston Globe* a week before the fight. "That's 100 percent for sure."

Micky's assessment was dead-on accurate. Veader could give Micky credibility or he could take it all away from him. A win for Micky could show people that he was back and ready to be a factor in the welterweight division, but a loss would prove that his best days were long behind him. Some people in boxing may have thought of him as a dinosaur, too old and too slow to survive. But Micky was only thirty. He wasn't old. He was experienced. "My whole career, I fought the best," Micky said. "It's time [Veader] fought someone like me. There's a hell of a lot of pressure on him now. I remember what that was like. He has everything to lose. He's in the position I was in years ago when I fought Harold Brazier and Charles Murray back-to-back. If he wants to go up, he has to get by someone like me. There's no pressure on me now. I've been on the bottom. The only place I can go is up. I really don't think he has any idea who Micky Ward is, but if he's watching the old tapes like against Murray, he's not seeing who he's going to be in with. That guy didn't care anymore. I was burned-out. I'd lost my self-confidence by then. I'd lost all faith in my ability. It was a combination of my hand problems and my personal problems and just being burned-out after taking too many tough fights in a row. After I lost my big fights, I just felt like I was getting used. But I'm mentally ready for this fight. He's never been hurt and had to fight back to win. He's never been hit and felt like he was in Disneyland for three rounds and come out of it standing. I know about that. It seems like a lifetime since I walked into the West End Gym with my brother. It's so long ago, I don't remember if I liked it or not, but I must have because I kept coming back. I been through a lot since then. For a while, my mind wasn't there and it wasn't fun no more. I kept asking why I was there. Saturday I'll know why I'm there."

Saturday was April 13, 1996. Six thousand people paid their way into the FleetCenter to see a seven-fight card featuring Ward–Veader and Rosenblatt–Davis. Borges was there, and he ran into Micky and Mickey entering through a side door.

"Tonight, the other guy's gonna find out what it means to be a professional," Borges said to Micky.

"That's what I'm counting on," Micky said with a grin.

It was a much nicer welcome than Veader received as he entered the arena that night. Although he was a fellow New Englander, Veader was treated as an outsider. His popular Irish opponent was going to have a significant advantage in crowd support fighting in Boston.

"Some of Micky's people got up in my face and started swearing at me right away," Veader remembers. "I knew it would be his home-field advantage, but he had an even bigger crowd with him than I expected. I was never treated like that. I did most of my fighting in New England, and people either knew me, or at least respected me."

Ring announcer J. J. Wright got the evening started, "Good evening, ladies and gentlemen. Are you ready for some action tonight or what?"

The partisan crowd wanted action. They booed Veader and cheered wildly for Micky during the introductions. Micky acknowledged the fans, but focused on staying loose and shaking off some nerves by bouncing up and down. Veader kept his head down and moved slowly from side to side in his corner.

"I can't say I've fought the toughest opponents, some decent fighters," Veader said during a pre-fight interview with ESPN. "But I'm ready to take the step up. I'm going to win the fight that Micky Ward never won."

When the opening bell sounded, Micky bounded out of his corner and went aggressively after Veader, landing several left uppercuts and a few body shots. It was more of an onslaught than Veader had ever experienced. He tried to keep his distance, but Micky continued his encroachment. Still, Veader's boxing skills were immediately evident. Veader had talent. His footwork was fluid, graceful, and in perfect balance, and his hands were fast. His jab was effective. Veader was in a new place, in front of a large crowd and an angry man, but he was not intimidated.

"When you're in tight, watch for that left hand," Prout told him between the first and second rounds. "Tie him up in there and let the ref break you apart."

Prout was worried about Micky's power. The plan was to make sure that Micky couldn't set up camp on the inside where he could fire his left-hand body shots at will. Early in the second round, Micky landed a stinging left jab and moved in close. He was able to get inside without paying a price, and once inside, he opened up a cut over Veader's right eye. It was a sizeable gash, one that could force a stoppage.

"He caught me just right," Veader said later. "It wasn't a hard shot, but I got a good-sized gash. . . . That was new for me. I was never really cut before."

Unfortunately for Micky, referee Gerry Leone said the cut was caused by a clash of heads. Leone was wrong about that. Leone and the fight doctor looked closely at the cut between rounds. Veader's corner worked feverishly to close the cut and ensure the fight would continue.

"Put your head back," Prout told his young fighter. "You gotta box, baby. Just a little graze, it ain't nothing." Then, pleading with the doctor, Prout said, "It's early. It's early. Let me work, Doc, please. Close your eyes. See, I got it closed, Doc."

Desperation inspired Veader in the third round. In the final minute of the round, Veader landed a big right-hand body shot that hurt Micky. That renewed Veader's confidence, and he was able to land several more power shots before the end of the round. Micky was surprised by Veader's power.

"I'll be honest with you," Micky said after the fight. "He's a good puncher. I got hit there in the third round, and it threw my heart rhythm off. My heartbeats got screwed up. I couldn't catch my breath. That's why I stepped back. I tried to wait around to try to catch my breath, but I couldn't. I was getting scared. I didn't know what to do. But I was not going down."

Micky survived the third-round assault, but while his heart recovered, he lost the third, fourth, and fifth rounds. Fans unaware of his physical ailment and remembering the end of Micky's first career were concerned about Micky's sudden return to inactivity. It was as if the clock had turned back five years, and once again Micky wasn't throwing punches. In the sixth, Veader landed a solid combination that hurt Micky again. This time, however, the barrage served to invigorate Micky. Micky pounded his chest and yelled, "C'mon!" Veader accepted the invitation and moved in. Micky stopped him in his tracks with a hard left. Then he doubled up with two more lefts that stunned Veader. It wasn't enough for Micky to win the round, but it might have been enough to make Veader nervous. "You got him," O'Keefe said after the sixth round. "You got him right where you want him. All you have to do now is take your time. Once you're inside, *tap, tap*. Take the step, and let it go! This guy's never experienced the likes of Micky Ward!"

O'Keefe was right, but he had to be worried about the score-cards. If this fight went the distance, it would be difficult for Micky to win, because he had given away so many of the middle rounds. After a fairly even seventh round, Micky was behind by one point on two of the judges' cards, and the third judge had him ahead by one. O'Keefe made no secret of the fact that the bout was slipping away. He told Micky it was time to go for it all.

"The left, Micky. It's time to land that left!"

It happened quickly. With thirty seconds to go in the eighth round, Veader was sliding with his back along the ropes when Micky hit him with a left hook. It was a shot that stunned Veader more than it hurt him, but he looked confused. He wondered if Micky thought he was hurt, and if he would pounce on him or pull back. While he was wondering, Micky landed two quick shots to his ribs. Veader had been able to fend Micky off for the entire fight, but now as Micky had put it, "He was in Disneyland," and he had to make it through two more rounds. Veader countered, but Micky ducked low. Then, from out of his crouch, Micky rose quickly and brought a hard left hook with him. The blow landed flush. Veader was down in an instant, sprawling against the lower ropes. It was as good and clean a shot as there is in boxing, and it put Veader on his ass. To his credit, Veader got right up. He indicated to the ref that he was okay. Leone believed him and signaled to Micky to return. There were only ten seconds to go in the round, and Veader was able to survive. "Now, you've got him," O'Keefe reiterated. "Go right after him. Double up. Don't let up on him. He's gonna need more time to recover. Now don't get careless. But go get him, Micky. Fucking go get him!"

Micky emerged for the ninth round and quickly put Veader up against the ropes. Veader ducked and bobbed and weaved. He threw harmless jabs in an attempt to keep Micky away. He was on the defensive. Micky began throwing his punches with pinpoint accuracy. He hurt Veader with another left hand. Veader bounced from one set of ropes to another, and the punishment continued. The punches were coming from everywhere. Veader fought courageously, taking the abuse and refusing to go down. Finally, just when it appeared that Micky had tired and his barrage had subsided, Leone jumped in and gave Veader a standing eight-count. At first, it appeared to be an advantage for Veader. It would give him time to recover. But it also gave Micky a chance to catch a breather.

"Are you all right?" Leone asked Veader, and Veader responded with a head nod. Leone allowed the fight to continue.

With Veader's back still against the ropes, Micky threw wildly. He couldn't seem to finish off the wounded warrior in front of him. Micky, exhausted from his incessant, all-out attack leaned against Veader who, exhausted and dizzy, leaned against Micky. The two battlers appeared to be holding each other up, but Micky was merely sizing his opponent up. He had been trying to knock Veader out with head shots, but the head of the Viper had proven to be too elusive. So, Micky fired one more left into Veader's ribs.

"The kid crumpled," O'Keefe said. "It was over, and Micky was the champ."

Veader rested momentarily against the lower rope and picked himself up. But he was met by the referee who waved off the fight. Micky raced over to his corner, dropped to one knee, and thanked God for this moment—his moment. He'd done it!

O'Keefe sprinted into the ring and, operating on pure adrenaline, lifted Micky into the air. They had done this together. Micky raised his hands in exultation, and O'Keefe lowered him down just a bit and kissed him on the cheek. Micky returned to the corner of the ring and dropped once again to one knee.

By now, Micky's mom had entered the ring. She waited for him to rise, and then she hugged her bloody, sweaty son. Micky had finally won the kind of big, important fight that had eluded him so many times in the past.

"I've been through a lot of tough fights and fought some of the best in the world," Micky said after the fight. "I take my hat off to this kid. But I've been waiting a long time for this. I've paid my dues. I knew he was hurt once I went upstairs and then went downstairs. You don't get up from those."

Veader agreed, "The ones that knock you on your butt are the ones you don't see. And I didn't see that one, and the next thing I know I was on the canvas. It was all Micky Ward. He took the fight to me. He deserved to win it. He caught me with a shot, a hook, dropped me on my ass. He hit me on the jaw. I was still dazed and then he hit me with a body shot, and I went down and that was it. It's plain and simple. I'll take this back to the gym and maybe I'll learn from it. But I'll be back definitely."

Micky, who had left the big time behind five years ago, was back. He didn't just win. He won by a knockout. He beat an undefeated fighter in front of six thousand people at the FleetCenter.

"I knew Micky had a lot of heart," said Joe Lake. "Mickey O'Keefe had him in tremendous shape. He's losing every second of every round, but in the ninth round he hits him with that body shot, and the fight's over. Now all the people who thought Micky was done, they start crawling back into the picture."

That included Top Rank promoter Bob Arum, who witnessed the fight. And that could only mean better fights and bigger money.

"I can remember at the end of the eighth round," Valenti says. "Veader's corner was looking at me, and they're saying, 'You tricked us!' I didn't trick them. They wanted the fight. Next thing, the house goes berserk when Micky wins, and Arum was right up on his feet with them. He was ecstatic. He had abandoned Micky, and here he is stopping this 31–0 kid."

It was Micky's sixth straight win by knockout, and his sixth straight win without his brother or father around. They could only watch that night from their separate prisons, but Micky knew they were on his side. He told the ESPN audience after the fight:

"I just want to say hello to my brother, Dickie. This is for you, Dick. I love you. And for my father. I love you. And for little Dickie and my daughter, Kasie, who are watching, and I love you both."

After a few minutes of quiet reflection in the locker room, Micky showered, packed his bag, and left with Mickey O'Keefe. There was a party going on at the Highland Tap, and Micky stopped in to receive the congratulations of his friends, fans, and family. It was a good night. O'Keefe stayed for ten minutes and left unnoticed. He looked back and saw Micky smiling and laughing. He was the toast of the town, the best thing to happen to Lowell since, well, maybe since forever.

CHAPTER TEN

The real money in the junior welterweight division in the spring of 1996 was in the control of Oscar De La Hoya. The Golden Boy had already won titles in the super featherweight and lightweight divisions, and two months after Micky's stirring knockout of Veader, De La Hoya was scheduled to fight Julio Cesar Chavez for the WBC light welterweight title. If Micky could get the winner of that fight, he'd be looking at his first six-figure payday.

There was also the possibility that Micky would fight former WBC super featherweight champion Gabriel Ruelas on the under-card of another Dana Rosenblatt fight. Rosenblatt had earned the fight that Micky never could. He was going to fight Vinny Pazienza in Atlantic City. Rosenblatt suffered the only loss of his career that night, going down in the fourth round.

But both possibilities were long shots. Chavez and De La Hoya were probably looking for bigger and better things than Micky at this time, and Ruelas spent his career fighting at 135 pounds, and wasn't keen on moving up in weight. So, Micky reached for a sure thing. He accepted a rematch with Veader for thirty thousand dollars.

"That was my first negotiation," Joe Lake claims. "I negotiated with Top Rank and Ron Katz for the second Veader fight. They didn't want to pay him that kind of money, because they got him for next to nothing the first time. But Veader's people wanted the fight, because they thought Micky got lucky and that he would never do it again. So, we got Micky some money for what we figured would be an easy night."

The rematch would be held at Foxwoods Resort Casino in Connecticut three months after their first encounter.

"I took a couple of weeks off after that first fight," Veader says. "Then they came with the idea for the rematch, and I said, 'Yeah.' I wanted it. I always felt confident I could beat the guy. I knew I was doing all the right things in the first fight until he hit me with that shot."

Micky, who had been in the gym every day for ten months, also took a few weeks off after the first Veader fight. He arrived at the weigh-in the day before the fight a pound and a half over the limit. So O'Keefe brought him to a sauna in the hotel to sweat it out. After an hour, Micky had lost the pound and a half, and O'Keefe had lost closer to eight.

The fight was promoted as "The Redemption," which meant it had been hyped as Veader's chance to redeem himself. The fight title and promotional hook were more than a little disrespectful to the guy who had won the first fight. It turned Micky into a role player, someone who was just supposed to play a bit part in the career of another fighter. But every fight for Micky now was an attempt to atone for his own missed opportunities. He wasn't insulted by the focus on Veader. He was determined to make this all about his own redemption.

Micky walked out of his locker room at Foxwoods led by O'Keefe's good friend Danny Gilday, who was waving a large Irish flag. The crowd, already much more in favor of Micky than Veader, responded with raucous cheers. They were some of the last big cheers of the evening.

From the beginning, it was clear that this fight would not be waged the same way as the first one. Veader, who had been felled in the first fight by a couple of big head and body shots when either fighting inside or coming out of a clinch, was dead set on not letting that happen again.

"I knew the mistake I made in the first fight," Veader says. "He's kind of awkward. It was tough to box with him. He was tough to figure out. I was always second-guessing myself. Towards the end of the second fight, I just started going at him, and I remember thinking this is how I should have fought the whole fight."

Fans would like to have seen that, too. The first three rounds were identical to one another. Micky would either punch and jab his way inside or just walk through a couple of Veader punches. Either way, once he got inside, Veader grabbed hold of him, especially cognizant of tying up Micky's left hand. He definitely didn't want to get hit with that meat hook again.

Nothing changed in the fourth, and referee Steve Smoger was not happy about it. At one point, he admonished the fighters, saying: "I'm giving you guys the opportunity to work your way out of these clenches. Let's go. No more holding on."

It was a warning to both fighters, but it was meant for Veader. He was the guilty party. In the sixth round, Smoger reprimanded Veader again about the excessive holding. And in the seventh round, Smoger pulled Veader aside for a third time. Smoger was well within his rights to take a point away from Veader, but he did not.

"It's time to switch to southpaw, Micky," O'Keefe advised him before the eighth round. "If you turn that way, he'll have trouble holding the left. Come at him from a different angle and see how he handles that. Go for it, Micky."

The strategy worked. In the eighth, Micky was able to get inside and stay there long enough to land a dozen or so lefts. Finally, free to throw, Micky assailed Veader with assorted uppercuts, body shots, and hooks. A few of them seemed to hurt Veader, who quickly covered up. He was grabbing hold of Micky's right hand now, and the left was busy finding its target. Veader's plan to survive was backfiring badly. Each time Micky moved inside, Veader took a couple of blows before he could hold on, and those blows were taking their toll. The scorecards may have been close, but Veader was getting beat up worse than he had been in the first fight. Another cut had opened up over his right eye, and his face was growing puffy.

"You're the champion, Mick," O'Keefe said before the start of the final round. "You're the champion. Go out there and show him. You're the champion. The champion!"

Micky was the champion, albeit the WBC Continental Americas champion, for whatever that was worth. And he defended the title with a unanimous twelve-round decision. When the decision was announced, O'Keefe lifted Micky in victory once again, and the championship belt was draped around Micky's waist. Back in the locker room, Micky thought about how grateful he was for the opportunity, for the victory, for the second chance, and for Mickey O'Keefe. As Lake, O'Keefe, and Micky left the building, they were met by about two hundred people waiting for Micky, hoping he'd say hello and sign his name in assorted autograph books or on programs, shirts, baseball caps, and in some cases even cleavage. Micky did stop, and he signed for everyone there. He talked to every kid and made sure the fans got what they wanted. It took nearly two hours. Only then did Micky return to his room and fall instantly asleep.

There was no giant celebration this time, no ride back to the Highland Tap. Micky felt good, but he couldn't deny that this victory wasn't as sweet as the first one against Veader. Beating Veader was a nice payday for a struggling street worker, but it was not a brilliant career move.

Veader fought only once more, nearly a year later, beating a mediocre Daryl Lattimore at the Strand Theater in Providence. Veader finished his career with a record of 31–2. He was a pro fighter for seven years, but the twenty thousand dollars he took home from the two fights with Micky was the most money he ever made. It should have been different.

"I stopped because I just got frustrated," Veader says. "They kept me in limbo. . . . I had a daughter from a previous relationship, so I just had to start working. I made more money working. So I decided

I'm just gonna go back to driving a truck like I'd always done. Look, I never thought I was going to be this undisputed greatest fighter, but I always liked my chances against anybody I fought. . . . Obviously I wanted to win a title, but it just didn't happen. I feel I got a lot out of boxing. . . . And it was fun. But I did think I'd have more of an opportunity to make some money, not be rich, but just some money. And basically, I just walked away with nothing."

And that's the slim margin of difference in the world of boxing. Ron Borges explains it this way:

> Veader thought the first fight was his night to shine. He didn't know he was going to find out that he was in there with a different animal. Veader fought bravely that night. But in the second fight, he made a clear decision that he was not going to get stopped by this guy. If you're a halfway decent boxer, you can go a hundred rounds with Joe Louis. . . . You're not going to win the fight, but he's not going to knock you out. You have to be somewhat complicit in your own demise. I think [Veader] realized that if I can't beat this guy, I can't beat the top guys, because this guy isn't even among the top guys. And he wasn't. Micky was a top guy in certain things, his willingness to take the punishment, and his ability to take it, and of course the body punch. Plus, his resiliency in life. Most people would have crashed and burned, the people around him certainly tried. If Valenti hadn't come around when he did, Micky probably would have crashed. Micky needed somebody who cared about him a little bit. I'm not saying Valenti is Mother Teresa with a beard, but he wanted him to win some fights. He could make some money.

And Micky was ready to cash in, but he knew things needed to be different this time. He needed better management. Mickey O'Keefe was a wonderful friend and a great trainer, but he wasn't an experienced manager or a well-connected one. Joe Lake was committed to Dana Rosenblatt. And Micky still harbored a grudge against the guys at Top Rank.

This time Micky was going to take control. That meant surrounding himself with people he trusted, which made his next move all the more curious. Micky solicited the help of an unlikely suspect, a guy with no experience in the business of boxing whatsoever, a guy who ran a cab company in Boston, a guy whose greatest qualification was that he was friends with Micky's father. Micky asked Sal LoNano for help, and just like that Team Ward was under new management.

CHAPTER ELEVEN

"Sal LoNano wants you to believe he's connected to the mob. I don't think he's connected to his balls."

That was Danny Gilday's assessment, and one that Mickey O'Keefe shares. O'Keefe was suspicious of LoNano as soon as he started hanging around the gym when Micky was working out.

"What the hell are you coming around here for," O'Keefe challenged LoNano one day before the first Veader fight.

"I'm just making sure Micky's okay."

"Well, who the fuck are you?"

"I'm a friend of his father. He asked me to keep an eye on Micky."

O'Keefe wanted to throw him out. His years on the police force told him that the tall round man with the round face, black curly hair, and the large fingers was up to no good. But Micky didn't mind him being there, so O'Keefe kept his mouth shut.

LoNano was the owner of J. J. Automotive in South Boston and the Independent Taxi Company. He'd attended most of Micky's early fights and got to know Micky's father, George. Micky thought that he was a decent guy and a successful businessman, and at his father's prompting, Micky asked Sal to get involved with his career. Their meeting took place inside Micky's pickup truck in the parking lot of the Ninety Nine Restaurant in Lowell.

"You know something, Sal," Micky began, "other than Mickey, I just don't have any faith and trust in the people that I'm with. I feel like they're taking my money. It happened before, and I don't want it to happen again. I can't fight and worry about my money."

Micky was looking for an honest man in a dishonest world. He thought he'd found one to work with him and Mickey O'Keefe, so he continued.

"I'd like you to come on and be my top advisor."

LoNano had been in business for twenty-five years, but he admitted to Micky that he might be out of his element when it came to giving advice to a professional boxer.

"What does a top advisor do?" Sal asked. "I mean, Micky, I'm only being honest with you."

Micky didn't really know either. He only knew that he wanted Sal to stick around, to help guide him, and to be involved in the major decisions regarding his career. He also wanted Sal to keep an eye on the money trail.

Sal didn't agree to anything that day in the pickup truck, but he did call Bruce Trampler of Top Rank and, with Micky's authority, asked him to send a copy of all of Micky's checks. After a quick evaluation of the records, Sal discovered that twenty-five hundred dollars were missing that Micky didn't know about.

"They had taken twenty-five hundred dollars out, not once, but twice," Sal says. "I showed Micky and said, 'This is what's going on, buddy. This is what they're doing.'"

"Sal, I want you to manage me," was all Micky said.

Sal was floored. He immediately felt the pressure that comes with the fear of failure. He wanted to help Micky, but he was afraid of the responsibility. He would be entering unknown territory and if he failed, it was Micky who would suffer most.

"I gotta be honest with you," Sal said. "I'm a fight fan. I love the fights. I love you as a fighter and as a human being, but do you know what you're asking me?"

"Sal, I need someone that I can trust. I can train. And believe me, Sal, whatever matches you want to make, I'll fight. I'll fight anybody."

"Yeah, but buddy, it's not as easy as what you're telling me."

Sal accepted, and like Joe Lake before him, he sat down with Micky's mom to lay out the ground rules. Micky wanted him to be in charge, so he would be in charge. No questions asked. Once again, Alice stepped aside and gave Sal the go-ahead to navigate Micky's career.

Sal turned out to be a quick study. His initial apprehension was replaced by a nervous energy and acute curiosity. He asked questions of everyone. He wanted to know about Micky's diet and his training regimen. He introduced himself to all of the major players in the fight game, including promoters, managers, and other trainers. He eventually found one of the best cutmen in the business, Al Gavin, to begin working Micky's corner. And it was Gavin who gave him the confidence that he could be successful as a first-time manager.

"Don't worry about it so much, Sal," Gavin said. "You'll be a good manager, because you're not a fighter. If you were a boxer, and then you wanted to be a manager, the whole thing would be a cluster fuck."

And in just a matter of months, Sal delivered the goods, or perhaps more accurately, the goods were delivered directly to him. It was Labor Day 1996, five weeks after Micky's second victory over Veader, when Al Valenti received a phone call from Ron Katz.

"I'm gonna make Micky Ward and Chavez," Katz blurted.

"You're gonna make Ward and Chavez," Valenti repeated. "Wait a minute. Before you do anything, I did all the work bringing Micky Ward back, and now you're telling me *you're* making Ward and Chavez?"

"I'm just telling you that's what's going on," Katz explained.

"Where are you going to do it?"

"I don't know. Maybe in Boston."

"Well, that would be a nice consideration," Valenti said. "Then at least maybe I'd get to promote the thing."

A few days later, Valenti's phone rang again. This time it was Sal.

"Let me ask your opinion," Sal began. "Can you trust Ron Katz?"

"I wouldn't trust him as far as I could throw him," Valenti said. He was still upset about not being involved in the Ward–Chavez plans.

"Well, how much do you think Micky should get to fight Chavez?"

"Well, you're asking me a loaded question here," Valenti began. "Because if I throw out a number, you're gonna have that number in your head, and it's only my opinion. I'd rather not give you a number, but I will tell you it's worth money. It's not a title fight, but it's worth some real money."

Armed with this vague information, Sal negotiated with Bob Arum and Top Rank for Micky to fight Julio Cesar Chavez in Las Vegas for the biggest payday of his life—one hundred thousand dollars. Micky signed a contract to fight on HBO on the same card as James Toney and Montel Griffin who would battle for the WBU light heavyweight title. Micky was back in the big time.

Chavez may have been the best there ever was. He began fighting professionally in Culiacan, Mexico, in 1980, and he went fourteen years and ninety-one fights before experiencing defeat. Along the way he won and defended titles in the super featherweight, featherweight, lightweight, and light welterweight divisions. By 1996, he had fought in twenty-six championship fights and won them all. He finally lost a split decision to Frankie Randall when he was knocked down for the first time in his career and was penalized one point in both the seventh and eleventh rounds for low blows. He avenged the loss to Randall four months later, and he didn't lose again until Oscar De La Hoya bettered and battered him in June 1996, knocking him out in the fourth round. After that loss in June, Chavez was looking for paydays and contenders. He began by knocking out Maine's Joey Gamache in October. For that fight, Chavez earned 1.5 million dollars, all of which went to the

Mexican government to cover back taxes. He needed another payday and another contender, and this time he chose Micky Ward. It was the best moneymaking opportunity of Micky's career, and if he won, he could start thinking seriously about a title shot with De La Hoya.

Micky needed to be ready for this battle. He needed to prepare as he'd never prepared before. And since the fight would be in Reno, Nevada, Team Ward, now consisting of Sal, Mickey O'Keefe, and Jimmy Connolly, another trainer, went out to Big Bear, California, for six weeks.

"I'll never forget Big Bear," Sal says. "When we first got up there, you have to get used to the atmosphere. It's ten thousand feet above sea level. As soon as we arrived, we went shopping for groceries, and I was leaning on the cart, stumbling all over the place, trying to catch my breath. Micky's looking at me and he says, 'For Christ sakes, what are you, drunk?' I couldn't get my feet going. It took me a day to get used to it."

Big Bear was boxing heaven for Micky. The surroundings were beautiful, and there were no distractions. He wasn't in Lowell anymore. He didn't work a ten-hour shift and then try to squeeze a training session in late in the evening. No friends and family calling him all the time or invitations to go out drinking. In fact, there was no alcohol in the cabin where the four men stayed. There were no temptations; only the work mattered. This is what Micky missed in the first part of his career. This is what Ben Doherty and the men from Rhode Island had offered him when they wanted to financially back him as an investment. This is what the best and highest-paid professional boxers did to get ready for a fight. And Micky was right on the edge of breaking into that circle of great fighters. Beating Chavez would put him in the center.

So Micky got up every morning at 4:30 for his five-mile run. He returned for a healthy breakfast and a serious training session with O'Keefe and Connolly, who, as expected, weren't getting along. O'Keefe never warmed to the idea that Sal had taken charge, and he resented the fact that Sal had brought in another trainer to help. O'Keefe didn't think he needed any help.

"It was a fucking nightmare from the beginning," O'Keefe remembers. "You could feel something wasn't right. Sal's there telling me about the mother, and that he's gonna be the spokesperson. I knew then something was up. Then Jimmy Connolly says to me, 'I'm gonna have Mick doing this and this, and I need him to do that.' I says to him, 'Jimmy, did something change since last week. I thought I was the trainer.' And he says, 'Well, Sal wants me to do it.' Fuck that! I tell him, 'I don't care what Sal does. I don't care what you do. I know Micky better than any of you. I've been working with him every day. When nobody else is there, it's Micky and me.' So right off the bat, that set the tone. Thank God for A.A. I went to meetings every night just to calm myself down."

There was obvious tension in Team Ward. O'Keefe put himself on the outside of Sal and Connolly, but continued to keep his focus on getting Micky ready. Micky worked hard and tried to relieve some of the tension with some practical jokes.

"He put toilet paper in my shoes," Sal explains. "I had told him my feet were sore, and then the next morning I couldn't put my sneaker on. He says, 'You got the gout. We gotta take you to the hospital.' I believed him. So, I'm like sweating bullets, I'm so nervous. He's walking around saying, 'Sometimes they gotta cut the foot off with the gout.' I'm like, 'Don't they have some pills they could give me?' And he's like, 'Yeah, but sometimes it doesn't work, Sal. They might have to take the foot right off.' Then all of a sudden he says, 'Let's go to the hospital.' So, he goes to his room to get ready to leave, and I took my sneaker off. That's when some of the toilet paper comes out, and I yelled, 'You bastard!'"

Micky says he was fully prepared to take the prank all the way to the hospital. "That would have been great!" he laughs.

But the laughter stopped on December 1, five days before the fight. Chavez had pulled out. Chavez had been paid a half million dollars in advance by promoter Bob Arum, but he wasn't going to fight.

"One of the Chavez people was in the gym watching Micky work out," O'Keefe recalls. "And they're seeing this devastating left hook. I'm not saying Chavez would be afraid of that, but his people might be. If you see sparring partners going down and looking like they're gonna puke, it gets to you."

That's not the excuse Chavez gave, however. Chavez claimed to have hurt his hand during a training session. He delivered a doctor's note written in Spanish to Top Rank that, when translated, simply said "hand injury." But there were reports that if Chavez truly did hurt his hand, he hurt it while beating up his brother-in-law. Chavez was embroiled in a custody dispute with his wife, and he may have kidnapped his son. It was more likely personal problems that caused him to pull out of the fight.

Top Rank's Bruce Trampler delivered the news to Sal. Sal sat Micky and Mickey down at the kitchen table in the Big Bear cabin and simply said, "We're not fighting Chavez."

The room went quiet. Sal didn't know what to say next, and Micky and Mickey were too stunned to speak. Finally, after Sal gave a brief explanation of the reasons he'd been given, O'Keefe slammed both palms down on the table, stood up, and said, "Fuck it, Sal. Let's go home."

But it wasn't that simple.

"We can't—" Sal began.

"What do you mean we can't? It's easy. We pack up, and we get the hell out of here."

"There's the expense money," Sal said.

"What the fuck do I care about that?" O'Keefe shouted.

"We're gonna have to pay them back the twenty thousand dollars," Sal explained. Micky was just sitting there listening to his two handlers sort this out.

"Why would we have to pay that back?" O'Keefe was incredulous. "I thought that money was given up front. It's not our fault there's not gonna be a fight."

"No, they said we'd have to pay it back if there's no fight, but look, they've got another kid for us."

O'Keefe didn't like the sound of that. He'd come out to Big Bear and missed his wedding anniversary in order to get Micky ready for a fight with Chavez. Micky was ready. The strategy was in place.

Now, a few days before the fight, they were going to throw some-body else at them.

"Who's the kid?" O'Keefe asked.

"Manny Castillo."

"A Mexican?"

"Yeah, I think so."

"Jesus Christ!" O'Keefe exclaimed. "Are you kidding me?"

"So, he's Mexican. What's the problem?"

"Do you know anything about the Mexican fighters, Sal? Them Mexican fighters, they fight the fights so they can get in the gym and fight. They're tough. And they come to fight."

"We'll be all right," Sal said directing his comment more to Micky than to O'Keefe.

"We don't even know anything about this guy," O'Keefe argued. "There's no tape. What's his style? We're gonna throw Micky up against someone he's never seen or heard of before? It makes no sense."

It made even less sense the day of the fight, December 6, 1996. It was several hours before Micky was scheduled to enter the ring. Micky and Mickey were in the dressing room when Sal entered, clearly dismayed. The expression on his face was as if someone had died. It was the money.

"I'm sorry, Micky," Sal began. "There's nothing I could do. But they're not going to give you the one hundred thousand dollars for this fight."

"What the fuck, Sal!" O'Keefe yelled.

"Yeah, Sal, what are you talking about?" Micky asked.

"Arum just told me that we signed a contract to fight Chavez for a hundred grand. Now he tells me, 'No Chavez, no hundred grand.'"

"So, what are we fighting for?" O'Keefe interjected.

"Ten."

"Ten?"

"*Ten!*"

"That's bullshit, Sal! That's bullshit and you know it! C'mon,

Micky, let's get the fuck out of here. You and me. Like it's always been. You and me are walking out of here together right now!"

But Micky didn't move. He was watching ninety thousand dollars drain out of his bank account. In his mind, he'd already put the money in there. He was planning on buying a house, a nice one, in a nice neighborhood in Lowell, somewhere close to his mom and to the Highland Tap. There were some houses off Stevens Street that had some nice backyards. He'd thought about owning one since he was a kid, and he was close a few years ago. But when Laurie and Kasie left, he lost some of the desire to be a homeowner. And the money had gotten tight in a hurry. With rent and child support, there wasn't a lot left over from a road paver's salary.

Micky just sat there with his head down. He needed a moment to let his dream die. Micky was calm. O'Keefe was a wild man, ranting and pacing. And Sal began to sweat. Deep down he knew that O'Keefe was right. He knew he wouldn't allow a bait-and-switch maneuver like this to screw him in his other business dealings, but this was different. There was the twenty thousand dollars that was already gone that would have to be paid back. Micky and Mickey weren't going to do it. That would be on him.

"Christ, twenty K's a lot of money," he thought. But he couldn't tell Micky to fight. O'Keefe wanted to take that decision out of Micky's hands, but that's exactly where Sal put it.

"I'll fight him," Micky says.

"Of course you'll fight him," O'Keefe said. "You're Micky Ward. What the fuck else are you going to say? But this is crazy! We take this fight, and we're all a bunch of patsies. . . . Sal, you can't let him do this."

Years later Sal would say, "It was a bad business decision, but we took into play that Micky wanted to fight, and he was ready. It wasn't about the money. It was about beating this kid and moving on to the next fight."

"You're on such a high," Micky added. "Then the fight gets canceled. So you don't want to fight, but you want to fight because you're ready. You want the money, too. Ten grand is ten grand, you know? You're not fighting the big-name guy now, so the money gets cut. But what are you going to do? You still have to pay rent. I needed to make the money. I still have a daughter. You have to make money somehow. What am I gonna do, just come home and make nothing? He was a tough kid from East L.A. I fucking nailed that kid."

Micky took the fight, but it cost him. He lost ninety thousand dollars, and more.

"In the first round," Micky explains. "I throw a body punch at him. Right there, the tendon ripped off the bone. It was my left thumb, and it killed. It felt like an M-80 went off in there. I had to go nine rounds with that. My thumb was huge when I was done. Now, I've lost my left hand, which is my bread and butter. I kept throwing it anyway because it was numb. I couldn't feel it anymore."

O'Keefe was the first man in the corner that night with Jimmy Connolly working as the assistant. O'Keefe was aware of Micky's thumb injury as soon as it happened. He could read it on Micky's face, and it was confirmed when Micky didn't throw the left again for the rest of the first round.

"What's the problem, Mick?" O'Keefe asked as Micky sat down on his stool.

"My thumb. It hurts bad."

"Don't worry about it. We're gonna be fine," O'Keefe assured him. "This kid is gonna stick and move. He's not gonna stay around long enough to get hit. He's gonna stay away from you and slip. You watch. He'll plant that elbow to protect himself. So, get him upstairs."

O'Keefe was upbeat and positive for the one minute he had Micky's attention in the corner. But as Micky returned to the center of the ring for the start of the second round, O'Keefe spotted Sal in the front row, and gave him a look as if to say, "This is your fault, you son of a bitch."

"You know, between rounds you only have a minute," O'Keefe explained later. "But you really only need about fifteen seconds. You get him over there. You sit him down. You wet him up. You let him relax, take a breath. You get him ready, and then you say, 'Are you ready? All right, here's what you gotta do. He's throwing that jab. Throw the double jab. Get underneath, hook, hook, move.' Micky knows what to do. He just needs to hear it before he goes back out there."

Micky lost the first four rounds on all the judges' cards. This was going as badly as it could.

"Look at me," O'Keefe said to Micky between the fourth and fifth rounds, but Micky didn't seem to focus. "Look at me!"

Micky was still not listening. "Look at me. Focus on me. Forget about the crowd. I just want you to win this one round. Go out there and box him. Stop trying to take him out. Box him!"

Micky won the fifth round, and the sixth, and the seventh. He could no longer feel the pain in his left thumb, and he was throwing well with both hands. In the eighth, Micky dropped Castillo with a left hook. Castillo jumped back up clapping his hands together, smiling through his mouthpiece.

"It was like he was glad that I hit him," Micky said. "That kid was tough. I won, but I paid the price, because of my thumb, and the ninety thousand dollars gone."

Micky ended up winning the fight on a split decision, but there was little jubilation in Ward's camp. Micky had ruptured a tendon in his thumb, and he had struggled to beat an unranked, unheralded, unheard-of boxer. His big-money fight had been snatched away from him, and there was no way of knowing if he'd ever get another one. Micky was disappointed. Sal was worried. O'Keefe was pissed.

"Instead of making a hundred grand, Micky makes ten," O'Keefe states with some incredulity. "That's what they said. I'd like to know."

O'Keefe's anger and suspicion reached a boiling point after Team Ward had flown back home and landed at Logan Airport. O'Keefe, who had left for Big Bear about three weeks after the other three guys, including Connolly, needed a ride home, but he was insistent that he wouldn't take a ride from Sal.

"You coming home with us?" Micky asked.

"I wouldn't get in that fucking car with them if my life depended on it. No way, no how. I'm still too fucking pissed."

"Are you mad at me, too?" Micky said with a hint of school-boy in his voice.

"Yeah, I am, Micky. How could you let those guys do that to you? You're gonna fight Chavez for a lot of money, and you ended up fighting this other guy for chump change? How do you know for sure the hundred grand wasn't still out there on the table only somebody else picked it up?"

"Who? Sal? He wouldn't do that."

"I'm glad you can be so sure. I'm not. I've been a cop for too many years. Nobody's above suspicion, Micky. Nobody but you and me. Where were these guys for the past two and a half years when it was just you and me in the gym every day, and fighting for four hundred bucks? You couldn't find those little shits then, but they're around now. They're around to make money off of your blood and your sweat. Don't you forget that, Micky. Don't ever forget that."

There was a heavy snow falling, but the two men seemed not to notice. They stood there quietly for a moment, the silence broken by Sal blowing the horn as he pulled up in the car. It was time to part ways. Before Micky jumped in the car with Sal and Jimmy, and O'Keefe went off to call for his own ride, O'Keefe took a deep breath of cold New England air. He exhaled with a short, strong burst, shook off the cold, and said:

"Look, Micky. I'm not really mad at you. I just want to kill those bastards, and I'm trying not to say too much. Go home. Get some rest. Then we'll see about that hand, probably needs surgery, you know. Then we'll see when we can get you back in the gym."

"All right, Mickey. And just, you know, thanks for everything. And it's just that I didn't have a choice. I had to fight or I'd end up with nothing. Again."

The two men gave each other a quick hug and a slap on the back, and Micky got into the back of Sal's car. Sal avoided eye contact with O'Keefe, who remained on the curb long enough to watch the car pull away. There it was, both literally and symbolically, Sal was taking Micky away from him.

LoNano would be side by side with Micky from this point forward, but he was never made to feel welcome by the surrounding influences in Micky's life.

"I took money from my business to help this kid out," LoNano says. "And still I was getting shit on from the people of Lowell."

There were reasons for that, valid or otherwise. Sal was an outsider. He wasn't from Lowell, wasn't part of the inner circle, and had no boxing experience whatsoever. Even though Micky had asked him to guide his career, the public perception was that Sal had somehow weaseled his way in and forced O'Keefe out. It was a bad decision to fight Castillo, and Sal was held accountable. There was also the little matter of ninety thousand dollars that was a cause for great suspicion. The big stranger with the gold chains around his neck had only been in the picture for a few months, but already money was missing, O'Keefe was out, and Micky had a bad thumb.

"I got everybody pissed off," Sal says. "All of Lowell is ready to come down on me because O'Keefe is a Lowell cop, more popular than me. I came into his town and I erupted his world. It wasn't about Mickey O'Keefe, and it wasn't about Sal LoNano. It was about Micky Ward, and I had a job to do. I'm nervous, because I don't want to ruin this kid's career. I always said, 'I was with Micky Ward because I believe in him.' That's what drove me to stay with him."

Fortunately for Micky, Bob Arum also believed in him. Arum first brokered a deal with Chavez and promoter Don King to get back his five-hundred-thousand-dollar advance, and then he looked for a way to make amends for Micky's lost wages and missed opportunity.

"Maybe it will all work out for the best," Micky said hopefully. "Because putting me on this card was kind of a makeup to me from Mr. Arum."

The makeup date was April 12, 1997. After a short time off to have his thumb surgically repaired and healed, Micky would fight on the undercard of the Pernell Whitaker–Oscar De La Hoya welterweight championship fight at the Thomas and Mack Center in Las Vegas. As a way of making things right, it was a sincere effort on Arum's part to give Micky another opportunity, but it didn't quite make up for the disparity in paychecks four months earlier. Ward would be paid thirty thousand dollars to fight undefeated Alfonzo Sanchez. It was expected to be a severe test. Sanchez had won his first sixteen pro fights, fourteen of them ended in knockouts before the end of the third round. "Pancho" Sanchez was strong, very strong.

"Hey, look, I'm thirty-one years old," Micky said before the fight. "There's no point in taking easy fights at this stage. I need to find out where I am. This is a reality check. You can't keep fighting nobodies or you'll never know who you are."

Micky knew the truth. If he lost, he wouldn't be done. He could still make decent money as the opponent on the undercards of main events. He was talented and entertaining enough for that. But if he lost, he knew he might never be able to convince anyone that he deserved a shot at a legitimate title.

"Micky's got heart," Jimmy Connolly told the *Boston Herald* days before the fight. "He's been screwing around his entire career, but he knows every fight is an important fight now."

Connolly was the trainer chosen to talk to the press this time around, because for the first time since Micky began his comeback, O'Keefe would not be in his corner. That was emphatically decided one afternoon at the West End Gym in Lowell.

"Mickey," Sal said to O'Keefe. "I'm not trying to piss you off, but I thought you should know that we're gonna go with Jimmy as the first man in the corner. You'll be the second."

"What the hell are you talking about? Fuck that! I'm not the second man. I've been training Micky forever."

"I just think Jimmy's got more experience," Sal explained. "We could be on our way to the big time, and I don't want to take any chances."

"And what experience do you have, Sal? Who the fuck are you, anyway?"

"I'm a businessman, and I'm making a business decision. It's nothing personal."

"Of course it's personal. It's me and Micky. That's personal. Micky's a person, and I'm a person, and we've been in this thing for years. Now you come in here and start telling me I'm second? That's horseshit. I'm no second."

"Well, that's the way it's gonna be."

O'Keefe knew that this was Sal's big power play. Sal was trying to get him to quit. Truth be told, the growing tension in the gym every day wasn't good for Micky. It was making everyone uneasy, and it was nothing more than another nonconducive, unwanted distraction. But O'Keefe wasn't ready to quit, not without a fight.

"Did you know about this, Micky?" O'Keefe shouted as Micky finished pounding the heavy bag and walked over to officiate the argument.

"Yeah, Mickey. I'm real sorry about that. It's just that Sal thinks this will be better."

"Oh, that's what Sal thinks, is it? When the hell did you stop knowing how to think for yourself? Do you think it's gonna be better? You think having that guy talking to you between rounds is gonna be better? C'mon, Micky, who knows you better than me? Who can get you to listen better? Who knows your style and what works for you better than me? Who? These fucks?"

Micky didn't have answers for any of those questions, at least not any that he could express at that moment. In his heart, he knew that O'Keefe was his most loyal and trusted friend. But loyalty had never been especially profitable for Micky. O'Keefe was an inspirational leader and a great motivator, but Sal was getting things done. After all, he was about to make decent money, and the promise of much more was right there in front of him if he won. He didn't want to hurt O'Keefe, but he felt that he had to listen to Sal's advice. He was going with his gut this time, not his heart.

"Mickey, it doesn't have to be like this," Micky said to his friend. "You can still work the corner. I'll know you're there. I want you there. You know? I need you there."

"Well, there's no way I'm gonna be there if that guy's there," O'Keefe said without hesitation. Then he laid down the ultimatum, "Look, Micky, you have to decide. It's Sal or it's me. One of us is walking out of here right now. If it's me, so be it."

And so it was. O'Keefe didn't know it at the time, but Micky had already signed a contract with Sal. The contract made Sal Micky's official manager with certain rights and privileges to decide things such as who would be in Micky's corner. It was a preemptive move that Sal made in anticipation of a power struggle such as this one. In the end, Micky didn't have a choice, unless he wanted a legal battle. He'd been there before with Gagliardi, and he wasn't going through it again.

"I'm staying with Sal. I'm sorry, Mickey."

O'Keefe turned, grabbed his things, and walked out. In the next few weeks, he received several calls from Micky and his mother asking him to please come back.

"That's it for me," O'Keefe told them both. "Let Sal work the corner. He wants to be in the corner anyway. This is his big chance to be in the limelight. Let him have it. I'm out."

It wasn't easy for O'Keefe to walk away, but the right thing to do hardly ever is, and it was the right thing for him. O'Keefe knew who Dickie was, and certainly didn't want to deal with him when he got out of prison. He had enough experience with Alice to know who she was, and she had worn him down before. The writing was on the wall. Mickey O'Keefe stood to receive all of the blame, none of the credit, little of the money, and all of the bullshit. So he walked.

Micky was disappointed, but he moved past it quickly. Boxing was a rough game, and O'Keefe was a tough guy. He'd be fine. No sense worrying about what had already happened. It was time to focus on what was about to happen—the Sanchez fight.

For the ninth fight of his comeback, Micky entered the ring in an emerald robe with white trim. He was wearing green trunks as well. The white Irish kid who could fight was playing up his Irish heritage as much as possible for the national audience. Tonight, his fight with

Sanchez was leading off the broadcast. And with Whittaker and De La Hoya waiting in the wings, the number of viewers was sure to be in the millions.

In the first round, Micky circled the ring, making himself a moving and nearly unhittable target. Roy Jones Jr., a member of the broadcast team for HBO, said, "Sanchez looks like one of those heavy-hitting Mexicans who don't have a lot of speed, but have a lot of power."

Micky and his corner were aware of that reputation, and they weren't looking to find out the veracity of it in the first three minutes. The crowd at the Thomas and Mack Center didn't wait to voice their displeasure. They started booing Micky before the end of the first round. Micky landed just one of fourteen punches in round one.

"What I'm thinking is this could be one of those David Copperfield fights," HBO analyst Larry Merchant began. "You know, David Copperfield the magician. You wish he was here so he could make this fight disappear."

Announcer Jim Lampley summarily derided Micky for continuing to circle the ring, openly mocking him when Micky did stop long enough to engage.

"Oh, he threw a punch," Lampley said with mock surprise. "He threw a left hand to the body."

And Merchant wasn't finished. "Isn't the Boston Marathon coming up soon? As I watch Ward, I keep thinking of running and stuff."

It was an embarrassing two rounds. Micky may have been following orders, but he appeared to be running scared.

"This is dreadful, dreadful stuff," Lampley offered. "But it is the theater of the unexpected. Maybe by the end it will be a barn burner."

But round three was just more of the same.

"People are paying to be entertained, and they're not getting it," HBO fight analyst Harold Lederman said. "Mitch Halpern should call time. I mean, this guy's running away. It's awful. So, it's up to the referee really to get this guy to fight. And he should. He should just stop it, and say, 'If you don't fight, you don't get paid.'"

By the start of the fifth round, Micky had only landed a total of twelve punches. Perhaps, thinking it was time to stop running, Micky found what appeared to be an opportunity. He fired off a right hand, but it only grazed Sanchez. The attempt left Micky slightly off balance and unprotected. Sanchez countered with a booming left uppercut, and Micky dropped instantly to one knee. He stood up quickly, but Halpern gave him a standing eight count.

"Are you all right?" Halpern asked staring straight into Micky's eyes.

"Yeah," Micky said with a nod.

Micky didn't appear hurt, but he returned to bouncing and running around the ring.

"This is really one of the saddest kinds of fights in boxing," Merchant lamented. "Micky Ward is thirty-one years old. He's here because he needs the money. He's taking a beating. He's getting humiliated. It is part of the game that is in no way ennobling or uplifting."

Between the sixth and seventh rounds, Halpern did go over to Micky's corner and tell him he needed to start fighting or a point would be taken away, and eventually the fight might have to be stopped. Micky had lost all six rounds of a scheduled ten-round fight. There was no way he could win the fight on points. He'd have to earn a knockout, and if Halpern didn't see some effort in that direction, there really was no sense in continuing.

"C'mon, Micky! You're not going to get hurt," Connolly said. "Look, we're losing six rounds. They're gonna stop the fight. Is that what you want? You want me to stop it? I'm gonna stop this fight, Micky. I swear to Christ, I'll stop it!"

Micky reacted angrily, "Don't stop this fight. Don't you ever stop this fight!"

Micky stood up and pounded his gloves together. He couldn't hear Sal yelling from his position in the front row, "You gotta go out there and go to the body, Micky! You're running around too much! Don't run around anymore. Go to his body!"

Midway through the seventh round, Micky landed a hard left to the body. It went undetected by most of the people in attendance and watching at home, but Sanchez flinched. It wasn't obvious, but Micky noticed it. He saw just enough in that flinch to know he had hurt Sanchez. How much did he hurt him?

"Well," Micky thought. "I guess I'll just have to find out."

Ten seconds later, the fighters moved in close. For one of the very few times in the fight, they stood toe-to-toe. Micky tapped Sanchez in the head with his left hand, and then dropped it downstairs to the ribs. It was his patented move. The tap to the head served no other purpose than to make Sanchez forget about protecting his body for a moment, and the shot to the body served to remind Sanchez that he should never leave his ribs unprotected. It was a ferocious hit to the liver, and Sanchez went down in a heap.

He began crawling along the floor in agony. He looked like a soldier wounded in battle trying to crawl back into his foxhole.

"What am I looking at?" Merchant said while trying to take his foot out of his mouth.

Sanchez continued crawling around long after he was counted out. Sal jumped into the ring and gave Micky a giant bear hug, pure adrenaline helping him lift Micky high into the air.

"Unbelievable," Lampley said stunned. "It is the most unlikely knockout you will ever see. Now is that a lucky punch or did Micky Ward just make idiots of us all with a spectacular piece of strategy?"

Sanchez was still on the canvas, curled up in a fetal position for several minutes. Finally, the stool was brought to him, and he was helped onto it. Micky took a moment to kneel down in his corner to pray. He was left alone until he blessed himself with the sign of the cross and got up to see the crowd that had gathered in the ring behind him.

"This is one of the most extraordinary things I've ever seen in boxing," Merchant admitted. "You can't make it up, folks."

Ring announcer Michael Buffer put the period on the end of the sentence by saying, "Ladies and gentlemen, referee Mitch Halpern reaches the count of ten as the pride of Lowell, Massachusetts, climbs off the deck to win by knockout victory at 1:53 seconds of round number seven. KO winner, Irish Micky Ward."

Micky returned to the locker room, and before the reporters arrived to ask their questions, Sal had one of his own.

"Micky, you ran all freaking night. What was that all about? I mean, we told you to stay away for a few rounds, but not all freaking night."

"I know. I know," Micky responded. "Once I started doing it, though, it was hard to stop. When I was afraid you guys were gonna stop the fight, I knew I had to do something."

"That's why I was yelling to you, 'Go to the body! Go to the body!' I was just excited. What else was I gonna tell ya? I'm not a corner guy or a fighter or a trainer. I don't know what else to tell ya."

When Micky was showered and the reporters were allowed into the dressing room, Micky told them, "I'd hurt him with one left hook earlier, and I heard him grunt, so I knew I might be able to do it again, but I had to keep my distance because he's so strong. Heart and fucking soul, man. Never give up. My shoulder was a little sore and I couldn't get off, but I wouldn't quit."

Some twenty-five hundred miles away, a squinty-eyed man with a bushy mustache sat down in his living room. First, he had been up screaming at the television about whoever the hell it was who'd told Micky to run away for six rounds. Then he was up on his feet counting along with the referee Mitch Halpern. ". . . eight, nine, ten. He did it! Donna, he did it!"

Mickey O'Keefe stayed on his feet applauding long after his wife came in to see the many replays of the knockout. The happy couple stood there for a few minutes basking in the glow of another Micky Ward victory. Donna knew that her husband was part of it, even if he felt like he wasn't. While she was thinking, "Micky Ward wouldn't be there raising his hand in victory if it weren't for the man right here holding my hand," O'Keefe was thinking, "Look at that son of a bitch Sal. He's got no more right to be there than a pig's uncle. Makes me sick."

O'Keefe didn't stay up to watch Whittaker retain his title with a unanimous decision over De La Hoya. He went to bed, and he slept well that night. He had no regrets, unless regret was wishing things could be different.

CHAPTER TWELVE

A winner has options. Now, with nine straight wins, including two against formerly undefeated fighters, Veader and Sanchez, Micky was being viewed as a winner. He shed the label of journeyman and proudly slapped one on that read "contender." Of course, there was more than one path to a title fight.

A match with Vernon Forrest was the first option presented to Micky. Promoter and manager Lou Duva offered Micky forty thousand dollars to take that bout. Meanwhile, a Denver-based promotional company known as America Presents tried to gauge Micky's interest in a fight with Rafael Ruelas in July. Sal was ready to lunge at that opportunity, but he was getting a sense that a bigger fight might be dropped in his lap. He thought he had it when Micky was offered one hundred thousand dollars to fight Pernell Whittaker, but HBO vetoed the match. Micky was looking for something bigger, but so was HBO.

Finally, Arum showed up with an offer for Micky to fight Vince Phillips for the IBF junior welterweight title on August 16. The fight would either be in Atlantic City or at Foxwoods in Connecticut, and it would be televised on ABC.

"The winner probably fights Kostya Tszyu in Australia in December for some big money," Arum said.

Joe Lake was involved in the negotiations for the Phillips fight, finally settling for a fifty-thousand-dollar purse for Micky, but it was the last time Lake would involve himself in one of Micky's fights.

"Alice started calling me every night asking, 'What are we going to do next?'" Lake said. "It was every fucking night! I told her, 'I thought we already discussed this. I don't have a mouse in my pocket. We aren't going to do anything. I'm doing what I'm doing. I thought you were staying out of this.' And she's like, 'Well, I just want to be kept informed.' Jesus Christ, what a pain in the ass! It was exactly what I didn't want when I started with this thing."

Even if Lake could have withstood her involvement, he couldn't stand Sal's. Like O'Keefe, Lake was immediately suspicious of the new guy coming around the gym, and those suspicions never waned.

"Do me a favor, buddy," Lake told Sal during a workout one night at the World Gym in Somerville. "The kid's trying to work out. I've gotta get him through a workout. I don't need you fucking constantly in his ear. Step aside. You got someplace you can meet him somewhere, do that. Wait for him. When he's done and he's out of the shower, he's all yours. I don't even know you."

"I'm a friend of his father's," Sal said, repeating what he had told O'Keefe. "Why are you so concerned about me coming around?"

"Well, first of all, I run the gym, and I don't know you from a hole in the wall. And second of all, yeah, you're damn right I'm concerned."

Lake didn't believe it when Sal told him that Micky's dad wanted him to look out for Micky's best interests.

"I know George Ward," Lake says. "And he doesn't give a fuck about anybody. He doesn't care about his kids, or he would have taken care of them instead of being in and out of the joint. So I knew that was fucking bullshit, and Sal's a fucking con man. Sal was just a piece of shit, but at least then I knew what he was all about."

But for Micky it was all about the fifty-thousand-dollar fight, a title shot, and the tremendous potential for so much more. Truth be told, if Micky had fought Pernell Whittaker, he probably would have lost, and then he would have taken a few steps backward to smaller fights and smaller purses. Instead, he took on a more beatable opponent. He fought for a recognized title, and he held on to the possibility of taking giant steps forward with a large payday against Tszyu or Whittaker down the road.

Ron Borges wrote in June 1997:

> [Fifty thousand dollars] may not sound like much, and in the grand scheme of prizefighting it isn't, but for most boxers, a purse like that is as much a dream as a title shot is. It comes to far too few fighters, and Ward long ago grew to understand that. This is a fight about opportunity, an opportunity it seemed he might never get when he retired several years ago, his hopes beaten down by tough losses, bad hands, and the kind of family management that leads most fighters right where Ward was—driving a paving truck on hot afternoons.

Micky never seemed to mind the heat or the paving, and he went right back to it. The combined purses for Sanchez and Phillips would be eighty thousand dollars, but after expenses were deducted and Uncle Sam grabbed a piece of the action, there wasn't a lot left over. Micky still needed to earn a living. He was simultaneously rebuilding his career while helping to rebuild his hometown. In a strange reversal of fortune, the same city that had fallen and taken Dickie down with it was now making its comeback right along with Micky.

In 1993, during Micky's retirement years, Wang Laboratories declared bankruptcy and sold its world headquarters in downtown Lowell for a mere 525,000 dollars. During that same year, Lowell Police Chief Ed Davis began to realize that his department was up against street-level Dominican drug distribution networks run by people with prior military experience, which meant that SWAT teams were required to serve every search warrant. But over time, landlords evicted drug-selling tenants. Abandoned cars were towed. Broken windows were replaced. And Lowell began to look like a city making a comeback. Once the streets were safe again and the drug problem dissipated, life in Lowell began to improve. The former corporate headquarters for Wang, which initially couldn't find a permanent tenant because cars were stolen from the parking lot with such regularity, eventually became the new Cross Point Towers in 1996. And less than seven years after its initial sale, the eighteen-story building sold for 100 million dollars. Lowell's reputation as a safe and prosperous city was returning. The downtown area was revitalized, and its troubled past appeared to be just that—in the past.

And it wasn't just Micky and Lowell that were making comebacks. It was Mickey O'Keefe as well. If he was going to return, things would have to be different. Whatever the reason, Sal swallowed some of his pride and asked O'Keefe back.

"You can call the shots as far as the training goes," Sal promised. "And you'll be first in the corner."

"That's all I ever wanted," O'Keefe said. "I'll see you guys at the gym tomorrow night."

The gym these days was the Somerville Boxing Club. Upstairs were two boxing rings, three heavy bags, and two speed bags. It was newer and cleaner than most of the places in which Micky had worked out. And hanging on the wall, not far from the photos of champions like Roberto Duran, Hector Camacho, and Wilfredo Benitez, were the words: LUCK IS WHAT HAPPENS WHEN PREPARATION MEETS OPPORTUNITY.

This was Micky's opportunity, and he wouldn't mind if he had a little luck on his side. Vince Phillips was as tough an opponent as Micky had ever faced. Phillips was an immensely talented fighter who had squandered the early part of his career because of a drug addiction. His abuse of cocaine kept him out of the ring from November 1993 to December 1994. But he won his fight against drugs and went on to win the biggest fight of his career, stopping

Kostya Tszyu in a huge upset in the tenth round on May 31, 1997. It turned out to be *Ring* magazine's "Upset of the Year," and it occurred six weeks after Micky's upset victory over Sanchez. It made perfect sense to put two fighters together who had provided shocking knockout victories and see what would happen. Micky, of course, wanted the fight because when Phillips beat Tszyu, he became the IBF champion, and that was a title he would put on the line against Micky.

"Micky knows he was in a tough position in his last fight, and he's in a tough position now," O'Keefe explained. "None of these guys offering him fights want him to win, but he's got nothing to lose and I know if he's in shape, and if he hits you with that hook to the body he can take anybody out. It's like being shot by a bullet."

Sanchez knew that. Veader knew it, too. And so did a host of others who had stood in front of Micky. And O'Keefe was certain that Phillips would learn the same lesson.

"I believe this is his destiny," O'Keefe told the *Globe* the day before the fight. "Here's a kid that's worked harder than anybody. He's the best-conditioned athlete in New England right now, bar none. Micky Ward's put time and blood and heart and soul in it. When he wins, he deserves it, because when the darkest days came, he overcame it and he did it himself."

"I just stuck in there and did what I had to do," Micky added. "I took the fights, the ones I wasn't supposed to win. So it's nothing new to me now. I'm probably a big underdog going into this one. That's fine. I'll be thirty-two in October. If things, God forbid, don't work out for me in this fight here, I don't know. I don't know. Things don't look good, put it that way. This is a make-or-break. Do it now. This is a world championship fight. I have to do it now, or I'll probably never do it."

Indeed, destiny appeared to be getting involved in Micky's career once again. Days before the Chavez fight, he was told that there would be no Chavez to fight. Hours before the Saoul Mamby fight, he was told he'd get Mike Mungin instead. And so when the phone rang three weeks before the Phillips fight, Micky answered with trepidation. O'Keefe sounded very somber on the other end. Micky was nervous. He knew that Phillips had received nine stitches on his nose after his tussel with Tszyu and there was concern about the cut healing in time, so he figured he was about to lose his title shot.

"I've got some news for you, Mick, about the fight," O'Keefe began. "Are you sitting down?"

"Shit! What is it this time?"

"Well, things didn't work out scheduling-wise in Atlantic City, so . . ."

"What about Foxwoods?" Micky interrupted. "I don't care. I'll fight him anywhere."

"Anywhere?"

"Yeah, I'll fight him on the moon if I have to. You know that. What the hell are they trying to pull this time?"

"Well, they want you to fight him at the Roxy. Right there in Boston. How's that sound to you?"

"Better than the moon. Christ, you're a shit, you know that, Mickey. You had me scared to death."

"Yeah, I thought that was fun. You didn't think that was fun?"

"Well, maybe when my heart goes back up to my chest, I'll think that was fun. Right now, I think you're a shit."

"That's my boy. It's gonna be a big night at the Roxy."

"Helluva fight," was all Micky said as he hung up the phone, relieved and laughing. O'Keefe got him pretty good with that one. "The little shit."

The Roxy is an intimate setting that can only accommodate about a thousand people. It's a throwback to the days of club fighting. The inside of the Roxy is similar in appearance to the Lowell Auditorium or the Blue Horizon in Philadelphia. Each has a balcony surrounding the ring, and particularly at the Roxy and the Blue Horizon, the balcony hangs over the ring. It places a lot of people extremely close to the action and can create an excessively boisterous and rowdy environment. And that's exactly what you had when the

Roxy filled up with about 85 percent Lowell natives. The balcony was full, and there was standing room only on the floor. The fans were all there to see Ward get another shot at a title. The full bar was simply an ancillary benefit.

The room was dark except for the bright lights shining down on the ring. Micky appeared from the darkness wearing white trunks with a black stripe down either side. Thirty-four-year-old "Cool" Vince Phillips entered the ring in shorts striped in purple and silver. Phillips carried a record of 36 and 3, but he was unbeaten at 140 pounds. His only losses occurred when he moved up to welterweight. He and Micky both weighed 139 pounds for this fight.

Micky was already winning the first round when he landed two chopping overhand rights. The second one stopped Phillips in his tracks. As he paused to absorb the blow, Micky smacked him with a left hook to the jaw. It was a defensive lapse by Phillips, and it cost him. He came out in the second round a bit more cautious. By the end of the second round, however, Phillips started to find his range. He threw a vicious straight right hand that Micky seemed to catch on his forearm, but the force of the intended blow pushed Micky back against the ropes. Phillips followed in pursuit and started banging Micky with a cascade of lefts and rights. Micky blocked some. Others found their mark. Micky countered with effective lefts, but he received worse than he gave.

"Keep the heat on!" trainer Kenny Adams yelled at Phillips between rounds. "Don't let this guy rest. Keep the heat on! You're looking beautiful, baby. Beautiful. Just go out there and keep the heat on!"

Phillips stayed on the attack. Micky turned southpaw. That was his customary move, but this time it had even greater purpose. One of Phillips's losses was to a guy named Anthony "Baby" Jones out of Detroit who effectively switched to southpaw and managed to beat Phillips four years earlier. That was in Jones's backyard of Auburn Hills, Michigan.

But Phillips wasn't confused by the switch at all. Instead, he pounded Micky's right ribcage with solid left hands, and continued to sneak in some powerful rights. Micky stood his ground, landing a few good countershots of his own, but the fight turned suddenly with about fifty seconds remaining in the third round.

"Oh, and there's some blood over the left eye of Micky Ward," fight play-by-play man Dan Dierdorf exclaimed.

"And he's bleeding badly. You see it dripping on him," Alex Wallau of ABC's *Wide World of Sports* said. "He pawed at it once."

The gash was nearly two inches long, spanning Micky's entire left eyebrow. Micky continued to fight. He was sure his corner would be able to get the bleeding under control between rounds. But with twenty-five seconds still to go in round three, Phillips landed another straight right hand directly on the cut.

"That really rocked him," Dierdorf commented.

The referee, Dick Flaherty of Massachusetts, stared at Micky's cut for a few more seconds, and then decided the ring doctor needed to take a look at it. He called time-out and brought Micky over to see Dr. Patti Yoffe, one of the few female ring doctors in boxing. She pointed a small flashlight at the cut while O'Keefe wiped the blood away with a towel.

"He's fine," O'Keefe said hopefully.

But when O'Keefe used a Q-tip dipped in adrenaline hydrochloride to try to close the cut, Yoffe wasn't so sure. She saw the loose skin lap over the cotton swab and flinched. The cut was deep. She continued to examine it, looking very concerned and shaking her head. Micky knew what she was thinking.

"Let me go on. Please," he implored. "Let me go."

"It's too deep," Yoffe said over the crowd that was growing restless. "It's too deep."

"I don't care. Please. One round. Let me go one more round!"

Yoffe shook her head. "No. You can't go on," she said to Micky, and then she looked over at Flaherty and said, "This fight should be stopped."

O'Keefe fired the towel to the ground and shouted, "Oh, come on! Let him go! This is bullshit! He's fine! C'mon, he's fine!"

Barely two minutes had passed since the cut first opened up, and only five minutes ago, Micky was winning the fight. Now, it was over. He threw his hands down in disgust and walked toward the center of the ring. There he was met by Phillips who wrapped his arms around Micky's waist and lifted him into air. But Micky's disappointment and Phillips's jubilation would have to wait. By now the crowd had realized what had happened, and several loyal Lowell supporters began throwing cups and bottles of beer into the ring. A few chairs were tossed toward the ring as well, but didn't get that far. Micky was first to recognize the danger. He jumped out of Phillips's arms and began beseeching the crowd to stop. He raced over to the ropes and yelled at the instigators in the balcony, most of whom were friends and family, and ordered them to stop.

"Sal got hit with a cup of beer," Micky recalls. "My stupid fans. It was mostly my family up above. Phillips didn't deserve this. He's a world champion. He comes into my hometown. Why do this to him? It ain't his fault."

Meanwhile, O'Keefe the cop pushed Phillips to the ground and used his own body to provide cover for him.

"They were all throwing things into the ring," O'Keefe said. "I'm covering guys so they don't get hit. I'm not gonna let anything hit him. I don't give a shit what it is they're throwing. You don't know what you're gonna get hit with."

The potential for riot, at first real, was quickly suppressed. Fans stopped throwing things into the ring and simply chanted, "Bullshit! Bullshit! Bullshit!"

Meanwhile, Micky's cut was no longer bleeding. It had only taken a few minutes, and already the trickle of blood stopped. That would lead to speculation that if Micky were allowed to get to his corner, the cut could have been controlled, and the fight could have continued. After all, there were only eleven more seconds to go in the round when Flaherty stepped in.

"He couldn't go on," Yoffe said. "It was a bad cut, so I'm the bad guy. His vision was already blurred."

It didn't take Micky long to realize that Yoffe had done him a huge favor. When O'Keefe brought Micky to nearby Massachusetts General Hospital, the attending physician let them know that the cut would require eighteen stitches, twelve on the outside and six on the inside.

"At first I didn't agree with the stoppage," Micky recalls now. "But when I went to the hospital to get stitched up, the doctor said, 'If she didn't stop the fight when she did, you might have lost your eyesight. Your eyes might have been messed up for life.' The damage is a millimeter away from muscle. Once you get into muscle and cut into there, your eye could get dislodged. So, in hindsight, it was good that she stopped it."

Meanwhile, in the immediate aftermath of the fight, promoter Bob Arum was blinded with fury.

"She panicked!" Arum blustered. "You don't stop it on the first cut! If this fight was in California or Nevada or New Jersey, they wouldn't have done that. If it opens again, then you stop it. You ask why so many fights are in Nevada or New Jersey and it's because you get competent people. Sure, next round it's probably over, but you let him go back to the corner and give them a chance to stop the bleeding. Vince Phillips was cut worse in the Tszyu fight. There's a different standard in a title fight. I really have to question whether we should have women doctors at ringside."

Arum not only questioned the use of female officials in a male sport, he also vowed never to bring another title bout to Massachusetts.

His views were not shared by the Massachusetts state boxing commissioner, Bill Pender, who said, "Arum is woefully inadequate to judge a medical situation. Dr. Yoffe is one of our better ring doctors, who doesn't waste any time getting right in there to attend to injured boxers. I probed the cut myself, and it was long enough, deep enough, and actively bleeding, with approximately one centimeter of exposed bone, to convince me the bout had to be stopped. I totally agree with Dr. Yoffe, and I would do exactly the same thing. Also, this thing about female doctors disturbs me, and I believe Arum could be sued for what he's said."

In the end, the squabbling and second-guessing after the fight didn't matter. Micky had lost. He lost this fight and the opportunity for the next one, which could have been his first six-figure payday against Tszyu. That was the frustrating part of boxing that nagged at Micky. Each loss seemed to hurt twice.

Micky thought about why he returned to boxing. At first, it was because he was dissatisfied with how his first career had ended. That led him back to the gym where he hoped he could one day make some decent money. But the further he got back into it, the more he realized that he was in this for a championship. He wanted to know how far he could go, and he wanted to go to the top. The paper championship he won against Veader wasn't the top. That wasn't even close. He wanted a real title, and it crushed him to watch another one slip through his grasp.

Just as he had lost the USBA light welterweight title to Frankie Warren, the IBF Inter-Continental welterweight title to Harold Brazier, and the USBA light welterweight title to Charles Murray, Micky had lost another shot at a legitimately recognized championship. But even more than the others, this was a fight Micky was sure he could have won. He was never much of a bleeder. His face tended to just swell up, rather than open up. But fate had intervened on his night at the Roxy, when he suffered the worst cut of his career. It felt like his real destiny was to always be tantalizingly close to realizing his dream.

He thought about these things while the doctor stitched him up at Mass General. O'Keefe, sitting in the corner of the room, thought about these things, too. He knew how hard Micky had worked, and he thought that the kid deserved better.

"How's it look?" Micky asked about the black stitches and the purple welt over his left eye.

"Geez, and I thought you were ugly before," O'Keefe teased. "But this is almost unbearable."

"I'm gonna end up looking like you," Micky responded. "That sucks."

CHAPTER THIRTEEN

Dickie sat alone in his prison cell. His eyes were closed. His head leaned up against the cold cement wall. And his hands clutched several pieces of paper. They were letters written to him by family members. One of the advantages of having seven sisters and a brother is that when you go to jail, mail call is something you can look forward to.

Dickie's eyes were closed because he didn't have to read the letters anymore. He had read them so many times, he knew them all by heart. The pages were filled with the typical news about marriages, kids, and jobs. There was gossip about friends who had gotten into or out of trouble. There were stories about Dickie Junior's T-ball exploits. But mostly, the letters were about Micky's career: who he had knocked out, how he got screwed by the ring doctor, and who he was going to fight next.

Most of the information in the letters was redundant. Dickie had heard it when his mother and son came to see him. The visits were a little less frequent now that he'd been moved to the Plymouth House of Corrections almost ninety minutes from home, but he saw them often enough to know all about Micky's prospects and about Sal LoNano.

"Why'd you let Sal get his claws into Micky?" Dickie had asked his mom during visiting hours once.

"Micky wanted him because his father wanted him. What can I tell you? Things seem to be going pretty well," Alice said.

"You really think so? Christ, Ma, from where I'm sitting, all I can see is Micky beating a bunch of stiffs and then getting robbed by Chavez or Sal. Who knows what happened there? And then he gets a title shot, but no real money with it. He should be doing a helluva lot better than this. And he would be if I was with him."

The last sentence just hung there for a while. Alice was unsure how to respond. Her impulse was to bark at Dickie and tell him, "First of all, you can't be with him, because you screwed up so royally and now you're in here, and second of all, things weren't so great when you were with him the last time." But Dickie looked so good these days. He was all cleaned up. He had put some weight on. And he was being permitted to leave the prison every once in a while to talk to troubled kids. So Alice thought better about berating him.

"You're right, Dickie," she said. "Once you can start training him again, I'm sure he'll go right to the top, and you'll be right there with him. It'll be wonderful."

That was the singular thought that pushed Dickie daily. When the walls closed in on him, and he grew so emotionally fatigued that he could barely roll off his cot in the morning, he thought about getting back into the gym with his brother. His dream to make Micky a champion gave Dickie a purpose. In fact, he dreamed it so often and so hard it already seemed real, and that made him smile as he folded up the letters from home and put them neatly in a shoebox under his bed.

"Just a little while longer," he thought. "With good behavior, I'll be out in another year or so, and then it'll be me and Micky— straight to the top. It could have been me, but it'll have to be Micky instead."

There were several letters from Micky in Dickie's shoebox. In fact, there were more letters than visits. Micky didn't come very often, which suited Dickie just fine. He didn't like his little brother seeing him in the crack houses, and he didn't like Micky to see him in jail either, but it bothered him less and less as his physical condition improved and as he moved to minimum-security prisons.

"In jail he was always talking about how good he felt," Micky remembers. "And you could see it. You could tell from his body, because when he first went in there he looked awful, like a skeleton or something. Skull face. That's what crack does to you."

When Dickie was feeling good, everyone around him felt good, too. He had that kind of infectious personality, energetic and quick to laugh. He was smart, sharp-witted, possessed a keen memory, and he could read people. He couldn't get a read on Sal just yet, but he liked that Micky was with Mickey O'Keefe.

"That was a good move, Mick," Dickie told him. "He's a good guy. He don't drink, and he's got you in shape. He's good for you now, and then I'll get out and take you the rest of the way."

But it was after the Vince Phillips fight that Micky had to tell Dickie that O'Keefe was once again out of the picture. Sal and O'Keefe were able to put their differences aside for only a short period of time, long enough to get ready for Phillips. After that, there was more palpable tension during workouts, more arguments about what the best move for Micky would be, and more problems with the power structure within Team Ward.

"I'm the manager. You're the trainer," Sal constantly reminded O'Keefe.

"Then what the hell do you have Connolly and all these other guys hanging around for?" O'Keefe would ask.

"They're all good for Micky, and as his manager, I say they stay."

"Let 'em stay. I'm outta here."

This time, O'Keefe was out for good. There'd be no coming back.

"I went home and told my wife, Donna, when he's done with his career, I'll be there," O'Keefe says. "Until then I don't want to be around. I left right before the Mark Fernandez fight. Sal and I fought about him being in the corner, and he says to me, 'I don't want to work the corner. That's not what this is about.' You tell me. Was he in the corner?"

Eventually, yes, but Sal was not in the corner the night Micky fought Mark Fernandez at Foxwoods Casino Resort in Connecticut. It was April 14, 1998, the same night Andrew Golota knocked out Eli Dixon as the main event, and the same night that twenty-year-old Zab Judah improved his record to 15–0 with a second-round knockout of Angel Beltre.

Fernandez was merely a tune-up for Micky who had been inactive for eight months and was scheduled to fight Judah in June. Judah was an unbeaten and untested young star on the rise. He wanted to fight Micky in order to remove the "untested" label, and Micky wanted to fight Judah because it was a title shot, albeit a less prestigious title. Micky and Judah would vie for the vacated USBA junior welterweight title. It was a perfect match, but it took a while to come together. Sal was taking Micky away from Top Rank and doing most of his negotiating with Main Events promotions instead.

If Micky beat Judah, he wouldn't need Top Rank to find a significant payday, and he didn't plan on losing to the soft-hitting, though lightning-quick southpaw from New York. Still, waiting for Judah and watching other fights fall apart had left Micky inactive and potentially rusty. So when the fight with Judah was rescheduled for June, he grabbed the Fernandez fight on short notice. And despite having fought just three weeks earlier, Judah did the same. That put Micky and Judah on the same undercard just two months before they would be opposing each other as a main event.

Of course, the fight with Judah and the twenty-five-thousand-dollar payday that went along with it could be in jeopardy if Micky didn't take care of Fernandez first. Fernandez was nearing the end of a long, unspectacular career. He was thirty-seven years old and entered the ring against Micky with nine losses in his last twelve fights. Simply put, Micky couldn't afford to lose to this guy.

In Micky's first comeback fights, he weighed between 142 and 148 pounds. Since then, he had been tipping the scales very consistently at 140 pounds even. For the Fernandez fight, Micky was as ripped and muscular as he had ever been. He was a sinewy 143 pounds. His training with O'Keefe had gone well, and he continued the program long after O'Keefe left. He was ready for this fight and had another friend back with him in the corner. Richie Bryan was the second man in, and he squirted water from a bottle into Micky's mouth while the referee, Johnny Callas, gave the pre-fight instructions.

"Obey my commands at all times, and above all, come out fighting."

Micky obeyed. Wearing white trunks with kelly-green trim, Micky found early success with his left hand. Fernandez moved clockwise around the ring, running as Micky had done more than once in his career, but Micky wasn't chasing. He stayed in the center of the ring, occasionally landing a shot against his moving target. Fernandez moved well, mostly out of a southpaw position, and when he stopped long enough to exchange punches, he gave as good as he got.

Finally, with just over a minute to go in the third round, Fernandez threw two right-hand uppercuts, and then paused, waiting to unleash a third. During that pause, Micky struck.

"Oh! Fernandez goes down! Out of nowhere here in round number three," play-by-play announcer Al Albert said with great surprise on the *Fox Sports* telecast.

The left hook had the appearance of every other left hook Micky had landed to the midsection of Fernandez, but it landed where the others did not and it had a dramatically different effect. This one left Fernandez crumpled up on the canvas writhing in a kind of pain he'd never felt before. Micky watched Fernandez fall and walked away calmly, only glancing back once to survey the damage he'd inflicted.

"You don't get up from those," he would say later.

". . . six, seven, eight, nine, ten!" Callas yelled clearly as Fernandez struggled to get up.

"A left hook, a body shot to the liver," analyst and former boxer Sean O'Grady said. "You hit a man in the liver and he drops. The pain lasts, and it is excruciating pain. It lasts about ten or fifteen seconds, and then you're fine."

The pain lasted longer than that for Fernandez. He spent the next several minutes on the stool in his corner being treated by the ring doctor. When Fernandez finally did rise, he walked over to congratulate Micky.

"That shot was too good," he said. "I couldn't get up. It hurt too much. I felt like I was gonna die."

That made Micky laugh. He hugged Fernandez, ruffled his hair and wished him luck his next time out. That was Mark "The Cobra" Fernandez's fifty-second career fight. He would have six more, losing five of them, and he would never be hurt as badly as he had been the night he faced Micky Ward.

Zab Judah was watching from the locker room at Foxwoods, and he vowed to himself right then and there that he would not leave himself open to a Micky Ward body shot. Judah had already seen the tapes of Ward landing that vicious left hand against Sanchez and Veader, two previously undefeated fighters like himself. Judah knew that Micky was being placed in front of him as a stepping-stone. His handlers expected him to beat Micky, and they expected that victory to elevate him quickly in the junior welterweight division. Micky knew it, too. He also knew that stepping-stones work in both directions.

"I love these kinds of fights," he said. "There's no pressure on me; it's all on him. They put me in there because they expect me to lose, but it ain't gonna happen."

Micky, concerned about Judah's significant advantage in hand and foot speed, entered the ring in Miami, Florida, several pounds lighter than normal. He was a trim 137 pounds, not nearly as bulked up or buffed as he had been in a few of his previous fights. He worked himself into quite a sweat in the locker room before coming out, and he continued bouncing on his toes and throwing punches in his corner while waiting for the fight to begin. He was hoping to get off to a quick start against a very quick fighter.

Judah was a natural southpaw from Brooklyn, New York, who had shown amazing hand speed on his way to winning eleven of his first fifteen fights by knockout. His superiority over each of his opponents was evident in the fact that he had never lost a single round on any judge's scorecard. He had fought forty-five professional rounds and won them all.

Judah came out in red trunks. Micky was in white with green trim. Both fighters began by snapping off jabs. Judah avoided Micky's. Micky took Judah's on the chin. Judah was by far the quickest opponent Micky had ever faced. Micky whiffed on several punches because when he let go of his punches Judah would be standing in one place, but by the time the punches were completed, Judah would be somewhere else. He was that quick.

Through five rounds, Judah had landed 103 punches to just 29 by Micky. Judah's corner was growing more confident and telling Judah to be more aggressive.

"Throw more punches, Micky!" Rubert Brown, Micky's latest trainer hired by Sal, ordered him between rounds. Brown had helped Livingstone Bramble for many years, leading him to lightweight and light welterweight titles. "You've got to wear him down, or he won't be tired when you need him to be. Now, get out there and get busy!"

Micky picked up the pace. In the eighth round, he finally landed a good, hard shot square on Judah's ribs, but Judah appeared to shake it off. But he didn't shake off the next one. Midway through the round, Micky doubled up with a left hand to the body, and it nearly doubled Judah over. Judah took the shots and stayed bent over at the waist for a few moments. He was in an awkward position, down so low that it was hard for Micky to find a place to hit him. Judah stayed that way, as if he were taking a deep bow, for a few seconds and that bought him enough time to partially recover and then bounce away. Judah was still hurt, and he needed more time. He was also afraid of taking another shot like that any time soon. So he ran. He circled the ring with tremendous grace and speed. Micky did his best to cut off the ring, but Judah was too agile. Judah merely stayed on his bicycle and tossed out a few harmless jabs to give the impression that he was still fighting, but he was running. Finally, Micky stopped his pursuit and said to Judah, "Are you gonna fight or run?"

Judah answered by running until the end of the round.

"Something very important has happened here," ESPN announcer Al Bernstein said during the broadcast. "Ward is landing punches that he couldn't land earlier in the fight, because Judah has slowed down a little bit in his reflexes and is maybe a little tired."

At the start of the final round, Micky and Judah met in the center of the ring, and Judah said, "Great fight. Let's finish it."

This was the last round of yet another big fight in Micky's career. It was the final three minutes, and Micky needed a knockout. He was opposed by a skilled and lightning-quick fighter but not an especially dangerous one. The conditions were perfect for Micky to fight aggressively, with reckless abandon, and with desperation. But he didn't. He fought the final round much the same way he had fought the previous eleven, even though he had lost ten of those eleven rounds. Judah played it smart and rode out the twelfth round. When the bell rang, Micky threw his right hand down in disgust. He was upset with himself for not doing more to win the fight. He was angry that he had lost to a showboater who never hit him hard enough to leave a mark. And he should have been upset that he was put up against a guy he really had little or no chance of beating.

"That was a bad match with Judah," Borges explains. "That was a chance to grab a little money. But it turned out to be a bit of a turning point in Micky's career, because he may have realized that he couldn't outbox these speed guys at the top of his division. So, he turned himself into a brawler. That was his best chance to win. He was a boxer earlier in his career, but gave it up to fight inside almost exclusively after the Judah fight. It was the only way he could beat a guy with great hand and foot speed. This was a lopsided fight because he couldn't land his body shot. Zab never stood still long enough. Micky's uniqueness is his ability to punch to the body with such damaging effect. It's such a great risk to punch to the body, because you leave yourself open. That's why most fighters don't do it anymore. Micky made a living doing it, but he couldn't do it if he couldn't take shots, because you're paying a price for it. In this day and age you don't find many guys willing to pay that price, or who can take those shots that Micky did."

Micky lost ten of twelve rounds on two of the judges' scorecards and the third judge said he lost eleven out of twelve. The final punch stats told the story, Judah landed 270 mostly soft blows while Micky managed to hit his quickly moving target only 90 times in thirty-six minutes.

The twenty-year-old Zab Judah won the USBA title, climbed the rankings, and won eleven more consecutive fights, picking up the IBF light welterweight title along the way. He stepped over Micky and into the big time. Micky went in the opposite direction. The loss to Judah was a terrible defeat for his career. Everything he had proved with his victories over Veader and Sanchez, all the respect he had earned in his defeat to Vince Phillips, and all the opportunities he had received up to this point in his comeback were wiped away, almost without a trace. Micky had to prove himself all over again. He had to earn respect and further opportunities the hard way, by starting over. It wouldn't be easy. So, Micky went back to Lowell where things were never easy. He went back to Lowell where he could start his boxing career all over again—with Dickie.

CHAPTER FOURTEEN

Back in Lowell, Micky's boxing career was in limbo as expected. The loss to Judah had convinced most promoters and matchmakers that Micky was no longer worth their time. Micky had lost two of his last three fights. He was nearly thirty-three years old, and he couldn't beat the top contenders, so he wouldn't be given a chance to. It wasn't long ago that he was being mentioned in the same breath as Kostya Tszyu and Julio Cesar Chavez. Big-money fights and title fights had been within his grasp.

Micky was scheduled to fight a New York kid named Darius Ford at the Roxy in December 1998, but he bruised his right hand during a sparring session a week before the fight and had to pull out.

Despite the injury and the lack of direction in his career, he was smiling these days. In mid-October 1998, he received a belated birthday present from the state of Massachusetts. After four years and seven months in jail, Dickie walked out of prison, clean and sober, fit, and ready to work.

"I decided while in prison that I was going to make something of my life and once I got out I was going to help others avoid the same mistakes I made," Dickie told John Vellante of the *Boston Globe*. "I remember saying to myself when I heard the sentence, 'Hey, I deserve some time, but not that much.'Anyway, the judge did me a favor. Those words, 'ten to fifteen,' helped turn my life around. I was shuffled from jail to jail and started chairing Alcoholics and Narcotics Anonymous meetings. In Shirley, I met Mary O'Connell, a substance abuse counselor, who was a big influence in my life. She and my mother, Alice, were always there for me."

Upon his release, Dickie kept his word about helping others. He began working with kids in the streets and in boxing gyms in both Massachusetts and New Hampshire.

He helped, not by lecturing or threatening the kids, but by simply telling them his story.

"I tell them, in the ring I had thousands of people cheering me on. In jail, I had nobody other than my family. I tell them that the things I do now to stay clean and sober aren't half as bad as the the things I did to get my drugs and alcohol. Drugs and booze became the most important things in my life. Nothing else mattered. My whole life was drinking and drugging, drugging and drinking. I'd beg, borrow, and steal. Life was the pits. . . . I remember some Lowell cops telling me I was going to die. They were always after me, always chasing me down. Now they see me and ask me if I can help someone else. I'll always be recovering, will be until the day I die, but I can't worry about or change the past. I think about and live only for today."

So Dickie was back training Micky, just as the two brothers had planned. It was inevitable.

"It's great having Dickie back in my corner," Micky said. "He's there more than ever before. I had a good trainer while he was away, but Dickie's a good influence. I'm proud of the way he's turned his life around. Everything is positive. He's busting my cookies big time, and that's something I need in my corner. He'll make a big difference."

"It tore me apart that I couldn't physically be there with him," Dickie added. "He needed me. I had a lot of bad days in jail thinking about him and how I could have helped him. But it's nice to be back in his corner. We are a bind and we have faith in each other."

Joe Lake also knew the brothers' reunion was a foregone conclusion.

"Dickie's love for his brother is immense," Lake says. "They both love each other dearly. They can call each other assholes all day long, but nobody else better say it. I think a lot of times Dickie got in the ring and kicked Micky in the nuts when he needed it. As a disciplinarian he was very good. I don't know if Micky always had the best strategy to win under Dickie Eklund, but he was in great condition."

And Mickey O'Keefe also knew that Dickie's return to Micky's corner was unavoidable. That, according to his friend Danny Gilday, was one of the reasons O'Keefe was prepared to walk away when he did.

When Dickie first got out of prison in October, Micky stayed out of the ring for several months to have his hand checked out by a doctor. Eleven years and 190 rounds of professional boxing after the cops smashed a heavy flashlight onto his hands, Micky was going to have surgery.

"My hand was so bad, I couldn't punch anyway," Micky said. "So, there was no downside to it. No risk. No worry. Yeah, it was the same hand that got hurt at the Cosmo. It started the injury. It wasn't that severe when it first happened. But I kept using it when I shouldn't have. The injury wasn't healed, and I'd start training with it. I never gave it a chance to heal properly or fully."

So, Micky went to see an orthopedic therapist in Lowell who referred him to Dr. Steven Margeles at the Lahey Clinic in Burlington, Massachusetts.

"What can I do for you, George?" Dr. Margeles asked, calling Micky by his given name, because that's how Micky had signed himself in at the doctor's office.

"My hand's killing me, Doc. I can't even punch with it anymore."

"And you punch with it a lot?"

"Yeah, Doc. I'm a boxer."

By that time, Margeles was inspecting Micky's hand and had noticed the swelling and the tenderness around the second and third metacarpal bones. X-rays were hard to interpret, so Margeles ordered a series of tomograms, which are slice X-rays. It was evident that Micky had arthritis, not the kind caused by disease, but the boxer's version, known as post-traumatic arthritis. Instead of a chronic, dull pain, Micky had a sharp and intense one whenever he hit with his right hand. Fusion surgery, or arthrodesis, was recommended.

"Here's what will happen, George," Margeles explained. "First, we're going to scrape some bone out of your hip . . ."

"My hip?"

"Yes. We need to take bone out of your hip and put it into your hand."

"I'm having hip surgery? Doc, it's my hand that hurts," Micky protested.

"Right. Let me explain from the beginning. What I need to do is take off the cartilage around the traumatized area in your hand. I'm going to scrape past the hard subchondral bone down to the inner bone, which is spongy and has a high healing potential. You'll be left with two raw ends of bone, and a space in between. We have to put something in that space, and that's going to come from your hip."

"It still seems weird that my hip bone's gonna be connected to my hand bone," Micky said with a nervous laugh.

"Well, the gold standard for fusing bones together is the ileac crest. That's in the pelvis. It's not the ball of the hip bone. It's where your belt sits. It's fairly easy to get there. I'll make a small incision and then I'll go in there with a trocar, kind of like an apple corer. I turn that, and then scoop out the scrapings with a curet. That's more like a melon-ball scooper."

"You fixing me up, Doc, or are you making a fruit salad?"

"Believe me, we're fixing you up. Surgery is the only answer for this kind of problem. We'll scrape out this hard reddish spongy stuff first. Then we'll scrape away at the hand, creating the space I mentioned, and then we'll pack in the bone from your hip. We'll pack it in good and tight, fuse it together with a couple of screws, put a Band-Aid on your hip, and I think you'll be as good as new in no time."

Margeles couldn't guarantee the outcome of the surgery, but he told Micky that he probably wouldn't be able to fight again successfully if he didn't take this chance. Micky spent a few days and restless nights worrying. The worst-case scenario was that his career would be over. But even without surgery, he was pretty close to the end anyway. He couldn't beat the top guys with a handicap. So, on the day of the surgery, Micky relaxed. This was the rightthing to do.

Margeles began by tying a tourniquet around Micky's upper arm. He felt only a little pain while the apple corer and melon baller scraped inside his hip. He saw the scrapings and thought it looked a lot like red sand. He was awake and alert during the process, but he chose to look away as Margeles used a bone tamp to pack in the "red sand." Still, he could hear the crunching sound as Margeles stuffed the space between the bones. Three screws were used, including a compression screw that pulled the two sides together.

"The screw goes from the normal intact bone, across the space and into the other bone," Margeles explains. "So you pack some bone in, put the screw in, and then pack some more bone in. Eventually it all fuses into one strong bone. It's as strong as any other bone would be. And the hip bone's not compromised at all, because it all grows back."

The surgery went well, and Micky put it to the test, first in the gym, and then when he returned to the ring on St. Patrick's Day 1999. It was an anniversary of sorts. The fight was exactly five years after Dickie had been sent to jail. Now Micky had a new hand and his older brother back on his side. He hoped it would be the right combination.

He fought a perennial loser from Coventry, Rhode Island, named Jose Luis Mendez. Three weeks before facing Micky, Mendez was held up for target practice for four rounds by Anthony

Chase of Providence. Chase won a lopsided unanimous decision that dropped Mendez's record to 3–11–1. He had no business climbing into the ring with Micky Ward, but he had the courage to do it. So Micky hit him until he fell in the third round.

Now what? That was the question for which Micky, Dickie, and Sal really had no answer. Looking at it realistically, Micky was in jeopardy of being tossed aside and forgotten. His big wins over Louis Veader were three years ago. Since then, it could be argued that he looked bad squeaking past the Chavez replacement, looked dreadful against Sanchez before landing a lucky punch, lost to Phillips on a nasty cut, lost nearly every round to Judah, and had beaten a couple of nobodies named Mendez and Fernandez. Why would any promoter want to pay big money to Micky Ward? The subpar results made him look old and unimpressive. Maybe his time had come and gone. And to make matters worse, his right hand was hurting again.

"This was a different pain," Dr. Margeles explains. "We took another X-ray, and you could see that one screw was too long. One of the bones that gets fused is called the capitate. The screw had gone through the capitate, and through the joint and into the next bone over called the hamate. You could see where it was irritating the bone there. That was easy enough to take care of. You just take the screw out."

That problem appeared to be solved, but there was still concern over the direction of Micky's career. Sal recognized this and decided that it was time to take a bold step. The cab company businessman who was asked to be an "advisor" and then morphed into a manager and part-time cornerman was going to become a promoter.

"When I was managing Micky Ward, there was a time when I hit the wall," LoNano explained. "All these other promoters wanted Micky to fight for a thousand dollars or twenty-five hundred, three thousand dollars. And he was getting paid, and nobody on his team was getting paid. I didn't get paid for nothing. I went a good solid five or six fights without taking a dime."

So Sal went for a walk. He parked his car at Revere Beach, got out, and walked the shoreline. A mile in one direction and a mile back. Then he'd do it again. He wasn't aware of the walking anyway. He felt the weight of responsibility. Micky, who worked so hard and had so much talent, had turned to him for help. Something had to be done to turn things around. But what?

"I didn't want to waste his time," Sal says. "And I've got a family. So, I said to myself, 'What are you going to do, Sal? It's time to step up.' So I started thinking about promoting. I promoted my own business for thirty years. I knew I could promote, but I didn't know the businesspeople in boxing. So I went after Al Valenti."

Sal arrived at the Valenti Ticket Agency on Canal Street in Boston in April 1999. He was instantly intimidated as he looked around the outer office and saw a picture of Al's grandfather, Rip Valenti, and several signed photographs of great fighters, including Muhammad Ali. This was clearly where people who really know the ins and outs of boxing worked. When Sal walked in, he addressed an elderly gentleman reading a newspaper.

"I want to talk to Al Valenti," Sal said.

"He's over there," the man said. "What do you want, kid?"

"Kid?" Sal thought. "I'm over forty years old."

Al came out and invited Sal into his office.

"What can I do for you?"

"Look, I've got Micky Ward," Sal began.

"Micky Ward's done!" the man shouted from the other room.

"I'm not really promoting anymore," Al informed Sal. "I'm in retirement."

"I really only need a few minutes of your time."

"That would be a waste of my time. My dad out there is right. Micky Ward, he's nothing. He's the one who should retire."

"He's not ready to do that," Sal said, defending Micky. "I'm his manager, and I can't go nowhere. I need you to show me how to promote. I'm not looking for your money . . . and any promotions you help me with, you and I will split everything 50–50. You have the knowledge. I have the money. I just need to know how to put this all together."

"Micky Ward's all done!"

This time the proclamation by Al's father from the other room was followed by a hearty laugh.

Al looked at Sal, shrugged, and said, "There's really not much out there. And for me to get involved with Micky Ward would be like, it would take a catastrophic occurrence. I'm really not interested. I'm just not interested."

Sal stormed back onto Canal Street. He was angry and not sure in which direction he should go. He walked quickly up the road and took a left on Causeway Street in front of the Old Garden. This was the same path Tony DeMarco had taken on his way from his home in the North End when he fought Carmen Basilio for the welterweight title in 1955. DeMarco lost that night, but he was a big star at a time when boxers were among the biggest stars. Sal still wanted that kind of fame and fortune for Micky, and he still believed it could happen.

"Fuck him," he thought. And he turned around and walked back into the Valenti Ticket Agency.

"Listen, you got a half hour?" Sal said, speaking loudly this time. "I know you got thirty minutes for lunch. I'm gonna buy you lunch. Let's go next door and get something to eat. But I want you to listen to me this time."

Sal didn't wait for a response. He bolted out of the office and stepped into the sandwich shop next door. And he waited. He sat down at a table and waited to see if Al Valenti would follow him. He hoped curiosity, or at the very least hunger and the promise of a free meal, would persuade Al to hear what he had to say. Five minutes passed before Al finally sauntered in.

"Are you gonna listen to me this time?" Sal asked as if it was a command.

"Yeah, I'll listen," Al said, but before he had a chance to sit down, Sal stood up and said, "I can't do this here. Let's go back to your office."

Again, Al was forced to follow Sal, and he didn't even get lunch out of it.

"He was thinking he was better than me," Sal explains. "And now I've got him jumping around. So I've got his attention now, and I tell him what I want to do."

By the time Sal finished his sales pitch, Al and his father were both leaning back in their chairs smoking cigars. The smoke rings lingered in the air along with Sal's final thought.

"Look, I've really got a feeling about Micky. He's never really had a manager. You won't have to deal with Alice. You won't have to deal with Dickie. You just deal with me directly. So, what do you think?"

It was clear to Al that Sal really believed in Micky and that he was prepared to put his money where his mouth was. So he started at the beginning and tried to explain how boxing works.

"First of all," he began. "You have to have a little synergy. You have to have a vision of where you want to go with this situation. You have to have a venue. You have to have a date. And at this stage of Micky's career, it has to be a TV date, because if you don't have the revenue from ESPN or FOX then you just can't do it."

Sal listened intently. Ideas were running through his mind, but he wasn't sure any of them could work. How would he go about securing a venue like the FleetCenter or even the Roxy, and how would he get ESPN to broadcast a fight when he still didn't know who Micky's next opponent would be. The worry and confusion showed on his face.

"All right, look," Al continued. "I've been toying around with this idea for a long time. Last summer, I did this amateur boxing show at the beach up in New Hampshire. It was a Tuesday night in June. It was drizzling. And we still drew. We had about twenty amateur fights. If that can work, and if I can convince ESPN to do the show, I'll see if I can get a date. If all that happens, we'll make a fight. Remember, if you can get some money together, you can get a good fighter. But Micky's gonna have to win, or it'll be over in a hurry."

Sal was ecstatic. He had just watched Al Valenti go from "not interested" because "Micky Ward is done" to potentially making him the main event on a big fight card in New Hampshire. It didn't matter to Sal that Al had chosen to investigate possibilities in New Hampshire because he was no longer permitted to promote fights in Massachusetts.

A year earlier, Valenti promoted a show at the FleetCenter and had gotten into a beef with the Massachusetts State boxing commissioner, Mark DeLuca. By rule, there aren't supposed to be any children under the age of sixteen ringside for a fight, but DeLuca brought his two children, ages eight and nine, up to the front row with him. Valenti might not have cared except that those seats were being saved for Marvin Hagler, who was being honored that night.

"I see those kids, and I tell DeLuca to get them out of those seats because that's Hagler's row," Valenti recalls. "Hagler's gonna come down to those seats and that's it. When he gets there, I don't want him to have to deal with little kids."

DeLuca refused to leave, or to move his kids somewhere else. In his mind, he was the boxing commissioner, and he wasn't going to be told what to do by some two-bit promoter. Valenti didn't back down, and it turned out to be his undoing, because a week later, he had his license revoked.

Valenti, it so happened, owed the commission thirteen hundred dollars. The money added up because the Commonwealth of Massachusetts receives 4 percent of a fight, including sales tax and licenses. Valenti had bounced three checks attempting to pay what was owed. It wasn't a lot of money and, generally, that sort of thing was taken care of with a letter reminding the promoter that he was in arrears. A good check would be written and no further action would be taken. But this time DeLuca pounced upon a valid, though generally insignificant reason to take out his vengeance on Valenti. One of the boxing commissioners, Skeeter McClure, recognized the injustice and pettiness of the punishment and resigned the next day.

"They suspended Al's license over thirteen hundred bucks," future commissioner Ben Doherty laments. "I've gone to Al and told him, 'Just pay it. It's chump change.' But he won't pay the thirteen hundred bucks. I've written him letters and told him there'd be no prejudice. He'd get his license back and start making money here, but he won't do it, just to save face. DeLuca had a valid reason and he used it instead of looking the other way and waiting for the thirteen hundred bucks."

So Al was expelled to the north. His first call after Sal left his office was to Russell Peltz, the new East Coast boxing coordinator for ESPN. Al explained that boxing at the beach had drawn a good crowd before, and he was sure it could do so again. Peltz had an open date on July 16, but he wasn't sure he wanted to give it up for what Al was offering.

"This is my date," Peltz said possessively. "I'm gonna have to put some of my guys on it. What are the finances gonna be? How are we gonna make any money?"

"Russell, all I can tell you is I saw the amateur show work there, and this will be better. This is a pro show with Micky Ward."

"You didn't say anything about Micky Ward. Why are we using him? I thought it was all over for him."

"That's why I didn't mention him right away. I knew what you'd think. But we're gonna bring Micky Ward back."

"I don't know," Peltz responded, still not convinced. "Who's he gonna fight?"

"I don't know," Al had to admit. "We'll work on that. Just tell me I've got the date and then I'll sit down with Sal LoNano, and I'll sit down with Micky, and I'll explain how it's gonna work, and I'll make sure everybody's happy."

What at first seemed like a long shot all fell into place rather quickly. The Hampton Beach Casino was available. Peltz made a great match with Jermal Corbin, a twenty-five-year-old tough guy with only two losses in nineteen professional fights. And Sal put up the money.

"It was rough for my wife and my family," Sal says. "I had to put up my house to get the money. I took money from my mother-in-law, and money from my house. That was about twenty-five thousand dollars. Then there was money I took from the cab business, maybe a hundred thousand. I put up a hundred and twenty-five thousand dollars. That's a lot of money. My wife just looked at me."

The night of July 16, 1999, was a hundred years and a day from the exact date that the Hampton Beach Casino had first opened. It was a two-and-a-half-story building that ran 190 feet along Ocean Boulevard. It featured open porches running the entire length of the building on both the first and second levels. It could accommodate about three thousand people for a boxing match, and Sal did his best to make sure every ticket sold. By his own account, he lost about a thousand dollars that night.

"But it was worth it," he adds.

Micky wasn't the main event that night. That distinction belonged to Bryant Brannon and Demetrius Davis who were scheduled to fight for the USBA super middleweight title. But Brannon withdrew for personal reasons on the afternoon of the fight. That meant Micky would be bumped up to the featured fight of the evening, and Dickie saw that as an opportunity.

"We were going to make two other guys, James Butler and Merqui Sosa the main event," Peltz recalls. "But we decided to give it to Micky because he was the local guy."

But Micky and Dickie didn't find out until minutes before they were going to head to the ring. Micky was prepared to come out at nine o'clock, but that's when Butler and Sosa were summoned to appear instead. That's how Micky and Dickie found out they were the evening's main event. Moments later, Peltz heard there was trouble in the dressing room.

"Micky ain't coming out unless we get more money," Dickie told Peltz and the promoters. "He's the main event now, so he should get more money."

Micky didn't say a word. He just sat there with his gloves on, still sweating from the warm-up he'd done while still expecting to go on at nine. Micky appeared to be not listening while the people running his life decided what to do next.

"We were really on a serious time schedule," Peltz said. "I mean Dickie really had us by the balls. We needed Micky to come out and fight. So Al decided to give them more money. Micky was supposed to get five grand, and he ended up with seventy-five hundred. How could we argue with them that close to fight time?"

Sal watched all this with great concern. It was his money on the line. He had crossed over from manager to promoter to investor. He sure as hell needed Micky to fight, and he needed him to win, too.

Micky's mother, father, seven sisters, and daughter watched as Dickie encouraged Micky in the corner between rounds. They could all see that Micky's nose was bleeding profusely and that his white trunks were covered in his own blood. That was of no concern to Micky. A referee wouldn't stop a fight unless the cut was dangerous or the blood was affecting a fighter's vision. Micky was fine. And he was dictating to Corbin how this bout would be fought. Corbin was taller and had a longer reach, yet the entire fight was being waged with only a few inches separating the combatants. That took Corbin's height-and-reach advantage away, and gave an edge to Micky.

"You don't want to stay inside too long," ESPN fight analyst Teddy Atlas said about Corbin. "You're letting Ward, who's a stronger guy, the more experienced fighter, the better body puncher, you're letting him have his way."

The fight did not lack for excitement. Both fighters connected with several hard shots during the third round. They threw only power shots, overhand rights and lefts, hooks and uppercuts with both hands. They stood too close to jab. They were ear-to-ear and wailing on each other. More than once, when Micky landed a left to Corbin's ribs, Corbin flinched noticeably. His body bent over at the waist for just a split second before he righted himself again. He was either reacting to real pain or real fear. Either way, he kept on fighting, but those body shots had to be taking their toll.

"Corbin shouldn't be in there," Atlas assessed. "He should be outside using his jab."

Midway through the fourth round, Micky landed his patented vicious left hand to Corbin's rib cage. The thud could be heard throughout the casino. It was the kind of thunderous blow that had crumpled many a fighter before, but Corbin stood tall. Thirty seconds later, he absorbed another one. Ten more seconds passed, and Micky delivered a right hand to the center of Corbin's abdomen. Corbin spent the final twenty seconds of the fourth round in his own corner ducking and blocking an endless flurry of power shots. When the bell sounded, Corbin stood with his shoulders slumped, exhausted. Micky walked away to the far corner supremely confident that this fight wouldn't last much longer. Nobody could keep taking those punches to the body.

"The only punches Ward needs to throw now are to the body and the uppercut," Atlas advised. "The body punch will make him lean forward, the uppercut will bring his head up. And then go up top. It looks like Corbin is falling apart here a little bit."

As Atlas spoke, Micky pinned Corbin up against the ropes and began another ferocious assault.

"This is what Ward planned on for this fight," Atlas continued. "Get in the kitchen. Bang to that body. Micky's thinking this guy might have more talent than me on the outside, but inside he doesn't have the talent, the physical makeup or maybe the resolve to hang with me."

With twenty seconds to go in the fifth, Micky landed back-to-back shots to Corbin's ribs. Corbin barely had the energy to wince. His legs were gone. The body shots had done their job. The round ended and there would not be another one.

The referee visited Corbin's corner between rounds, and Corbin let him know he did not want to continue. Upon hearing the announcement that Micky was a winner with a fifth-round technical knockout, Sal jumped up from his seat in the front row, slipped through the ropes, and wrapped Micky up in his arms. This gamble had paid off.

"We took this fight hoping to show that Micky can fight, and now we're hoping for someone in the top five," Sal explained after the fight. "We think he can still fight for a title."

Unless they considered themselves either friends or family of Micky, not many others agreed with Sal's appraisal. Who was Corbin to raise Micky to the level of contender? He was a transit cop who fought a bad fight. Russell Peltz didn't seem very impressed when he said, "I thought Corbin was a nothing fighter, and it was just a good win for the local guy."

That was the prevailing opinion of the day because Micky's losses were just as memorable as this victory. Even Micky wasn't offended when *Ring* magazine offered a critical evaluation following the Corbin fight, "Ward, impressive win against Corbin, but a big loss is just around the corner."

The experts weren't expecting much from Micky Ward, and for his part, Micky wasn't surprised by his doubters and detractors. He would say the same things about a fighter who had lost title shots against Frankie Warren, Harold Brazier, Charles Murray, Vince Phillips, and Zab Judah. He had to admit it was a long list of failures.

"Hey, it's true. Every time I've stepped up, I've come up short," Micky said honestly.

But with the help of a new member to Team Ward, that was about to change.

CHAPTER FIFTEEN

Cutmen are like umpires and offensive lineman. The only time you notice them is when they're not doing their job. Al Gavin always did his job. Born in Brooklyn in 1934, Gavin picked up the sport his father loved, even had twenty amateur fights before he realized that his skills didn't match his passion. So he put down his gloves and picked up an endswell, an ironically named hunk of metal used to reduce the swelling on a boxer's face during a fight. Al Gavin eventually became one of the best cutmen in the business.

Gavin was a landscaper and gardener for the New York City Parks Department by day, and a student of blood and cuts by night. He got his education at Stillman's Gym on West Fifty-fourth Street in Brooklyn. Stillman's was the center of the boxing universe during boxing's golden age. It was the place where anybody fighting at Madison Square Garden trained before the fight. It was where Rocky Graziano smoked a cigarette in between rounds of his sparring sessions. It was where Jersey Joe Walcott and Joe Louis pounded the heavy bag for hours. It was where everybody stopped what they were doing when Sugar Ray Robinson did anything.

Boxing's elite hung out at Stillman's. They spit on the floor, smoked cigars, and then went over to the Neutral Corner bar for a few drinks. That's the environment in which Al Gavin learned to ply his trade. For a student, this was definitely old school. Gavin rubbed elbows with and observed the truest professionals in the sport: tough guys with hard edges, but who went to work every day and who respected the sport of boxing. Gavin learned from some of the best cutmen and trainers in the business, guys like Chickie Ferrara, Freddie Brown, and Whitey Bimstein. These guys knew what they were doing, and by the time he graduated from Stillman's, so did Gavin.

"As for what I do, I just have a feel for it," Gavin once told *USA Today* columnist Thomas Hauser. "It's a combination of art, science, and luck. Time is important. If there's a problem, I go to work as soon as the fighter reaches the corner. I don't get excited. I know where to put the pressure. Pressure is the most important element. That begins the process of stopping the bleeding."

The art of the cutman is in the dexterity, the speed, and the calmness under the pressure in which he operates. The cutman gets less than a minute to work. He needs to assess the severity of a cut, determine a course of action, and get to it. Like the boxer he treats, the best cutman is the most prepared. He has petroleum jelly smeared on the back of his hands that he can apply to the fighter's face to loosen the skin and help prevent cuts. He has long Q-tips in his mouth or behind his ears that have already been soaked in adrenaline hydrochloride, a chemical that decreases the flow of blood. He drapes a cold, wet towel around his neck, which he can use to wipe blood away, and carries a bottle of Avitine, another common coagulant that can be placed inside a cut. The job of a cutman is to prolong fights that might otherwise have to be stopped.

"If you can't stop the flow, then you go," Gavin repeated often.

Through the years, Gavin worked with champs and chumps. He patched up heavyweight champion Lennox Lewis, and he made twenty bucks helping kids in four-rounders. His reputation grew to the point where everybody wanted him. Team Ward wanted him, and they got him.

"If you're gonna be the manager for Micky, at least let me have a little say in what goes on," Al Valenti told Sal when their partnership was just forming.

"Done."

"Good," Al continued. "Now, the first thing you're gonna have to do, because I don't want to have to deal with Dickie Eklund, is you gotta bring in a good guy. I have just the guy. I have the utmost respect for him. He's everything boxing should be. He's honest. He's sincere. He's hardworking, and he's knowledgeable."

"Who is it?"

"Al Gavin. I already talked to him about coming on board, and you know what he says to me? He says, 'All right, for Micky Ward I'd do anything.' How's that for something? He's a big fan of Micky's, says he likes the way he fights and how he conducts himself. That's what he said, 'how he conducts himself.'"

"How much does he cost?" Sal wondered.

"He takes the standard 3 percent. Don't worry about that. He'll be worth every penny."

Al Valenti felt better immediately. Even though all indications were that prison had mellowed Dickie, Al wanted to make sure Micky had a calming influence in the corner during his fights. Gavin would be that influence. Things seemed to finally be falling into place. Micky had good management in Valenti and LoNano. Dickie was back doing what he did best—getting Micky into shape. Gavin was on board. And Micky was a popular, marketable fighter who had just won a TV fight in convincing fashion. Team Ward was ready to make the next fight.

Valenti and LoNano began by pursuing Ray Oliveira, a thirty-one-year-old out of Fall River, Massachusetts. Oliveira was once a legitimate contender, but like Micky, his career had had its ups and downs. Six years earlier, he was given back-to-back title fights against Zach Padilla and Jake Rodriguez, and he lost them both. He was then relegated to fighting a bunch of no-names in places such as

Warwick, Rhode Island, and the Host Inn in Sturbridge, Massachusetts. His career started to take off again when he beat Charles Murray for the lightly regarded NABF light welterweight title, but the success was short-lived when he lost back-to-back fights again, this time to Reggie Green and Vernon Forrest. So he returned to pulling down a couple of hundred bucks fighting at the Rhodes-on-the-Pawtuxet in Cranston, Rhode Island.

Oliveira was still on that comeback trail when talks between his management team and Micky's started heating up. Even though Micky could have been looking beyond Oliveira and trying to land a top-ten fighter, Sal and Al were thinking about a smaller step forward. Sal had just formed SNL Boxing to begin working as Micky's manager and promoter. With Al's help, they planned on returning to New Hampshire to put on another show, this time with Micky and Oliveira headlining. The fight would sell out, they believed, as two New Englanders fought to shove past one another in order to climb up the ranks of the junior welterweight division.

ESPN's Russell Peltz said he'd put Micky back on TV in October if Sal and Al could find a venue and an opponent. The venue was easy. Al suggested staging the fight at the Icenter in Salem. It was a small ice rink just over the Massachusetts border, but it could easily be converted into a boxing venue. Once they had the television date and the location secured, Sal and Al began negotiating with Oliveira's manager Jimmy Burchfield. That's when things started to fall apart.

"If this fight's gonna happen," Burchfield told Sal and Al, "I want to be the promoter, because I want to figure in on the upside."

"What upside?" Valenti protested. "ESPN's gonna pay you fifty grand. You're gonna give Micky and Ray twenty-five or thirty grand apiece. You've got a building that's costing ten thousand. You haven't done the undercard yet. You haven't got the officials. You haven't paid for insurance. What upside are you thinking there's gonna be?"

"Well, if there's no upside, what are we making the fight for?"

"For the next one and the one after that."

"And if there's no upside, why do you want to promote it?"

"Same reason. Plus, we've already done the legwork. We got ESPN. We got the date. We got the building. We came to you. This is our deal, and we're going to see it through."

The conversations with Burchfield went on like that for weeks. The two sides fought over which fighter would be paid more, and whose name would appear above the other name on the fight posters.

"Jimmy Burchfield hemmed and hawed, saying he wanted the lead, and for Ray's name to be on top of Micky's. That matters to the fighters," Sal explained. "Micky Ward, after beating Corbin isn't about to look at a poster with a big shot of Ray Oliviera and a little Micky in the background. Ray Oliveira is not Micky Ward. Plus, I'm making this fight. And my fighter is going to be on top. No way is Ray gonna get the same money as Micky Ward either. We're giving Ray a shot. They should be thankful for the shot."

Burchfield either didn't see it that way or he didn't really want to make the fight. Finally, a frustrated Peltz called to find out why Sal and Al didn't have an opponent for Micky yet. When he learned of the difficulties getting Oliveira, Peltz started throwing out other possibilities. On the list of potential opponents was Reggie Green. Sal and Al couldn't believe it. Green was ranked seventh in the world. He had just lost the WBA junior welterweight championship fight to Sharmba Mitchell in a majority decision. One of the judges had scored the bout even. That's how good Green was. If he was willing to fight Micky in Micky's backyard in a fight promoted by SNL Boxing, Sal and Al were all for it.

"Go get me Reggie Green," Sal told Peltz. "I'm ready to jump up to another level, and I'm gonna cut Burchfield's legs out from under him just for being an asshole."

"Are you serious?" Peltz asked seeking confirmation.

"You bet I am. Make the fight with Reggie Green. Give him the same offer. And tell Burchfield, 'Thank you very much.'"

Peltz called back ten minutes later with the news that Micky Ward would be fighting Reggie Green on October 1 at the Salem Icenter on ESPN. Micky was back on national television fighting a contender for twenty-five thousand dollars, and Micky got every dime of that purse. Sal covered all the expenses. His new company, SNL Boxing, promoted the fight, and he just gave flat fees to everyone involved. Gavin and Dickie were given their appropriate percentages, but their money didn't come out of Micky's end. And Sal received absolutely nothing as Micky's manager; however, as the promoter, when he was finished handing out all the checks, Sal claims he was left with about a three-thousand-dollar profit.

"You won't find a member of Micky's family that likes Sal," Joe Lake says. "He tried to keep everything hidden about how much money he made. His battle cry was always, 'I made no money.' That was false. I know he made money with Judah, because why would you put Micky in there with a guy he couldn't beat for short money. Micky got twelve grand for that fight. It doesn't make any sense unless you're getting money on the side."

Lake explained how it could work, and how he suspected it did work with Sal.

"By you being the agent, you're making your own side deal. It's easy for you to say 'How much money is in this fight?' Once you know how much money is in the fight, you tell the fighter something less, maybe ten thousand, twenty thousand less. He agrees to the fight and the amount, and you get the money off the side."

That's just speculation, of course. For his part, Micky needed only to know that he was getting paid, and he was being handed a golden opportunity.

"If I can't beat a world-class contender like Reggie Green at this stage of my career," Micky said honestly, "I don't deserve another title shot."

Four days before his thirty-fourth birthday, Irish Micky Ward came bouncing out of the locker room at the Icenter accompanied by bagpipes. Fifteen hundred people heard the Irish music and knew the night was about to begin, but they couldn't have known they were about to witness a terrific and bloody fight between two men with hearts of lions.

Micky was more active than was his custom in the first round. He was trying to get off to a quick start against Green, who was known as a sharpshooter and a counterpuncher. Green's style was to Micky's liking, however. Green was a skilled boxer, but he stood much more flat-footed than someone like Judah. Green wasn't going anywhere. He was going to stand and fight, just like Micky.

Pow!

The shot came straight up the pike and landed square on Micky's kisser. It was a hard right hand that knocked Micky backwards and almost down. Micky wobbled, but he didn't appear hurt. He appeared angry, upset with himself for letting that one through. While he cleared his head, he took a flurry to the body. Once he had recovered, he fired back with fury. A counter left hook found its mark on Green's ear. Then a big right hand spun Green around and off-balance. Green recovered quickly, but he had clearly yielded to Micky's will. Green the boxer was brawling.

"You're getting strong! He's getting weak!" Dickie shouted above the roar of the crowd while Micky sat in his corner after the second round. "I know he's got heart, Mick, but forget about it! Hands up. Three or four punches. Deep breaths. He's a good fighter, Mick. Forget about it! You're better. Three or four. Mick, Mick, Mick, you're following him, Mick. Let him go. Cut the ring off. Be patient. Cut the ring off! Three or four. Mick, you're hurting him. Everything you throw, you're hurting him. Deep breaths."

Micky sprinted back to the center of the ring, gloves attached to his forehead protecting his face as he stepped inside. Green blasted him on his way in, but Micky was willing to take one to give two or take two to give one. He just wanted to be close enough to Green to land the big one. In the final minute of the round, he threw a double left hook. The second one landed hard to the side of Green's face.

"I think this fight breaks down fairly simple in certain strategic ways," Teddy Atlas said during ESPN's *Friday Night Fights*. "Ward wants to get in, and he has to be careful he doesn't get caught coming in by Green. And when Ward's inside, he wants to go to the body and the uppercuts, and I think Ward can get opportunities catching Green when he's stepping out."

Ward was winning the round right down to the final twenty seconds. That's when both fighters simultaneously rose from their crouches and fired hard left hands. Green's landed. Micky's did not. Micky's did not because by the time it would have reached its mark, he was already sprawling into the ropes.

"A counter left hook hurts Ward!" exclaims blow-by-blow announcer Bob Papa. "Ward is still hurt. He's trying to hold on. He eats an uppercut. A fighter cannot be saved by the bell in any round."

"Ward should stay still," Atlas observed. "It's obvious his legs aren't under him."

If it weren't for the ropes, Micky would have found himself in the front row. Somehow he managed to remain standing. Green was on him in an instant, and Micky was looking to survive. Only fifteen seconds remained in the round. Could he hold on? Micky was out on his feet. He was stumbling around the ring. Fortunately, his awkwardness served to protect him. Mercifully, the bell rang.

"Ward, bloody mouth, is out on his feet," Papa said. "And they have one minute to revive Micky Ward."

Perhaps stunned by what had just happened, Dickie was slow to bring the stool into the ring. Micky stood dazed in his own corner for ten seconds before he was finally able to sit down. His eyes wouldn't focus, and his ears couldn't hear. Dickie struggled to get the mouthpiece out as he guided Micky on to the stool.

"How do you feel, Mick?" There was no response.

"You all right?"

"Yeah."

Then Al Gavin took over, "Let me see your mouth. Move to the side, Dickie. Let me see the mouth."

Dickie obeyed and Gavin leaned in to inspect a wound on Micky's lower lip. What he found was a gaping hole that he could put his finger through. If Micky wanted to brush his teeth, he wouldn't have to open his mouth.

"Uh oh!" Dickie reacted with alarm.

"He can go," Gavin said as he went to work on stopping the bleeding. Then he added, "But you've got to fight this round, Mick. This is a bad cut."

What Gavin was saying was that he could get the cut under control for the next three minutes, but beyond that, he couldn't be sure. Micky needed to get himself together at least enough to defend himself from any further assaults on the one-inch hole in his lip, and perhaps enough to go after a knockout.

But Micky didn't hear any of what was being said. He was still in a complete fog. Dickie noticed and yelled, "Wake up, Mick!" Then with increasing urgency, Dickie repeated, "Wake up! Wake up!" And for added emphasis, he slapped Micky hard and stood him up from the stool.

Time was up. It was time to return to battle. The mouthpiece that was so difficult to get out was shoved back in. Dickie jumped up and down and encouraged Micky to do the same, but Micky did not. He was going back into the ring with a trained professional, a man well versed in the art of knocking people out. "The worst I've been hurt in a fight was the third round of the Reggie Green fight," Micky said years later. "When he caught me with a left hook and tore through my lip, I could stick my tongue through it."

Green's corner was aware of Micky's condition, and they sent their guy back out with one simple directive, "Take this guy out."

As the bell rang to start the fourth round, Micky took a step toward the center of the ring, and a noticeable bounce had returned. He approached Green quickly and then sidestepped him. He was moving well and keeping his distance. Green seemed startled by Micky's resilience, and it must have worried him. He responded by working cautiously, throwing a few jabs and allowing Micky to stay away. A minute passed and neither fighter had landed anything substantial. That was enough time for Micky to recover.

"I think Green is making a mistake," Atlas offered. "I don't know how this fight is going to go, obviously. But right now, he's allowing Micky to recover a little bit. . . . He knows Micky is a veteran who's been hurt before, knows what to do when he's hurt, but he's being a little too cautious right here. . . . Ward doesn't care if he loses this round, he just needs to get through this round and recover a little bit."

Gavin went back to work when Micky returned to the corner. The hole in Micky's lip had not been damaged any further, and the bleeding was under control. Gavin's abilities were the primary reason Micky was able to continue fighting. Whether that was a good thing or inadvisable had yet to be determined.

Micky had lost that round. Then he lost the fifth and sixth rounds as well. He was no longer hurt, but he was most definitely losing and continuing to take punishment. Green leaned on Micky so hard that he was actually able to push him backwards while he was throwing punches. Micky leaned back, but was most effective when he stepped back and to the side, freeing up some space for him to land some solid punches. In the final minute of the sixth, Micky caught Green with a left hook to the chin. The sheer force of the blow knocked Green off balance, but he did not appear to be hurt, and Micky did not increase his activity at that time.

"Come on, Mick! Head, body!" Dickie yelled from his corner. Then he began answering questions from Bob Papa and Teddy Atlas during a live in-round interview for the ESPN broadcast.

"Do you think Micky got a break in that fourth round when Green really didn't come out and press the action after Micky got hurt?" Papa asked.

"Micky was banging him to the body, wearing him down, too," Dickie explained. "So, you know what I mean, he's dead tired himself. I told Micky to keep working. Stay to the body. You know what I mean? He's giving him too many breaks. He's switching lefty and he's getting caught, and I don't want him to."

"Why does he do that?" Atlas interjected. "Every time he switches he seems to get hit with a clean right hand."

"Because Green's a smart fighter. If I was fighting Micky and he turned lefty, I'd be banging the right hand. You do that for a split second, and then you get back into your righty stance. Mick, head body, right there! Head, body! Ah, shit!"

And the interview ended there. "All right, thank you very much, Dick. Best of the luck the rest of the way."

Micky was already contending with the hole in his lip and had been swallowing a disgusting amount of blood since the third round. He also had developed considerable swelling under his left eye that Gavin was trying to keep from opening up.

"Mick, you're letting him work all over you," Dickie criticized. "He's tiring you. You should be tiring him. Micky, go for the gusto! You gotta work, Micky. You gotta work!"

"You've got to go for the body," Gavin interjected while treating Micky's cuts. "Two punches, not one. Two!"

Bloody, battered, and bruised, the two fighters persisted. They were exhausted, but they could rest tomorrow. Each round was replete with punishing power shots. Micky was getting the worst of it. Green had fought within inches of Micky most of the night, and another hard left hook to the jaw in the ninth round reminded him to keep a safer distance. Late in the ninth, Micky and Green connected at the same time. Left hooks together. Green took more than he gave. Micky sensed it and stepped up his intensity. As he went in for the kill, Green landed a counter left hand. Bam! Just like that, the momentum shifted back in Green's favor.

"Throw a hundred punches, whatever you have to do!" Dickie exhorted his brother. "Spit. Can you swallow a little bit? You're still fighting real good, Mick. Keep your hands up. Let's go, Mick. You need the knockout. Go get it!"

Micky came out for the tenth and final round looking to land a knockout blow. He knew that was the only way he could win this fight. He was too far behind on points. So, he threw haymakers at Green's head with both hands, and he threw body shots in combinations, but Green kept coming at him. Then halfway through the round, Micky landed one of those patented left hooks to the ribs that caused Green to jump up in the air. It was a full-body flinch. When Green came back down, Micky hit him again in the same spot. This time Green nearly doubled over, but he willed himself upright. He backpedaled to safety, but his hands were low as Micky swooped in. Micky hit him with a left hand to the head. That wobbled Green. Micky hit him again. Green stared straight down at the canvas. He didn't move until another head-body combination sent him across the ring. Green looked as if he wanted to keep backing up forever, but the far ropes stopped his retreat. Micky was on him in a flash, but he didn't throw any punches for a moment. Instead, while the crowd was on its feet, roaring as if they were in the Roman Coliseum, Micky patiently waited for the right opening. Only one minute remained in the fight. The next sixty seconds would determine where Micky's career would go.

Micky banged Green with a left uppercut that shot his head back like a gunshot victim. Green moved to the center of the ring and bobbed his head up and down like a drunk who is unsure if he just dropped his car keys.

"Green is in trouble right now. He should tie Ward up. He should tie Ward up right now," Atlas yelled into his microphone.

With thirty seconds to go, Green was moving on instinct. He was fighting courageously, but he was wobbling and unable to defend himself. Just as Micky was about to inflict further damage, the referee came in to separate the fighters. As Norm Vellieu approached, Micky landed one more left hook. This one sent Green sprawling against the far ropes. He managed to stay on his feet, but Vellieu waved off the fight.

"That's a bit controversial, because as the ref was stepping in, he kind of blocked Green's view and Ward caught him a good clean shot," Atlas said.

Bob Papa added, "That's bad refereeing right there, I think, Teddy."

"I didn't like that. I didn't like the way that ended, I'll be honest with you. Because as he was stepping in, Micky might have stopped him anyway, but he made it controversial. As he stepped in and put his arm in, he distracted Green. Green let up a little bit and then Ward threw a punch. I'm not saying Ward wouldn't have got to him, but it shouldn't have been that way."

But Green could not argue with the stoppage. He had no fight left in him. He was exhausted and beaten, and so was Micky.

"That truly was fighting," Atlas would tell Ron Borges of the *Boston Globe*. "That was not entertainment. That was not business. That was fighting. This is a barbaric thing at the core of it. . . . Like the mobsters say, that was a real guy up there. When it came down to what a fighter is about, Micky Ward was it. . . . You don't see it too often no more."

Green held his head high and his chest out; he'd fought with as much courage and pride as Micky had. Green went back to his dressing room, packed his things, left the bloody hand wraps on the floor, and headed out to the parking lot. He shuffled slowly and accepted help from a man on either side of him. It was evident that his ribs were causing him intense pain.

Before he got in his car to drive over to the hospital, Borges stopped him and asked, "Reggie, are you all right?"

"Did you see the fight?" Green asked.

"Yeah, I saw the fight. What happened?"

"The other guy happened. I've never been hit harder, and I have never hit anyone harder than Micky," Green said. "I honestly don't know what kept him up. No one left me busted up like Micky."

"I had the will," Ward would say. "He dazed me once, but with my heart I wasn't going down. I knew the body shots were getting to him. Even the ones on the elbows were takin' a price. I think he just said, 'Enough.' I knew I had to push it that last round. I knew I was down, behind in points. I was in good shape for it. I felt a little rusty. He's sharp, he's very elusive. It's hard to hit him with one clean shot. He moves around a lot on his punches, so it's hard to catch him square. But I just wanted to keep pressuring him, and I knew if I kept the heart and God's will, I knew I would come out on top. It took me ten rounds, but hey, it's a win."

Micky was the winner, but you wouldn't know it by looking at his face. He was left with a huge swelling under his left eye and a two-inch gouge on his cheek that bled intermittently for the last five rounds. When Dickie lifted Micky into the air upon the culmination of the fight, his satin shirt was smeared with his brother's blood.

In the locker room after the fight, Micky slumped on a metal folding chair. He was clearly exhausted. He asked for some water, and Dickie handed him a plastic bottle. As soon as the bottle came in contact with his lips, he cringed and cried out in pain. He dropped the water bottle and put his hand to his sore mouth.

Just fifteen minutes earlier, he was still getting punched in the mouth, but he gave no indication that it hurt. Now that he was no longer in that other mental place where fighters have to go, he was just like anybody else. He felt pain.

"People ask me all the time," Borges said. "'How come boxers don't feel the punches?' They do feel the punches. They make choices that the rest of us don't make. But as soon as Micky was in a civilized setting, he couldn't make that choice anymore. Soon after that, his girlfriend comes in and hugs him and goes to kiss him, and she gets the same reaction as the bottle. He was willing to get punched in that lip by Reggie Green for as long as it took to win the fight, but he could not be kissed on that lip. That says all you need to know about what it takes to be a fighter."

Teddy Atlas knows what it takes. Recognized as one of the best trainers, Atlas was a fighter himself until a spinal injury forced him to retire.

"Micky was in there with Green, who was more athletic, just as experienced as Micky, and had better skills than Micky," Atlas expounded. "Green had more speed and had more options in the ring. He was winning the fight handily. He was doing more than winning the fight. Micky was taking a beating. He was there. He was not caving in at all. People cave in to degrees. The key with Micky was that he didn't cave in to degrees. Some people get credit for being stout because they're still there, but they become game quitters. They're not really looking to win, they're just accumulating punishment. They get credit by uneducated people in the sport by thinking they're at the same level of stoutness as somebody else, and they're not, because what has to be included in that effort is trying to win, not just surviving, not just enduring. That's what allowed Micky to stand out and to win the fights. He did not submit to that point where he was just enduring and not trying to win. That's why he gets credit for being stout at a higher level than somebody who just exists and just lasts. He did not make those solid contracts to just survive. The fight with Green was an example of that.

"Micky had ability that people don't understand. We register ability by things that are flashy, that are digestible to us and what we think are more tangible or easier to feel comfortable with, things that are loud. If somebody has fast hands, we notice. If they knock somebody out, we notice. But we don't notice the other things that are just as important and that are talents that have to be developed. And one of those talents is being dependable. Micky had that talent. . . . You don't see it the way you see those other things, but they serve you, and they can make you special. He had that talent of being dependable, of being steady, of being able to be within himself and see things under pressure. And sure enough, he changed that left hook angle to throw it inside the elbow, and he hurt Green. So after all that punishment, such a long night, and such a one-sided night, all of a sudden right there, he turned the fight around. And to do that, that meant that he had never capitulated—*ever*—during the course of that night. A lot of people might have still endured, but they would have capitulated. . . . But he never did. That's what allowed him to have that opportunity. He turned it around and stopped Green. He pulled that fight right out of the fire, a fight that looked to be gone."

It was the turning point of Micky's career. The kid from Lowell, who was being promoted by a guy who couldn't promote fights in Massachusetts, managed by a guy who had never managed before, and trained by his brother, the former crack addict, put on a remarkably entertaining performance with a dramatic climax, and he did it in front of a national television audience. Sal LoNano immediately knew what it meant for Micky's future. That's why when Micky was applying the finishing touches on Green, Sal ended up on the floor. Sal had jumped up in excitement and came crashing down on his ringside chair, breaking it. He ended up sprawled out on the ground and needed assistance from the New Hampshire boxing commissioner just so he could see the end of the fight.

Sal was ready to celebrate, but he knew that Micky wouldn't be. So, he played traffic cop in front of the locker room preventing Micky's friends and family from barging in. Micky's seven sisters took turns cursing him out, but Sal held his ground.

"Micky thanked me for it," Sal says. "You have a warrior who just went through a war, and he doesn't want to see friends and have family hugging him. He needs to be alone, to cool down. Let the cutman and the doctor look at him. Give him some water. What was inside that door was a kid who really respected me, and he thanked me for what I did. Give him ten minutes. That's all I wanted to do."

When it was time to go, the post-fight celebration spilled over to the Coliseum, a little Italian restaurant. Sal took over the kitchen and prepared food for about sixty people. Reggie Green came over from the hospital, still sore and very hungry. It was a wonderful night that lasted until the wee hours of the morning. But Micky never showed up. Sal didn't see him again until the next morning for breakfast at the Holiday Inn.

"Hey, where'd you go last night?" Sal asked. "Everybody was asking about you."

"I had to go get stitches," Micky said.

"How many?"

"Sixty," Micky said flatly. "What's good here? I'm starving."

Sixty stitches. Micky had fought seven rounds with a hole in his mouth that required five dozen stitches. That's why Al Valenti called Gavin "the miracle worker."

"He plugged him up," Valenti said. "And give credit to Dickie. He kept working on his calves and his head. He got him back in the fight. In the fourth round, Micky's legs came back."

The two guys in the corner had a hand in it, but it was Micky's left hand and his lion-sized heart that did the rest. It was his miracle comeback. He took the punishment. He refused to quit. It was Micky who had survived to fight another day.

CHAPTER SIXTEEN

"In the long run," Al Valenti summarizes, "Micky's epitaph will be that he was a fighter. He was a fighter in life, and he was a fighter in the ring. He should have been a loser, but he turned out to be a winner. When you consider what he was born into, and how he came out of that, it was like the odds of winning some of those fights that he won after starting out so far behind."

Micky did start out in the back of the line. No money, no education, no discipline at home, no positive role models, and not much of a chance. But when you're on the bottom, there's really only one way to go. And that's where Micky was going. Up.

His inspiring victory put a lot of possibilities on the table, including a chance to fight the WBC champion, Kostya Tszyu, in December. Micky could have been a co-headliner with the Fernando Vargas–Winky Wright IBF light welterweight title fight on HBO, but the injuries he sustained in the Green fight wouldn't be healed in time. So Micky had to pass.

Sal and Al had thought they'd have a chance to make the Julio Cesar Chavez fight finally happen, but the day after Micky beat Green, Chavez took a beating at the hands of lightly regarded journeyman Willy Wise. And so, three years after Chavez would have represented Micky's big break, Micky had actually moved beyond perhaps the greatest light welterweight of all time.

There was also plenty of talk about Micky taking on Arturo Gatti, the former super featherweight champion who was ready to move up to the light welterweight division.

In 1997, Gatti was badly hurt in the fourth round by former world champion Gabriel Ruelas, but he knocked Ruelas out in the fifth. And in 1998, Gatti and Ivan Robinson traded leather for ten rounds before Robinson was awarded a split decision. Both of those exciting battles were recognized as "Fights of the Year."

Now, it was 1999 and Gatti had only fought once, knocking out Reyes Munoz in the first round. He was inactive, but not forgotten, and a battle with Micky Ward promised to be a classic matchup.

"I love that fight," HBO's Lou DiBella said.

But it didn't happen. Not then. Sal pushed the discussions as far as securing a date, March 11, a location, the FleetCenter in Boston, and an undercard that would include WBU champion Shea Neary against Ray Oliveira. But as that deal fell apart, primarily because Gatti demanded too much money, another intriguing possibility began to materialize.

"After Reggie Green we should have gotten a lot of offers," Valenti concluded. "Micky's won two fights on TV. He's exciting. He can draw a crowd. But we're not getting anything we really want. Time passes, and we're into the New Year, and I'm at the Golden Gloves in Lowell with Sal. My cell phone rings and it's the big-time promoter Cedric Kushner and he asks me, 'Who's got Micky Ward?' I said, 'I'm sitting right next to his manager, Sal Lo-Nano.' So he says, 'Well, what do you think about going to England and fighting Shea Neary?' 'I don't know,' I says. 'Let me get back to you.'"

There wasn't a lot to think about. Valenti said, "Offering Shea Neary to Micky Ward was like offering a steak to a tiger. This guy was undefeated with twenty-two wins, but he'd only fought in Europe.

Anybody who fights in Europe is not giving themselves the opportunity to show what they've got. So, we called back and Cedric talks to Sal and we make the fight."

Kushner's first phone call to Al occurred in late January 2000, and the fight was scheduled for March 11. Everything fell into place that quickly, in part because Kushner had been working with Neary and his management team for more than a year, trying to find him a strong American fighter to raise his profile and his bank account. Micky was not Kushner's first choice, but he was the first one to say yes, and he was ready to go on relatively short notice. Six weeks would be more than enough time to prepare. Furthermore, the fight had a natural, easily promotable hook built right in.

Neary was born and raised in Liverpool, England, but he was of Irish heritage. In fact, his nickname was "The Shamrock Express." To Cedric, Sal, and Al, a good old-fashioned bout between two tough Irishmen sounded like a perfect match. More important, HBO concurred, and Micky would get his first six-figure payday. He agreed to fight Neary at the Olympia Grand Hall in Kensington, England, for one hundred thousand dollars, by far the biggest purse of his career. He would fight outside the United States for the first time. He would make his HBO debut, and he would fight for the WBU light welterweight title. He was getting his chance to be a world champion, just as Dickie had promised and boldly predicted. It was all coming together.

"It didn't make sense for Neary's people," Valenti figured. "The minute I called Al Gavin to talk about it, he was just as excited as I was. We could assess the fight fairly accurately. We figured it would be a tough fight, but one that Micky could win. And Micky knew then that if he fought a marginal guy, so what? He wanted to fight the best guy out there. His window of opportunity was closing. He figured Reggie Green's resume was a lot more impressive than Shea Neary's, and he'd already beaten Green."

Team Ward, which included Micky, Dickie, Sal, and the two Als, Valenti and Gavin, traveled to England one week before the fight. They received twenty thousand dollars for training expenses which would cover the hotel for the entire party, food, and sparring partners. According to Sal, "The weather was lousy. The food was bad. The coffee, I hated." He was miserable, and he was worried that if he couldn't please himself, he wouldn't be able to please Micky.

"Part of my job was to make sure everybody was satisfied," he said. "If I can't keep the trainers happy, then Micky's not gonna be happy."

The odds in England against Micky winning the fight were 5 to 2, and there were betting establishments all over the place willing to take some action. The two Als went out for a walk on Thursday, a day before the weigh-in, two days before the fight. They went on for about eight miles ducking into gambling halls all along the way. In each place the conversation was the same.

"How much will you take on the Neary fight?" Valenti said with his very American accent. "Will you take a thousand?"

The guy in the betting window would then make a phone call and tell Valenti that they would only take a hundred.

"He could tell I'm from the states, and if I'm looking to lay that kind of cash on Micky Ward, then I must know something," Valenti deduced. "They got nervous. They'll take the loss on 5 to 2, but not for a thousand bucks. So, we walked a little bit further and placed a few more hundred-dollar bets at a few different windows."

As a tough kid who did most of his fighting close to home and on the East Coast, Micky was used to having the crowd on his side. But even though there was a large Irish community in Liverpool because so many people had come over from Ireland during the potato famine of the 1920s, they would not be cheering for Irish Micky Ward. This was Neary's turf, and the Shamrock Express was a real fan favorite. They would be eleven thousand strong at the Olympia Grand Hall, and nearly all of them would be in Neary's corner.

"He tried to intimidate me in his hometown," Micky recalls. "I said, 'No way.' I don't care where I am. You can have the whole country behind you, but it's only you and me in the ring."

Micky was first to enter the ring with the sound of Whitesnake's "Here I Go Again" blaring over the sound system. He was sporting a goatee for the first time in his career, and wearing yellow boxing gloves and white trunks with black trim. He stood and watched Neary come out with musical accompaniment from the Wild Irish Rovers. Green lights flashed throughout the Olympia, and Neary, wearing green gloves, pounded himself in the head with surprising force. This was as big a night for him as it was for Micky. He was a national hero performing for the first time on an international stage, and he was putting his undefeated record to the test.

"We think that's an empty record," Dickie told HBO. "He hasn't fought anybody."

Micky went forehead-to-forehead with Neary as referee Micky Vann delivered the pre-fight instructions with a thick cockney accent.

"Come out when you hear the bell. And don't mess about."

The fighters obeyed and as the fight began, they immediately went back to standing forehead-to-forehead. This time, however, they were exchanging blows. There would be no graceful movements around the ring in this fight, no Ali shuffles, no stinging jabs. These guys were prepared to lean on one another, plod around the ring, and pound away with power shot after power shot. It was how Micky liked it, and how Neary liked it.

Neary was nearly Micky's twin. The two men were built the same and had similar short, reddish hair. And they fought the same. They threw hard punches and they took hard punches. In many respects, Neary was the perfect opponent for Micky. He wasn't especially fast with his feet or his hands, and he stood right in front of Micky, which allowed Micky to be extremely accurate with his punches. It was an odd strategy for Neary, because he had invited Reggie Green to England to spar with him before the fight. Green had used the "stand in front of the guy and take those body shots" style, and it didn't work. Now, Neary was doing the same thing.

"All right, if we take him out early, we take him out early," Dickie said after the second. "Knock him out. We don't need to go to a decision. All right, keep your hands up. None of this moving around like that. Pump the double jab. It's been good for you. Jab him. Jab him. Double jab!"

Neary's cornerman, Judas Clottey, offered the same advice, saying, "Keep working the jab. You're looking great, but you've got to keep that jab going. Don't let him dictate the pressure."

Back on the other side of the ring, Dickie blessed himself and took the stool out of the ring with him. As he stepped off the apron, he handed the stool to Sal, and they sat down together.

"Sal wanted to be in the corner for the Neary fight," Dickie said. "We didn't need him. Al Gavin's there. I'm there. What do we need Sal for? He's clumsy and in the way. I banged into him once going up to the apron, killed my knee. I don't need that when I'm trying to get to Micky."

Although Sal was admittedly nervous and struggled to keep his hands from shaking when Gavin asked him to unscrew the top of the Vaseline jar, he maintains that there was a perfectly valid reason for an inexperienced man to be in the corner during a championship fight.

"I was there to cope with Dickie," Sal said. "He's crazy. I have to be a calming influence. Plus, I put myself in the corner, because being a manager, it goes to the chief second. Micky wanted me there to make sure Dickie didn't throw in the towel. That's a tough decision for his brother to make."

That decision was almost necessary in the third round. According to the punch stats for the fight, Micky had connected on half of his punches through the first two rounds, an inordinately high percentage for any fighter, and especially high for Micky. Neary was an easy target. But that changed in the third. Micky, who had already switched to a southpaw stance twice in the fight, did so again. This time he paid for it. The lefty position left him open to a right-hand lead, and Neary connected with it. Micky was hurt.

"Ward wobbled there by a right cross from Neary," HBO commentator Jim Lampley exclaimed. "Neary goes to the body and to the uppercut as he tries to finish Micky."

Micky lost his balance like someone who has forgotten there's another stair. He almost fell down trying to figure out how to get both feet on the canvas at the same time. He immediately covered up on the ropes, and Neary went into full attack mode. He pressured Micky and pounded him with vicious body shots. Micky's instincts told him to fire back, but he took several more shots to the head. Finally, Neary missed on a wild right cross and an equally inaccurate left cross. After the two whiffs, Micky leaned back against the ropes. His reaction said, "Whoo! That was close!" Those punches could have done serious damage, not only to Micky's brain, but also to his career. Getting knocked out in the third round against the English Irishman would be another major setback.

As Micky worked his way off the ropes, he raised his hands with pride and some sense of relief that he had regained his senses. The signal was to himself, his corner, to Neary, and to the crowd. He was letting everyone know he had survived. Neary needed to know it, too, so that he would worry about what kind of man stood in front of him. Who takes shots like that and celebrates only a few seconds later?

Micky backed Neary up with a couple of shots, but then late in the round, he dropped his gloves and Neary connected with a hard left hook. Neary dropped his hands, and Micky hit him with a short right hand on the ear.

"This is like a movie fight. This is like *Play It to the Bone*," Lampley said.

It was an amazing round, and when the bell sounded, Neary stared at Micky in disbelief. Micky looked back and smiled. He put both his hands on Neary's head with respect, and turned away still smiling. But as he returned to his corner, he heard this from his brother.

"Listen, Mick, don't take unnecessary punishment. You're not a punching bag. This guy, you can tear his head off if you keep your hands up. Why are you letting him abuse you? Defense. All right. If you can let him hit you with your hands down, you can destroy him with your hands up."

There was more close-range fighting in the fourth. Each man took the other's shots. First, Neary to the body and the head, then Micky with an uppercut to the chin.

"They are trying to hurt each other with every punch," HBO's Larry Merchant observed. "This is a test now of will, strength, and conditioning."

In the fifth, Micky worked his way off the ropes by landing four consecutive uppercuts, two with each hand, popping Neary's head. Another body shot from Micky reminded Neary of just how much the last one hurt. Then another one. Ward's left to the body was laying the groundwork. Those are the shots that take a fighter's legs away.

"You're in there close, short punch. Short punches," Dickie encouraged his brother. "You know what I mean. Head, body, head. Remember that in your mind. Head, body, head. This kid's gonna go! But if you let him hit you, you're gonna get banged up. You don't need to get hit. You're not a punching bag for nobody."

"Your hands are much faster than his," Gavin added flatly while he worked on a small cut on the bridge of Micky's nose. Gavin never raised his voice, but Micky could hear him. He stood and stared across the ring. Neary stood, too. He was bleeding from the mouth. His cheeks were red and swollen. Both fighters had red welts all over their sides and midsections. The punches they had thrown and the punches they had received had taken a lot out of them. But Neary was winning on the judges' scorecards.

"The way this fight is going," Merchant began. "Ward is going to have to do something dramatic late in the fight as he has before, because it's going to be very difficult for him to get a decision in Neary's home country and hometown."

Dickie and Gavin concurred, and they admonished Micky in the corner.

"You've got to remember, Mick, you're in his country," Gavin cautioned.

"That's right," agreed Dickie. "We've got to take him with a knockout. We've trained hard for this, Mick. Don't let him punch you when you don't need to. He's tireder than you."

Micky started throwing punches with more force and aggression, and in the eighth round, he found what he was looking for.

"Oh! Big uppercut by Ward!" Lampley screamed as Neary tumbled over backward. "I told you he was putting more mustard on the uppercut, and that one lands Neary on his butt. First time in twenty-three professional fights that Shea Neary has been down."

Micky had hurt Neary with another shot to the ribs, and as Neary bent over from the force of the blow, Micky hit him cleanly on the chin. Neary stumbled backwards until his ass hit the canvas and his legs flipped up over his head. He was up immediately, but his eyes were glazed over.

The referee, Micky Vann, gave him a standing eight-count and then invited Micky over to try to finish the job. Micky approached lackadaisically and then unleashed a hard left-hand uppercut. Direct hit. A left cross. Direct hit. A left hand to the body. Neary was backpedaling the whole time.

"Ward lands a huge left hook and another uppercut, goes to the body with the left hook, lands the uppercut again. Neary down for the second time. Micky Vann's gonna stop it right there. Irish Micky Ward with a big eighth-round TKO," concluded Lampley.

"He's done it again," Merchant said respectfully. "He's done it again."

The last shot sent Neary sprawling out of control until he landed with his head crashing low on the belt buckle in Micky's corner. Dickie jumped over the fallen warrior, ran out to the center of the ring, and lifted Micky in his arms. When he finally let Micky down, he grabbed his head with both hands and said, "You're the world champion. You're the champion of the world."

Micky circled the ring looking for an empty space. He found it in a neutral corner where he knelt to say a quick prayer. Dickie joined him there, and the two brothers thanked God together. Their dreams had come true. Micky was a world champion, and Dickie had helped get him there.

"Ladies and gentlemen," ring announcer Michael Buffer said. "A round of applause for two Irish warriors who put on one helluva show here in London. The official time 2:55 of round number eight. Referee Micky Vann calls a halt to the fight. The winner and new WBU light welterweight champion of the world, Irish Micky Ward!"

Micky heard it and let it settle in his mind for a moment. What a long hard road it had been to get here. Every boxer makes sacrifices, spends hours in the gym, and feels the pain of blows to the head and the stomach. And almost every boxer does it without reward. For every champion, there are thousands more who try and fail. Only the rare and extraordinary get to wear the belt of a champion. Many people credit Micky's heart.

But Teddy Atlas disagreed. "Heart is a word for the uneducated and uninitiated when it comes to boxing," Atlas scolds. "It's confidence. It's mental toughness. It's discipline. It's something that's developed. Micky didn't want to take the punch. He tried to block it, but when he had to take it, he had the temperament of a fighter. He was going to behave like a fighter. He wasn't going to allow taking a punch to stop him. If that's what he had to do, that's what he would do. Taking a punch, the physical part, you want to have a strong neck, a shock absorber so to speak, but the mental part is the most important part. You have to make up your mind that you're going to deal with it in the proper way, and that is to not allow it to bring you to a point where you can't go on. It takes tremendous concentration. It takes tremendous understanding. It takes understanding and to be in that mindset that when you get buzzed, which everyone does, that you're not going to allow yourself to drift, not to allow yourself to go to a place where you can't come back, where you're gone. You have to understand that and be willing to make that stand. Micky was always willing, more than willing. It was part of his makeup that he'd make that stand."

Micky took that stand when he was out on his feet against Reggie Green and again when Neary hurt him in the third round. Taking that stand was the difference between Micky and almost every other boxer. It may even have been the difference between him and a champion like Neary. The Shamrock Express had never been asked to take that kind of stand before.

"The saddest part of that night is that Micky literally destroyed Neary as a fighter and as a man," Al Valenti says. "He was 22 and 0 and a heckuva fighter, but after Ward, he only fought two more times. Both were European guys, one from Northern Ireland and the other from England. And he was done. Micky broke him that night. I remember how devastated he was."

George Foreman said during the fight that Neary was the better fighter, that he moved better and had a better jab. But the better fighter lost, perhaps because the tougher man had won.

"I won it. I trained hard for it. It was long overdue," Micky told Merchant in the post-fight interview. "I started in 1985 on ESPN shows. I thank Teddy Brenner. He's passed away. He gave me my shot. He started me off at Top Rank, and I just kept going. But it was all that combined, all the stuff I went through, the losses. It was just heart. I fought the best in the world. When you fight Zab Judah, ain't nobody better than that. I don't care what anybody says, there ain't nobody better than that man. . . .

"I've taken a lot of punches from a lot of guys, and I knew I could do it. . . . I hit him with a lot of flush right hands and some double jabs, and then bang over the right. I have to thank Dr. Margeles from the Lahey Clinic for getting my right hand back."

Micky closed out the Merchant interview, saying: "This is what it's about. It took longer than I wanted, but I got it. I just hope it puts me into better things. He's a great fighter. I'm not saying I'm a better fighter. I'm not better than anybody. I just come here to do my job. I do the best I can do. I was the better man tonight. I take nothing away from him. I want to say 'Hi' to my daughter and to my Mom who couldn't be here. 'I love you, Ma.'"

Back in Lowell, Alice Ward smiled and waved at the television. "I love you, too, Micky," she said.

Micky returned to the locker room with his WBU championship belt draped over his shoulder. He held the belt high over his head and gazed at it. It was beautiful. And it was gone a few minutes later.

"They put the belt on Micky," Sal recalled. "And we went to the dressing room, and we all took turns taking pictures with it.

Then the belt disappeared. There were supposed to be two belts there, but the WBU president, John Robinson, only had the one belt. So, they gave it back to Neary and told us they'd send us one of our own."

Never having been a champion before, Micky was unaware of the appropriate protocol. So, he was understandably shocked and upset when Neary's handlers walked into the locker room and retrieved the belt, claiming that it was the ex-champion's personal possession.

"I didn't know what was going on," Ward told the *Boston Globe*. "I said, 'Hey where you going with that belt? That's mine!' Then they told me that when you win a title you get your own belt to keep. The new champ gets the belt in the ring, but the ex-champ gets it back later. Too bad, because it was a nice fit, it felt good. I would have loved to have brought it home to Lowell."

But Micky went home as a champion albeit without a belt. He put a down payment on a new house on Upham Street in Lowell. He swam in his new pool, played with his dogs, and trained for his next fight. Five months later, he still hadn't received his championship belt. Sal wrote the British Board of Boxing Control, which was in no hurry to ensure that the man who took the belt from their favorite son got one of his own. Still, finally, the belt was shipped from London to Glen Feldman at the WBU headquarters in Connecticut. The belt changed hands a few times and ended up at the West Farms Mall in Avon, Connecticut. So Sal and Al drove down to pick it up and delivered it to Micky personally.

"Here. We thought you needed something to hold your pants up."

That was a good day in a career filled with hard days and a life filled with bad days.

CHAPTER SEVENTEEN

It was good to be Micky Ward, and that hadn't always been the case. He was a world champion living in his new home, and he was in love. He met Charlene Fleming, a Lowell native, through an acquaintance of his father. She was a natural and gifted athlete in her own right with more medals than Micky. Hers were won in track and field in which she was a stand-out high jumper. Now, she was Micky's girlfriend, back from an exciting trip to London and living in Micky's new home on Upham Street.

After the Neary fight, Sal recalls Micky telling him, "Now you're gonna get paid." But Sal says he responded, "No. Let's wait for the next one. I have a house and an automobile. I'm okay with finances. And here you are, always working hard in your life. I want you to be able to buy a house and feel what I feel. I want you to feel all the good of being a professional athlete."

And now it was time for the next one. Once again, discussions centered on the possibility of Micky fighting Arturo Gatti.

"Yeah, if the money's right," Sal told the *Boston Herald* at the time. "Let's face it. Micky's the world champion now. He has some leverage. That's what you become champion for. HBO vice president

Lou DiBella told me he'd love to make a Ward–Gatti fight at the FleetCenter. I'll get together with DiBella and Cedric Kushner Promotions and see what's in store, to see what's best for Micky."

HBO is where the money is in boxing. Micky owed much of his success to ESPN and Top Rank, but his earning potential on basic cable was limited to the tens of thousands of dollars. HBO and pay-per-view boxing matches brought the ceiling up to six and seven figures. DiBella and Kushner were part of the group that helped make the Ward–Neary fight on HBO, and Sal was looking for them to do something like that again. The problem, however, was that DiBella was no longer with HBO.

In May 2000, DiBella walked away while being pushed out the door. HBO bought him out of his contract for a few million dollars, and gave DiBella the right and the opportunity to sell programming to HBO. Basically, he was given some dates. All he had to do was go out and make the fights.

Just prior to DiBella's split with HBO, it was announced that Micky was going to return to London to fight Eamonn Magee on the undercard of the Lennox Lewis–Francois Botha fight on July 15. Three newspapers in London and one in Dublin reported the news that was news to Micky and Sal.

"All of a sudden I'm getting calls from all over the world," Sal told George Kimball of the *Boston Herald*. "I don't know how they could announce a fight over there when we'd never even talked about it. We'd been negotiating for possible fights with Philip Holiday and Antonio Diaz for later this year, and there was briefly the possibility of Micky filling in against Kostya Tszyu on July 15 if [Julio Cesar] Chavez couldn't make it, but they didn't offer enough money. Right now I'm planning on putting Micky on a July 14 ESPN2 show at Hampton Beach. We're not fighting Magee, and we're not going to London."

They didn't go to Hampton Beach either. Instead, Micky went to a large bingo hall at Foxwoods Resort Casino in Connecticut and fought Diaz, a twenty-four-year-old Mexican American from California. Diaz suffered a couple of defeats early in his career, but hadn't lost in more than four years. He also held a share of the IBA light welterweight title. At the time, there were five championship belts, and the IBA's was the weakest and least prestigious of the group. Micky's WBU belt was fourth on the list.

Neither belt was on the line that night. But Micky had to give his up because WBU president John Robinson wanted Micky to defend the title against a British contender, someone like Magee. Instead Micky took the Diaz fight for nearly double the money and was stripped of his belt. Ward–Diaz was on the undercard of a "Prince" Naseem Hamed fight on HBO's Main Events pay-per-view broadcast, and it was worth 175 thousand dollars to Micky.

"In my way of thinking," Sal explains, "we're gonna get a good half-million-dollar fight. Right now, we're going after money. We could have held on to the belt and fought in England for one hundred K, or we could go after Diaz and get De La Hoya."

A cash grab was exactly what Micky wanted, too. He told Ed Gray of the *Boston Herald* a day before the fight, "I want to get something out of boxing after all the years I've put into it. I don't think it's a game. Any fight can be my last fight. I look at things realistically. I'm thirty-four. I'll be thirty-five in October. I didn't start fighting fifteen years ago when I was nineteen. I started when I was seven. There's a lot of wear-and-tear."

Despite neither championship belt being on the line, the August showdown was billed as a "Battle of Champions." Diaz came out in a brown-and-gold robe with matching trunks. He was booed lustily by the pro-Ward crowd when ring announcer Michael Buffer introduced him. Micky, voted the "Comeback Fighter of the Year" in 1999, was welcomed with loud cheers. He acknowledged the support by punching vigorously in his corner. He was in white trunks with black trim, still sporting a reddish goatee.

Micky came out swinging. He was snapping off more jabs than usual. Diaz did the same, and his left jab was more effective. He showed good head movement, but his feet were relatively still. Micky did not park himself on the inside as he had done in recent brawls. His respect for Diaz's punching power was evident. Micky was less willing to take his power shots. He wasn't gambling with this kid who had won twenty-six straight fights, eighteen of them by knockout.

"Micky, you gotta punch more," Dickie said after Micky had lost the first two rounds. "When you're on him, you've got to punch. Don't take unnecessary punishment. Move your head. Push his head down. Be mean. This is your life right here."

Diaz wasn't wincing or flinching the way other opponents had done when stung by Micky. Instead, he stung right back. Diaz was 34–2. Micky was 35–9. That's a combined eighty fights of experience and plenty of acquired toughness.

In the fifth round, Diaz began to put on a boxing clinic. His jabs were right on the money. He followed straight rights with hard lefts. He was throwing combinations of punches and each one was hitting its mark. Finally, Micky landed a big right hand. The final minute of the round was a wild display of aggression. Dozens of punches were thrown by both fighters. First Micky hit Diaz three or four times. Then Diaz returned fire. The crowd that paid to see violence was getting its money's worth.

"We may see a standing ovation at the end of the round," the broadcast announcers said during a verbal exchange. "This is exquisite stuff, in terms of the energy of both fighters. It's amazing. . . . These guys are like wind-up toys. They just keep going."

As the bell rang, the crowd did, in fact, stand in appreciation of two warriors who had just exhibited what boxing, toughness, and courage are all about. Both corners thought that their fighter finished the furious flurry with the advantage.

"He's tired," Joel Diaz told his son. "Listen to me. He's tired. He gave it all he had in that round. He's done."

Meanwhile, Dickie put his face within inches of Micky's, looked him straight in the eye, and said, "This is your game! All right. This is it. You're the champion. All right. He thinks you're old. You're washed up. You get fresh now, Micky. He is dead! He is dead! He has nothing. He's a little boy now. He's dead!"

Diaz won the first four rounds on the outside. But by the sixth round, he was in the brawl. Micky made the challenge, "Can you take everything I'm willing to take?" And Diaz chose not to back down and went toe-to-toe.

"I'm beating him up the middle," Micky told Dickie in one of the few times Micky ever spoke in his corner.

"I know you are," Dickie answered. "Stay right there. Shoot up the middle. Boom, boom, boom! All right? Big hooks to the body, not so wild."

In the eighth, Diaz leaped off his feet and brought a stinging left uppercut with him. Micky's head snapped back violently. Blood immediately began flowing from Micky's nose. A right and a left hand followed from Diaz. Micky was hurt. His nose was probably broken. This was when it became evident that Diaz was the fresher fighter. Micky's punches had lost a little of their steam. Micky's nose was gushing blood for the final two minutes of the eighth round. The cut above Micky's nose just above the bridge looked deep enough to require stitches, but Gavin got it to stop bleeding.

"I know you're tired, but suck it up!" Dickie shouted without compassion. It is the appropriately emotionless pronouncement that this situation called for and when Micky heard it, he knew his brother was telling him the truth. It reassured him.

"I wasn't 100 percent for Micky last time, only 20 percent," Dickie admitted before the fight. "Now that I'm back, I'm giving 110 percent. I do everything I can do for him. That's why I run with him, spar with him. I missed out. Now I do it all for him. Fighting's a lonely game. When you have someone to do stuff with you, it's a plus."

Micky clubbed Diaz with an overhand right on top of his head. Diaz swung with a wild left hand and fell to the ground. It was ruled a slip, not a knockdown, and it happened because Diaz threw a punch while he was still dazed.

Smoger called time and asked for a towel. He dropped to his hands and knees and wiped up the wet spot left by Diaz's sweat-soaked body. But it wasn't enough time for Diaz to recover. When Smoger summoned the fighters to return, Micky leaped in and landed a hard left followed by a big, big right. The bell sounded. Diaz was woozy, but he found his way back to his corner. His father sprayed him with water while the blood from a deep cut over his left eye raced down his face.

"He's dead tired, Mick," Gavin said before the last round. "You're the champion."

Dickie added, "This is where you come through. Do it!"

Dickie slapped Micky in the face and Micky shook his head vigorously to pump himself up. He was summoning everything he had left. Diaz was doing the same.

The tenth round opened quietly and finished with a bang. With two minutes to go, Micky and Diaz started firing unceasingly at each other. Each landing a series of blows. They paused a few times, took deep breaths, and then fired again. Micky seemed to be scoring more. None of his punches were especially damaging, but they were landing. It had been a very close fight since the fourth round, and if Micky won the tenth, it could be the deciding factor.

As the bell rang ending another bloody battle, Micky and Diaz hugged each other. They had earned one another's respect. Smoger stepped in and with three heads touching, he said, "Oh boy, did you guys put on a great fight. God bless you both."

Micky put his arm around Diaz's shoulder and escorted him back to his corner. Then Micky ambled slowly over to his own, where Gavin continued to work on the cut above his nose for several more minutes. Dickie sprayed water on Micky's face and into his mouth, and they all waited for the decision. The winner of this classic battle was very much in doubt.

Finally, Michael Buffer grabbed the microphone and moved to the center of the ring.

"After ten grueling rounds, once more let's have a round of applause for these two warriors in the ring. . . . We go to the scorecards. Tommy Kaczmarek scores it 96–93. Glenn Feldman has it

95–94. Melvina Lathan has it 96–93. All for the winner by unanimous decision, Antonio Diaz!"

Micky had fought bravely, but he had lost. It seemed like a fair decision, though it could be argued that Micky lost the first four rounds, and then won four or more of the final six. Still, Micky lost gracefully, and Diaz won the same way.

"Micky!" Diaz called out, approaching Micky for another hug. "Great fight. You're a champion."

Blood was still dripping from Micky's cut as Larry Merchant made his way into the ring for the post-fight interview.

"It was tough," Micky began. "That's what it's about though. I don't get no easy fights. He don't get no easy fights either. I mean this is it. They pay to see us fight. They pay the big guys all the money. What do we get? We fought the best fight there is."

Merchant, oblivious to the steady stream of blood that was flowing even more freely down Micky's face, asked Micky what would be next for him.

"I don't know. We'll sit back and see. It's a tough loss. I trained hard for it. He was the better man tonight. I give him all the credit in the world. No hard feelings. He's a good man, good fighter. I wish him all the success in the world. And I'll be back maybe. We'll see. I don't know."

It was a loss. And the feeling in boxing circles had generally been, if you lose on HBO, you don't get back on HBO. But Micky was still an enigma. He was tough and talented. And he was someone that people knew and appreciated and would pay to see. "When we lost to Diaz, man, you want to see a sick manager," Sal said. "I knew all of Lowell was going to bust out. Everybody was going to come down on me like the world was coming apart. We gave the belt up and lost the fight."

But moods throughout Lowell improved as the offers started coming in. Ultimately, Micky turned down a one-hundred-thousand-dollar payday when he bypassed an opportunity to fight John-John Molina on a Lennox Lewis undercard. Instead, Micky agreed to challenge the WBC junior welterweight champion, Kostya

Tszyu, in February 2001. Micky would make 235,000 dollars and his debut on Showtime. And even though the fight was tentatively scheduled to be held in one of the Connecticut casinos, Micky and Sal planned to train for five weeks in Big Bear, California.

A month after the fight was announced, however, Micky was pushed aside. Tszyu was simultaneously negotiating with Sharmba Mitchell for a junior welterweight unification bout, and that fight fell together before Micky's fight with Tszyu was finalized.

"If Micky had beaten Diaz, he probably would have gotten Kostya Tszyu—which wouldn't have been good for him," Al Valenti figured. "The path he wound up on was the right one."

Russell Peltz would not have recommended the Diaz fight to Team Ward, but he had already been squeezed out of the picture. Instrumental, even vital, to getting the Reggie Green and Shea Neary fights, Peltz was dismayed to learn that Al and Sal had cut a new deal with Cedric Kushner.

"You put us on Broadway," Peltz said to Valenti. "And now you give it to Cedric, just because he's got the show. What did you do?"

What Al and Sal did was try to partner Micky with the guys who could bring in the most money. Kushner acted quickly getting Micky the Diaz fight, and it looked like a good money move at the time. Peltz says he would have done things differently.

"Things got a little touchy between me and Al," Peltz recalls. "I told Al, 'Diaz is a bad fight. Don't take the fight. You can't win this fight.' So of course, Micky goes out and fights a better fight than I thought he'd fight, but he loses. And afterwards, Al blames it on Micky's girl. He says he was spending too much time with her, and he wasn't properly prepared. But I told him not to take that fight. It was a stupid fight."

Kushner had helped Micky earn 275,000 dollars for two nights work, but instead of pushing Micky into another big-money fight, Kushner helped get Diaz a title fight on HBO against Shane Mosley. Diaz was knocked out in the sixth round and never fought another contender. History would reveal that Kushner had backed the wrong horse.

The Ward–Diaz fight was in August 2000, and the following month, Al Valenti went to Sydney, Australia, to attend the Summer Olympics. Upon his return, he learned that there was nothing going on for Micky. Valenti had plans to do another show at the beach in July, and he was confident that he could get Micky a good fight, something on par with Reggie Green, but that would be eleven months of inactivity. He needed to find something before that.

Foxwoods Resort Casino had an open date on May 18, 2001, and Micky was welcome to fight there for the fourth time in his career, but Valenti still needed to find an opponent.

"I come across the name Steve Quinonez," Valenti said. "And I call Sal and I tell him about the kid. He had a good record. He'd be good for TV. So I went to ESPN with Quinonez. They really weren't too thrilled with it, but it was Micky, so they went for it. I went to Foxwoods and I made the deal, and we're set."

The choice of Quinonez served several purposes. It was a payday, albeit small—thirty thousand dollars. Quinonez had a record of 23–5 that would look good when ESPN flashed it on the screen. Valenti expected Quinonez to be an easy mark for Micky. And, Quinonez was a lefty. Both WBA champion, Sharmba Mitchell, and IBF champion, Zab Judah, were southpaws, and Team Ward still had those fighters in their sights.

Quinonez, a thirty-year-old from California, was not known as a big puncher. Of his twenty-three victories, only ten were by knockout, a relatively low number given the low quality of his opponents. Compare that to Micky, who counted twenty-six knockouts among his thirty-five victories. Still, Quinonez had a dream.

"I was just visualizing [the fight] all night," Quinonez said. "I could see him in the first round . . . coming after me, and starting the first punch with that big left hook, and I make him miss. And I could see his head going down after missing, and I throw in the uppercut and hit him over the head and scoring that first knockdown. I just kept previewing it in my mind over and over."

Micky did come out and fire the big left hook, and Quinonez did make him miss, but there was no uppercut, and no knockdown.

Quinonez was a southpaw content to box from the outside. His feet were active. His jab fairly crisp. When Micky moved inside, Quinonez tied him up, and Micky's only option was to throw the left hand to the body. So, he did that several times. Then Micky switched to southpaw, and this time he didn't have to worry about a big right hand. Quinonez didn't have one. Now Micky could fearlessly slip his feet into position where he found himself staring at Quinonez's ribs from close range. *Boom!*

The shot seemed to literally lift Quinonez off the ground. Micky followed the first one with a second and a third. He was chopping away at the body. A minute later, with eleven seconds to go, Micky landed another shot to Quinonez's side.

"That was to the liver!" Teddy Atlas exclaimed as Quinonez dropped to both knees. "Devastating punch!"

And it was a punch that Sal LoNano missed seeing. He remembers walking in, and as he made his way to his seat, his son, Frankie, shouted, "He's down." Sal's first thought was that Micky was down, and he immediately said to himself, "Oh, my God! What have I done? I was trying to bring Micky back and now he's down?"

But as Sal turned to face the ring, he could see Micky standing patiently in a neutral corner and knew everything was all right.

It was amazing to witness. Micky threw with everything he had and landed his left square on Quinonez's ribs. Quinonez took two steps in the opposite direction, not yet feeling the pain, and then he collapsed. To indicate it wasn't a low blow, Referee Steve Smoger yelled, "Good shot! Good shot!" and sent Micky to a neutral corner. Then Smoger began to count Quinonez out while the fallen fighter writhed in pain.

". . . eight . . . nine . . . ten . . . Body shot. Good shot, good shot!" Smoger repeated. Later, Smoger would tell the *Patriot Ledger,* "That was a classic solar-plexus punch. He was paralyzed. Even though I gave him the count, I knew he was not getting up. He dropped like he'd been shot."

Quinonez was unable to rise for several minutes. The punch took the breath right out of him and put the fear of God into him.

"I thought I was going to die," he said. "As a boxer, I was used to feeling pain, but that was like someone putting a knife into you and turning it. It was the hardest punch I'd ever been hit with. You get hit a thousand times and then you get hit in that one spot. It was more like I was hit with a stun gun. It just froze me. The pain was so intense. I fell to my knees, and I just couldn't get myself back together in time."

The body shot has a lot to do with leverage. Micky was able to step to the side and deliver the punch with incredible force.

Ron Borges summed up Micky's talents this way, "He's a smart fighter in that he understands what people are trying to do against him, and he understands to some degree what needs to be done to combat it. But he's limited by his skill set. If he, for example, brought a bigger gun to the party, he'd have been champion for a long time. But if he didn't nail you to the body, he didn't knock out a lot of guys by hitting a guy in the face.

"Most people would rather get hit in the face than the body. It sounds absurd. I mean, who wants to get hit in the face? But between a big shot to the face or a big shot to the floating rib, hit me in the face. I don't care who you are, when you get hit in the body, you're going down.

"What happens is it takes a minute for all the air to get out of your body, and when it happens, you can't breathe. And it's not like you get the wind knocked out of you in the classic sense. It's completely different. You can't breathe, but the pain is unbelievable. Plus, you're paralyzed by fear."

The ring doctor put a light in Quinonez's eyes while he remained prostrate on the canvas. Meanwhile, Micky paced around the ring accepting congratulations from Sal, Dickie, and Gavin. When he saw that Quinonez was finally sitting up on the canvas, Micky went over to see if he was all right. Quinonez was now able to smile, but it was a painful one. He had just been victimized by the most devastating body puncher in boxing.

"What made Micky's body punch so good is that he committed to it," Teddy Atlas concluded after watching Micky for years. "He was going to find a way to get there. He didn't go away from it. The second thing is he found a way to make it happen. It's not by accident. He developed a technique, an art, a way that works for him that gave him an advantage over someone else to make it happen more than anyone else. He had a mechanism, a private genius. He would tap you on top first, with more of a snap in it than a full body commitment, so that he would be in position to quickly bring it back to the body.

"The conventional way is for people to go to the body first and then the head, but Micky turned it around. His technique was not to overcommit to that punch, just make it a little lighter, more of a snap punch, where he could quickly recoil it and go to the body. That's why he would get it in and get it in clean when he needed to. Micky developed this technique and it became his trademark, his forte, and it won a lot of fights for him. It put him in position to have the success later in his career."

Another win for Micky, and the same old questions: Where's the money? and What's next? It was Micky asking the first question, and he was asking it of Sal.

"I got accused of stealing Micky's money," Sal says. "Everybody on the outside thought Micky should have been making millions. His family got into Micky's head. I don't blame him. They were always telling him how I was screwing him. After the show, he challenged me. Am I supposed to get bitter? No, I said, 'I'm glad you challenged me. The only sad part is that you believed them.' And Micky said to me, 'I don't know what to believe, Sal. I'm hearing this from my mother and my sisters. I don't know what to think.'"

Tensions were eased and Micky's suspicions assuaged when Foxwoods opened the books and showed Micky where all the money went. Micky saw a detailed itemization, and according to Sal, "It proved that everything I friggin' told him was on that paper. I think I made five grand on that show. People told him I was making a hundred thousand. Fuck them! It never entered Micky's mind again that I would betray him. The family, however, remained unconvinced."

"That's the thing with family," Micky confirmed. "You just don't know who to trust. I love Sal, but when they take things out of you, you don't know what to think."

Meanwhile, the answer to the second question, what's next, was another day at the beach. He still didn't have an opponent, but Sal and Al were planning another end of the summer bash at the Hampton Beach Casino, and Micky would be their headliner. For Micky, who only had three fights in the last fourteen months, the summer couldn't get there soon enough.

CHAPTER EIGHTEEN

Boxing is a risky business, and it was time for Micky to take another risk. It had been two years since his epic comeback against Reggie Green. And in the past year, he'd lost to Diaz and thrown one incredible punch against Quinonez. HBO wasn't calling, Cedric Kushner wasn't calling back, and the champions of Micky's division, Zab Judah and Kostya Tszyu, were preparing to fight each other. Micky needed to make some noise in order to make some money. The best fighters still recognized that Micky loomed as a dangerous threat, so they weren't about to tussle with him unless there was serious cash on the table.

Micky was thirty-five years old. He couldn't waste any more time on guys like Quinonez. He needed to take on a well-respected, well-known opponent at whatever the price. He recognized that probably better than anybody.

"Micky, look, there's a handful of potential fights out there," Sal said to him in late June 2001. "I want you to pick one of the guys from this list, and I'll go after him whoever it is."

Micky looked at the list and pointed to Emmanuel Burton.

"Him."

"Micky, are you sure? There are some easier fights out there. We're not gonna make the money, buddy. You don't need a fight like that."

"Yes, I do," Micky corrected Sal. "How do you expect me to get back on HBO? Emmanuel Burton is the best. I want the best."

It was a risk, but the decision was made. For twenty-five thousand dollars Micky made his record-breaking twenty-sixth appearance on ESPN against hard-punching journeyman Emmanuel Burton, who took the fight on two-weeks notice.

"I expect another war," Ward told the *Globe*. "Burton has a walk-in style. I won't back up, and he won't back up. That's okay with me. I'd rather have a banger in there than a runner. I don't care about getting banged up. As long as I'm in shape, I can handle that."

The fight was Friday, July 13. It was approaching a hundred degrees inside the Hampton Beach Casino that night, and tempers were even hotter.

"First, we're in the locker room, and Dickie's calling me a fucking asshole," LoNano remembers. "He says, 'My brother's sweating his fucking ass off in here. You did this to him! And for what? Where's the money?'"

Sal tried to keep his cool, but he was sweating his ass off, too. When he walked away and entered the arena, he noticed a skirmish at ringside. His wife, Darlene, was in the middle of it along with Micky's mom and sisters.

"Why the hell do you get to sit here?" Micky's drunken sister Gail screamed as Sal approached.

"What's the problem here?" he said.

"You! You're the problem," Gail yelled. "You've got her sitting in the front row, and you throw us all the way back over there. Why does she get better seats than us?"

It wasn't the first time Sal had to deal with a hassle over seating arrangements. He didn't stay long enough to try to explain. He simply turned and walked away. As he did, one of the women doused him with what was left of her beer. Sal stopped. He didn't react, only paused and thought to himself, "What did I ever do to deserve this?" And he continued on his way. He regretted that later, because soon after he left, Gail cold-cocked Darlene with a straight hard right that would have made her brothers proud. It was the first punch of the night, and there would be twenty-one hundred more.

Micky entered the ring in white trunks with black trim, WARD spelled out in red lettering on the waistband. Burton was in red trunks with white trim. He came in with a pedestrian record of 24–17, but he began his career by losing more than half of his first twenty-three fights.

"Burton wasn't a hard puncher, but he threw a lot," Micky would say later. "That kid can fight like no tomorrow. He's probably the best fighter I ever fought in my life with that many losses. He could take a punch, too. Tough kid. A lot of his losses happened early in his career when he didn't train like he should."

On this night, both men appeared to be in excellent shape, and they would need to be in order to go ten rounds in this heat. In the opening moments, Micky got Burton on the ropes and began to slug away. This was Burton's plan—a courageous and potentially foolhardy strategy. He wanted to test Micky's strength. If he believed that Micky couldn't hurt him, he intended to slug it out with him on the inside. To that purpose, Burton spent the entire round in the corner with his back to the ropes. Micky wailed away at him. Burton threw only a few cursory flurries to keep Micky off and spent the rest of the time covering up. When the bell rang, Micky stepped back and smiled at Burton. Burton smiled back. The contract was made.

Burton returned to the ropes for the better part of the second round. Micky was throwing more punches than ever before and landing with increasing regularity. Burton responded with a pitter-patter of combinations. The first two rounds were all that Micky could have hoped for: he threw 101 punches in the first round, 89 more in the second, and he landed 53 power shots.

"You're doing great, Mick," Dickie said encouragingly between rounds. "Keep working him. This guy can't take this abuse much longer. Nobody can. Deep breath. Let's go home early."

In response to his own corner's instructions, Burton started the third with a commitment to boxing. He was fluid and graceful on his toes. He moved away from Micky fairly easily, changing directions around the ring, and throwing a few jabs to the body and to the head. It seemed that he could have been more in control of the fight from the outside from the beginning. As the bell sounded, Micky landed a decent right cross, and Burton fired back with three shots after the bell. Referee Steve Smoger jumped in quickly, and Burton rocked his head side to side with a big, crazy-man smile on his face. He was having a little too much fun for someone taking so much abuse.

The fourth round began with Burton switching positions, putting Micky on the ropes and going to the body. Burton was landing cleaner shots. Later in the round, Micky, clearly tired, threw a bunch of punches that missed, and Burton responded with a flurry that landed. For the final ten seconds of the round, both threw incessant lefts and rights. They were connecting. Hurting. Still throwing. As the bell sounded, Burton smiled again.

"Anybody watching this fight at home, in between rounds, call your friends up," Teddy Atlas said during the ESPN broadcast. "You're seeing something you don't see very often. Holy cow! Both guys inside making everything count. What a fight!"

The fighters combined to throw 256 punches in the fourth round. Burton outlanded Micky 57–34, and on Atlas's scorecard, the fight was even.

It had been nonstop action every second of every round, and it continued into the sixth. Another round with Burton on the ropes. Micky was relentless and effective this round. It was as if Burton had taken the round off. After three minutes of accepting punishment, Burton heard the bell and raised his hand in victory. It was an odd and premature gesture.

The heat in the casino was a factor. So too, were the number of punches Micky had been throwing. He had gotten tired sooner than usual, and his punches lacked that little something extra that might have been able to take Burton out. Also, Burton had fought two world champions in his career. He believed—and he was proving—that he could handle Micky's power.

"One thing I see right here, in his career, twenty-four wins and seventeen losses and four draws," Atlas said. "Burton sometimes has been convinced to do enough to lose competitively. He did not come here to lose competitively. He came here to win."

The seventh round was as frenetic as the previous, and in the final twenty seconds, both men started throwing bombs. Micky and Burton aimed and landed their punches with precision. Although they could see the return shots coming, they made no effort to stop them, too intent on landing shots of their own. They didn't feel the pain. But when the round was finally over, the exhaustion set in. This time when Burton returned to his corner, he was not smiling. He dropped down onto his stool and draped a towel over his shoulders. He looked like a beaten man, though he was not. He had landed 49 of 100 power shots in the seventh round.

So many punches had been thrown and had found their marks, yet neither fighter was seriously hurt. And there had been no knockdowns. Their combined wills had kept them on their feet. They had made that unspoken contract at the end of the first round, promising each other this fight would go the distance and the man with more stamina, more strength, and more consistency would win. With neither man backing down, the fight was as even as it could be.

"This is when Micky Ward gets strong," Dickie said affirmatively. "Don't worry about spitting. I'll mop the floor. C'mon Micky, plenty of time. Shoot up the middle, Mick. Don't take so many punches. You're taking too much punishment. Keep the hand in front of your chin and then shoot up the middle. C'mon Mick. This is your fight now. You're stronger than he is. You want it more."

The crowd was chanting, "Mick-y, Mick-y, Mick-y," as round nine began. Now, when Micky fired with his right, his left hand stayed on his cheek. When he fired with his left, the right hand stayed on his cheek. He was listening to Dickie's instructions. Midway through the round, as Burton stepped back to create a little space, Micky tagged him with a hard right. Burton took a moment to realize what had just happened, and Micky nailed him again. It looked as if it was a snapping left that initially got to Burton, and as he stepped back to recover, he put his hands down. Before he could take his fighting posture again, Micky hit him with that hard right. Burton was visibly stunned, unable to move for a full second. Micky went right after him.

"Burton is going defensive!" Atlas exclaimed.

Micky pursued. Burton instinctively started fighting again, but his mind wasn't right. He moved, but without purpose. Micky hit him with a left-right combination to the head. Burton threw a couple of big shots, but they didn't land. Micky tapped him on the head, and landed the body shot. Burton grimaced and dropped down to one knee in the corner.

"There's that body shot!" Atlas observed. "You saw a little change there. Burton went into that defensive posture, and Micky knew exactly what to do."

Burton took three deep breaths and stood up. He wasn't quitting. He had a contract with Micky he still needed to honor. Smoger rubbed Burton's gloves on his shirt and sent him back to the middle of the ring with forty-five seconds to go in the round. Fortunately for Burton, Micky was so tired, his shots kept missing, and Burton survived the round. It was a pivotal ninth round that could have tipped the scorecards.

"I had Burton up by one point going into that round," Atlas said.

Through nine rounds, Micky had thrown 1,007 punches. Burton had thrown 789. But Burton had landed 90 more punches, 358 to Micky's 268. If the fight went to the scorecards, the difference could be that knockdown, which made the ninth a 10–8 round.

"Here we go, Micky," Dickie shouted above the raucous crowd before the tenth and final round. "You hurt him there. He don't want to get hit by you no more. Go to the body. Deep breath. Keep your gloves up and go to the body. This is your fight. Three more minutes! Go!"

Entering the final round, Teddy Atlas had scored the fight 86–85 in Micky's favor. By the time the fight was over, Atlas had it even. Burton won the tenth because he had more energy and more power in his punches. Micky threw more than a hundred punches again, but they were slow and heavy. It hurt him to throw punches. His muscles were aching from overuse. Meanwhile, Burton was still landing shots that mattered. Whatever strength he had left was reserved to try to hurt Micky. But he couldn't.

"If you've never been to a fight before, if you've never seen what fighters look like, you're seeing it now," Atlas said respectfully. "Real fighters. A real fight. Nobody has to tell these two men how to act."

Even in the heat of battle, Micky and Burton knew what they were doing. They were staging a fight for the ages. They were in the midst of what would later be voted by *Ring* magazine as the "Fight of the Year." Neither took anything back to the corner with them.

"All you promoters out there, you don't always have the best funds in the world. Take all your money and give it to these guys. Give it to them," Atlas demanded.

With thirty seconds to go, Micky received a soft right hand to the face. It was not enough to knock over a chair, but Micky was so tired, the swat knocked him off balance, and he needed to take two steps back to right himself. Burton jumped out of the corner at him, but Micky was not hurt. The final fifteen seconds was all guts. The tanks were empty; they were fighting on the fumes. More leather to the face, more pain in the ribs, more aching arms and legs, more difficulty breathing, lungs gasping for air. Neither man expected anything less from himself or from his opponent.

"Oh my! Oh my!" Atlas exclaims. "Fight of the Year. Somebody give these guys a big payday. They've earned it."

As the final bell sounded, Smoger jumped in and grabbed both fighters around the neck. He pulled them close together and told them what a privilege it was to witness that fight.

"You both have a lot to be proud of," he said. "Good luck."

The final punch stats tell the story of human endurance. Micky threw 1,182 punches, landing 320 of them. Only a handful were jabs.

Burton threw 918 punches, but landed 421. Between them they absorbed 741 punches, and instead of collapsing on the canvas when it was over, they paced around the ring waiting for the three men with the scorecards to decide their fate.

The ring announcer, M. Mark Beiro, got everyone's attention by saying, "Ladies and gentlemen we have a unanimous decision."

Even that was a bit of a surprise. It could have gone as a split or majority decision or even a draw. The fight seemed that close to most observers.

"Judge John Stevens scores it 96–94," Beiro continued. "Judge Jim Fagan sees it 96–91, and Judge Mike Nolan has it 98–90."

A five- and eight-point difference? It was shocking. And it was alarming to both fighters. Those judges had seen something very different than everyone else. What was it? What had they seen, and who were they giving the decision to?

"All to the winner by unanimous decision," Beiro said, then pausing for some dramatic effect. "Irish . . . Micky . . . Ward!"

Certainly, a strong case could be made that Micky won the fight. Burton never protested. But to score it that unevenly was a surprise even to Micky's camp.

"The scoring was a little lopsided," Sal admits. "But Micky won the fight. Did he win by that much? I don't know, but he won. That fight was talked about for a long time."

Micky retired to his dressing room and collapsed onto a metal chair, announcing to those around him in a thick Massachusetts accent, "I feel like I'm hung ovah!" Later, after he was given a chance to reflect on what he had just been a part of, Micky said, "It's great to be involved in something like this. You look back at your career, and to have something like this, a classic fight, it makes you proud."

The Burton fight was "the" fight in Micky's career to that point. More than Neary and more than Reggie Green, the Burton fight put Micky in the national spotlight. Teddy Atlas was screaming for someone to give Micky a big payday, and people were listening— important people. Micky was getting toward the end of his career, and looking to cash in. The wheels were set in motion even before the Burton fight, and Micky did his part. He was supposed to beat Burton, which would put him back on a collision course with his friend from New Bedford, Massachusetts, Ray Oliveira. All Oliveira had to do was beat a guy named Ben Tackie for the NABF light welterweight title at Foxwoods in August. That was just three weeks after Ward–Burton. If Oliveira won, Ward–Oliveira was a likely undercard bout on a Zab Judah–Kostya Tszyu unification fight in November. The winner of that fight would then fight the winner of Ward–Oliveira.

"I only want two or three more fights," Ward was quoted as saying at the time. "I've been doing this since I was seven. I want to make some money and then go to work like a regular guy. I don't want to end up punch-drunk or looking like some guy who's had a thousand fights. It doesn't matter how much money you have if you're messed up. Ray is like myself. We've fought all the guys we had to fight. We fight our hearts out and don't say Jack. If we fight, it will be a business decision for both of us because we both know where the loser goes—back to work."

All the pieces were put in place, and Micky would probably earn close to a million dollars in the two fights. It was an exciting proposition for the two Massachusetts kids, but it never happened. Oliveira lost a majority decision to Tackie. It was a fight similar to Ward–Burton in that 2,729 punches were thrown, the third most in boxing history according to Compubox statistics. It was a stunning defeat that not only derailed Oliveira's career, but it put Micky in no-man's-land. He could have gone after Tackie, but Team Ward received a far more intriguing offer.

"I saw the Burton fight. I know you're not with Cedric Kushner anymore. So, I'd love it if we could get together and talk about Micky's future." It was Lou DiBella. So, in October 2001, Sal and Micky jumped on a train and headed for New York.

DiBella's office was in downtown Manhattan. His office window framed the New York skyline, featuring the Empire State Building. It was an impressive introduction to the really big time. In the past few years, Sal and Micky had had a few opportunities to dine at the big boys' table, but they only nibbled. DiBella was in a position to offer them a seven-course meal. And they were hungry.

"I know how hard you work with Micky," DiBella said to Sal. "It must be a real privilege. He's such a warrior. I don't mind telling you, Micky, I'm a big fan, and I'd really like to work with the two of you."

Sal recalls thinking that he was in Oz. "Wow! Wake me. Pinch me," he thought. Micky piped up first.

"Lou, I'll fight anyone. But I only want to fight two or three more times. So, I'm looking for some big fights. Big-money fights. I'm ready."

"I think so, too," DiBella agreed. "And I can get them for you."

"It's always been important to me," Sal said, "that we have a three-step plan. I like to have a couple of fights lined up after the next one, because it's important to have a game plan. We need to be flexible, depending on results, but we still need plan A, B, and C."

"Plan A is Jesse James Leija," DiBella said abruptly. "How's that sound?"

DiBella quickly explained that he was involved in putting together a fight in San Antonio in which Leonard Dorin would be fighting Raul Horacio Balbi for the WBA lightweight title. Leija was from San Antonio, and DiBella wanted to put him on the card. Micky was a perfect opponent.

"And as far as Plan B goes, Sal, that would be Arturo Gatti. Beyond that, who knows?"

It was everything Micky and Sal wanted to hear. With DiBella serving as advisor, Sal brokered a deal to fight Leija on January 5, 2002. Micky's take-home would be 250,000 dollars, the same money Leija would be making. Micky was ecstatic. Leija, who had been hoping for a rematch with Hector Camacho, didn't really want the fight.

"I'm getting about half the money I was getting for Camacho," Leija told boxing columnist Steve Kim. "I'm fighting a guy that is twice or three times as tough as Camacho. I have a bigger fight on my hands for less money. It doesn't make sense."

Leija's manager, Lestor Bedford, was equally upset about getting Micky as an opponent, but it remained the best money fight Leija could get.

"I'm very disappointed," Bedford said. "Micky Ward is a tougher fighter. I don't think there's any question that everybody perceives it as a tougher fight for James. Camacho's probably a little quicker, a little bigger puncher, but the thing is he can be hurt, and he is also subject to quitting. Micky Ward is neither one of those. He's got a lot more heart, which makes it a tougher fight."

Leija's camp was concerned. Team Ward saw Leija as a means to an end.

"When Lou DiBella talked about Jesse James Leija, that excited me," Sal recalls. "I felt as though if Micky beats Leija, we get Arturo Gatti. There wasn't any question in my mind. I knew about Gatti and his people. He was already on the radar screen. I always dreamt about Micky fighting Gatti, an Irish kid with an Italian kid. I couldn't see into a crystal ball, but it was my hoping and thinking that someday it could happen."

But the personalities and politics of boxing made it unlikely to happen, at least any time soon. DiBella and the chief operating officer of Main Events, Gary Shaw, hated one another, and there was no way they were going to sit down at the same table and negotiate a fight, no matter how much money was involved.

Russell Peltz, still with ESPN and Top Rank and formerly a promoter for Gatti, ran into Shaw at a Vinny Pazienza fight at Foxwoods, and Shaw told him, "Listen, I'll make the fight with you, but I won't make it with DiBella."

But Peltz couldn't help him at the time because he was no longer working with Gatti, and he was still on bad terms with Al Valenti and Sal LoNano. Peltz remained bitter that the men directing Micky's career had pushed him away in favor of Cedric Kushner, and then when Kushner abandoned them, they solicited the help of DiBella instead of coming back to him.

"When they made a deal with Lou to promote Micky," Peltz recalls. "I said, 'Al, why? You've got a fighter who's been on ESPN and HBO. Why would you go outside the family of me, Sal, and you? It's Kushner all over again. It's not necessary.'"

Then Peltz added, "Al should have known better. Al's a good guy, but his lack of the inner workings of the business really surprised me. Sal was complaining, but he would let Al handle things."

But Al could hardly be criticized for hooking up with DiBella, who brought Micky to San Antonio to fight Leija. It was a solid career move and a guaranteed moneymaker.

Team Ward was wildly optimistic. They believed that Leija was a perfect opponent for Micky. Leija was quick but not as quick as Judah. He could punch but not as hard as Burton or Diaz. He was a more natural lightweight, so Micky would be stronger, and if he could convince Leija to brawl with him, he would win. Then he would get Gatti. Plan A. Plan B. It was perfect.

"But you're fighting Leija in Texas, which is never a good idea," Valenti cautioned.

Valenti had a home in Hollywood, Florida, and he checked with the local realtor to see if there was another place in the same neighborhood that would be available to rent for a few weeks. So, a few days after Thanksgiving, Team Ward set up camp in a beautiful house right on the beach.

A long time friend of Valenti, Pat Burns, had a gym just on the north side of Miami where he trained professional fighters, including future middleweight champion Jermain Taylor and a Miami lightweight named Lamar Murphy. Burns was brought on board as a nutritionist, and Micky regularly sparred with Murphy. Dickie, not surprisingly, immediately felt threatened by Burns, but Pat's involvement was primarily out of convenience. He was there. He was friends with Al. He had something to offer. That was it. Still, he and Dickie never got along.

Micky got up every morning at 4:30 to jog along the beach. He ate what Burns told him to eat and did what Dickie told him to do. This was serious business.

"Micky was in the right place for this fight," Al says. "No alcohol during training camp. Training camp can be like going to prison. Very strict. Work hard, and when it's over, you have a beer. We didn't bring alcohol into the house, because if you see it, you want it. Out of sight, out of mind. Besides, one thing about Micky, you don't have to tell him what to do. Micky knows what he has to do. He'd get up on his own and go running every morning. You get up at six o'clock, and he's already on his way back from a run."

Team Ward returned home for Christmas before heading down to Texas a week before the fight, but before they left Hollywood, there was time for one big barbecue. Sal, the cook, went out and bought several pounds of prime beef.

"What's for dinner, Sal?" Micky asked.

"Barbecued steak," Sal said with pride. "I got some beauties. You're gonna love it."

"That's great, Sal, but we don't have a barbecue."

Sal was crestfallen but undeterred. He began walking through the neighborhood looking for a barbecue. He found one a few houses away, and following a quick inspection, determined that nobody was living there.

"So, I sent Al over there," Sal begins the story. "I told him I was gonna cook some steaks, and I tell everybody the owner of the home said I could use his grill. I got hamburgers, steaks, hot dogs, everything. Al says, 'I'll cook tonight.' I took the cover off the barbecue, and Micky says to me real quiet, 'Did you really get permission?' I says, 'No,' and we just started laughing. Al doesn't know any of this. Al's cooking and singing at the same time. He's having a great time when, wouldn't you know, the family shows up. Frankie, my son, comes running around the corner and says the guy next door is really mad. So, I go over there and Al's like, 'Didn't you tell me we got permission to use the grill?' And I said, 'Oh we've got the wrong house!' Long story short, we all sat down to dinner. He became our friend for the rest of the time down there."

After a short trip back home for the holidays, Team Ward was scheduled to meet down in San Antonio, but Al had business in Las

Vegas. He was part of the marketing team for the Andrea Bocelli concert at Mandalay Bay. After the show, he returned to his hotel room and felt like he was having a heart attack.

He called the front desk and got the number for Barbara Roach, the mother of Freddie, Joey, and Pepper, who was working out in Vegas as a boxing judge. Barbara gave Al the number of a doctor who told Al to meet him at the hospital. The problem? Kidney stones.

"I end up in the hospital for Sunday, Monday, and Tuesday," Al says. "Now everybody's in San Antonio; they don't know where I am. I'm on morphine the whole time. I told Barbara to call a couple of people. But word doesn't get to Sal and the rest. They didn't know where the hell I was. I finally pass the stone, and the doctor tells me I can go home tomorrow. I don't tell him I'm going to San Antonio, but that's where I went. You feel pretty good as soon as the stone passes."

Al was also given a full bottle of the pain reliever Vicadin, which Dickie begged him for more than once, claiming it was for his bad back. Al had a tough time keeping the narcotic away from the drug addict, and only managed to hold Dickie off by finally giving him a handful.

While Al and Dickie found relief from their pain, Micky felt as good as he'd ever felt. He was in a good place. His future was there for the taking. Beat Leija, get Gatti. Beat Gatti, get Tszyu. Beat Tszyu, get out of boxing a wealthy man and a champion. It wasn't just a dream. It was the plan.

"We'd like to match the winner of Ward–Leija with the winner of the January 26 Arturo Gatti–Terron Millett fight," HBO vice president Kery Davis told George Kimball of the *Boston Herald*. "Ward against Gatti is a fight I would pay to watch myself."

And if Micky could beat Gatti, he would certainly be in line for a title shot against Kostya Tszyu. Micky would be thirty-seven years old by then, and he could step out of the limelight as very few other boxers had ever done—with finality and with a championship belt. First things first, however. Everything hinged on getting past Leija.

"If I lose, I'm done," Ward told Borges a week before the fight. "That's why I got to win. I don't want that to come. If it does, I'll thank everyone who helped me and leave knowing I trained hard and never quit. Then people can judge me as they like. I know I never gave up in there."

Leija had a similar reputation. He was Micky's equal in many ways. Micky was thirty-six, Leija thirty-five. Micky had forty-seven professional fights, Leija, forty-nine. Leija was described in HBO's press release for the fight as "resourceful and relentless." Certainly, those were words that defined Micky as well. That's why the fight was considered a perfect match. It seemed destined to be a fight full of punches and counterpunches. Money would be at stake, but so would survival.

"The loser goes home, and he don't come back," Micky said. "I know he'll be tough. I know he's pretty quick and likes to counterpunch. It's in his hometown, so I know I have to make him respect me right from the first round. It's good to fight a guy like this. He's a pro. He's coming to win and I'm coming to win. I respect him, and I'm not afraid to admit it. That doesn't mean I'm afraid of him."

Micky wasn't afraid of anybody, and his respect for Leija was justified. Of Leija's five career losses, four of them came in championship fights, and Leija had stood up to the likes of Shane Mosely, Oscar De La Hoya, Gabriel Ruelas, Ivan Robinson, and Azumah Nelson three times. Leija's resume was sprinkled with some of the best names in boxing, just like Micky's. They'd both proven over the years that they were willing to do what it takes both before and during a fight. Now, they would have to prove it again.

Winning by knockout would be Micky's best option, because there was reasonable suspicion that it would be hard to beat a Texas fighter in Texas. Strange things can happen when a fight goes to the judges' scorecards.

"I'm definitely aware of that," Micky told Kimball. "Any chance I get to go in there and do anything, from the first round on,

I will. I know I have to beat him decisively to win down there, but on the other hand it *is* going to be on HBO, so everyone will see what happened."

But not everyone could see what transpired before the fight in Micky's locker room. Micky was sitting backwards on a metal folding chair getting his hands wrapped when the referee for the fight, Laurence Cole, walked in. Laurence Cole's father, Dick Cole, was the head of the Texas Boxing Commission, a fact that already had Team Ward more than a bit wary. Dick Cole wanted Leija to win the fight.

"You do the math," Valenti said.

Ron Borges and Al Valenti were standing with their backs against a far wall and heard Laurence Cole say over and over again, "I don't want to get involved." He said he knew that Micky liked to fight on the inside, and that he didn't want to have to get involved in either separating the fighters, giving warnings, or making rulings on whether a clash of heads was accidental or not.

"I want you guys to understand one thing," Cole said. "At the end of the night, I want to be the last person they talk about. I'm telling you, I don't want to get involved."

Borges heard him say it for the fifth time, and he turned to Al and said, "Well, one thing's for certain. He's gonna get involved."

Cole continued his nervous warnings in the center of the ring when he called Micky and Leija together. Micky approached Cole wearing white with black trim, Leija, black with gold trim.

"I gave you instructions in the dressing room earlier tonight," Cole told the fighters. "I want you to obey my commands at all times. I want you to watch your heads on the inside, and I want you to keep your punches in the front."

Cole was obsessed with the possibility of a clash of heads even though Micky had never had a stoppage due to an accidental head-butt. Leija, however, had had two. Six months prior to stepping in the ring with Micky, Leija lost a fight to Hector Camacho Jr. when Camacho suffered a cut from an accidental head-butt and refused to continue. The fight went to the scorecards and Camacho was deemed the winner after only five rounds. The fight was later declared a no-contest. Also, ten years earlier, Leija was cut by a clash of heads against Jose Luis Martinez. That was ruled a technical draw after nine rounds. Leija was known as a bleeder, and Cole was concerned.

Less than two minutes into the fight, Leija was cut. Micky had leaped in and landed a hard left to the right side of Leija's face. It was a solid shot that immediately opened a cut above Leija's right eye. The fighters grappled with each other on the inside, and Micky was able to land two more lefts to the same spot.

"Break!" Cole shouted as he separated the fighters. Then he looked at Leija's cut, and with some exasperation, he yelled, "Time!"

He told Micky to get in his own corner, and took a closer look at Leija's cut, which was not bleeding too badly. Then he did what he said he didn't want to do. He got involved.

"Accidental head-butt," he shouted to each of the three judges sitting around the ring. "Accidental head-butt. Accidental head-butt."

He repeated it three times to make sure each of the judges was aware that he was ruling that Leija's cut was caused by a clash of heads, but he was wrong. Micky's head never came in contact with the right side of Leija's face. *Never.*

"Leija is bleeding one minute and forty seconds into the bout," HBO's Jim Lampley said.

"What took him so long?" Larry Merchant asked.

Because Cole ruled it an accidental head-butt, if the fight was stopped because of that cut before the end of the fourth round, the fight would be called a technical draw. If the fight was stopped because of the cut after the fourth round, then it would go to the scorecards, and whoever was leading at the time would be declared the winner. Therefore, it was imperative for both fighters to try to win the early rounds. Aware of this, Leija became more aggressive in the final twenty seconds of round one.

"Now Leija starts to bomb Ward with his left hand, and lands a straight right-hand shot that backs Ward into the corner," Lampley exclaimed. "The crowd rises to its feet as Jesse James Leija comes alive at the end of the round!"

As Leija returned to his corner, the cut was visible, but the blood was not leaking down his face. His cutman was the experienced and highly regarded Joe Souza, so there was every expectation that Souza would be able to take care of the cut and keep it from becoming an issue.

"This is Texas, Micky," Al Gavin cautioned in the corner. "Don't give him anything."

"Pump the jab up," Dickie added. "As soon as you feel it, set, *bam!!* You have him. Now, c'mon! When your hands are free, hit him in the head, and hit him up the middle."

"He's right, Mick," Pat Burns chimed in. "You gotta touch him with the jab."

"Deep breath," Dickie continued. "Don't let the crowd get in the way of the plan. Feed off the crowd, Mick. C'mon, let's go! Feed off of the crowd noise!"

Leija returned for the second round with the cut clean and dry. Micky began by throwing more right hands than normal, perhaps trying to stay away from punching the cut and making it worse. Each time the fighters came together, Cole stepped in and pushed them apart. The fighters were clearly not tied up. They were still punching, and their hands were free, yet Cole yelled, "Break!" He was making it impossible for Micky to fight his most effective style, which was to brawl on the inside. Cole was intrusive and unwilling to let them fight their way out of holds and near holds, which they seemed inclined to do. Each time he separated the fighters, he took a moment to inspect Leija's cut. Two minutes into the round, Cole called "Time!" and summoned the ring doctor to look at Leija's cut. He was barely bleeding.

The doctor looked at the cut for a few seconds. Squeezed a gauze pad over the cut and shined a light into Leija's eye. He was satisfied and indicated that the fight could continue. Already, the crowd was chanting, "Bullshit! Bullshit!" And this was a home crowd. With ten seconds to go in the round, Cole separated the fighters once again and called time-out to scold Micky.

"You do not punch! You do not punch out!"

Cole was suggesting that Micky punched on the break. He did not. Micky managed to land an overhand right that rocked Leija just before the bell.

"He's walking backwards, James," Jesse Leija Sr. told his son in the corner. "Keep the pressure on him. He's not throwing back. He's not throwing when he's going back. You're too straight. More angles. Movement. Movement."

All the while, Souza worked on the cut. It appeared clean and clotted as the bell for round three sounded. Micky turned southpaw for a prolonged period to start the round. Halfway through the round, Leija was not bleeding. When Cole separated them again, he said to Micky, "Keep your head up." It was an accusation that Micky was leading with his head. Micky was winning the round with looping right hands and effective aggressiveness. By the end of the round, Leija's cut was bleeding quite a bit. The doctor looked at it again between rounds and allowed the fight to continue.

"Joe Souza is one of the best cutmen in the country," Al Valenti recalls. "He's from New Bedford. We all knew him. The cut was a good gash right above the eyebrow, you couldn't see it that well, because it was in the hairline. But as the fight goes on, the cut's getting worse. Joe's not making it better, he's making it worse. They're banking on a slow start by Micky and they're hoping to go to the cards."

"You've got to win this round," Leija's father said. "Ward won that round. So, you've got to win this round, James."

"What round is this?" Souza asked while squeezing the cut with two hands.

"Fourth."

"Is this the fourth round?" Souza asked with some surprise.

"When he comes in, uppercut this guy, James."

Again, the cut looked good as Leija came out for the fourth. Micky quickly landed a hard left to the area of the cut. Leija responded with a nice combination. Micky was not firing back, so he started up with another combination of his own. Micky was pushed up against the ropes, and Leija teed off with several body and head shots. Micky had no answer. Leija was throwing the uppercuts as he was instructed. This round the fighters were being allowed to fight in close. Micky's hair was turning red from Leija's blood. Late in the round, Micky connected with a couple of clubbing right hands to the top of Leija's head, but round four went to Leija.

Dickie was very calm in the corner. He didn't say a word for the first thirty seconds. Instead, he just rubbed Micky's chest and face while Gavin worked on some swelling over Micky's left eye. They had passed the fourth round, so if the fight was stopped on the cut, it would go to the judges.

"Jesus Christ, that is bad!" Souza says loudly in the opposite corner. And it was bad. The cut had gotten significantly worse the past two rounds, now extending the entire length of Leija's eyebrow. Very quickly into the fifth round, it began bleeding profusely. It could have been its severity. It could have been that it was not being treated well enough, or it could have been the left hooks that Micky continued to land. Leija was taking more than he was giving now. Micky did his patented double tap to the head and then dropped down to land a body blow. By the end of the round, Leija was a bloody mess. The eye was inside a pool of blood, and there was more blood up and down his entire chest.

"Oh, my God!" Leija Sr. exclaimed, referring to the cut, and then added, "You won that one, too. Give me the bucket. Jesus!"

Cole had again called time-out in between rounds to give the doctor time to inspect the cut. This time, the doctor did not give the go-ahead for another round.

"It's too deep. It's too long," was all he said.

Pat Burns was the first to recognize what was happening, and he started shouting across the ring, "He can go! He can go! Oh, c'mon. Don't stop the fight! He can go! Let him continue. He's a warrior!"

By this time, Micky realized what was going on, too. He bolted up from his stool and threw his hands down in disgust. Dickie was in the center of the ring, yelling at the ref and the fight doctor. Burns kept yelling, "He's a warrior! He's a warrior!" It was all to no avail. Cole commanded Dickie to get back to his corner, and barked, "You stay right there. You know what I'm doing. Okay? You know what I'm doing. I'm going to the scorecards. You know the rule."

Dickie spun himself in a circle and put his hands up to his head. He slammed his hands down on the top rope, acting out in frustration. He walked over to Micky and hugged him, telling him everything would be all right. Micky was visibly upset in his corner. He began to pace angrily. He knew his chances of winning a decision in Texas weren't very good. Before the fight he never thought about what would happen if he lost. Now, it was all he could think about. Lou DiBella could only help him if he helped himself by winning. This had potential disaster written all over it. Micky's mind was a blur. He glanced across the ring and noticed that Leija sat in his corner emotionless. He appeared to be content with the decision to stop the fight. Leija's complacency didn't go unnoticed by ringside observers.

"During that one-minute rest," HBO's Harold Lederman began, "Joe Souza was yelling at the doctor, 'Oh my god, it's too bad. You know the cut is too big.' I think that the Leija corner knew that they were ahead on the scorecard, and they're telling the doctor to tell the referee to stop the fight. The doctor told Laurence Cole to stop it, and he stopped it. I think Leija is just ahead in the fight, and I think they know it."

Emanuel Steward concurred.

"My point is this," he said. "I believe that if Leija's corner realized he was losing the fight, they would not have stopped the fight. And I will stand by that. I think the only reason they were happy with the stoppage and maybe encouraged the ref is because they felt they were ahead on points."

To be fair, it was a very bad cut. It was a quarter moon over his right eye, but it was not caused by a head-butt. Even slow motion replays couldn't find an instance in which Micky's head came in contact with that part of Leija's face.

While Cole announced to each of the judges that he was stopping the fight on an accidental head-butt rule, Micky and Leija met in the center of the ring and hugged. "It's not your fault," Micky said to Leija. But as they broke free from their embrace, Micky took a moment to survey the cut that had caused the fight to end prematurely.

"It's not even bleeding," he thought. "And it sure as hell wasn't caused by a head-butt."

If Leija's corner was trying to steal the fight by getting it stopped early with their guy ahead on points, they took an awfully big chance. As ring announcer Michael Buffer gave the scores, he said:

"Ladies and gentlemen, in round number one there was an accidental head-butt. The wound suffered by Jesse James Leija got so severe that the doctor advised your referee Laurence Cole to call a halt to the bout at the end of the previous round. We go to the scorecards. We will have a technical decision."

Micky shuffled his feet, took a deep breath, and listened to hear his fate announced.

"The scoring totals are as follows," Buffer continued. "Duane Ford scores the bout 48–47 for Micky Ward."

There was a smattering of applause. Micky put his head down and said a quick prayer.

"Ray Hawkins scores the bout 48–47 for Jesse James Leija."

The applause was louder this time, and now it was Leija who put his head down and hoped for the best. Micky tipped his head to the side as if to say, "Here we go!"

"Gail Van Hoy scores the bout 49–46 for the winner by technical split decision. . . . Jesse James Leija!"

Again, Micky threw his hands down in abject disappointment. Cole raised Leija's hand in victory, but Leija never smiled. He barely acknowledged the pronouncement, clearly more embarrassed than elated. He was not proud of this victory.

"I didn't stop the fight," Leija told Larry Merchant in the ring.

"I didn't say a word to the doctor to stop the fight. I don't think either one of us should have won the fight. . . . The fight was just getting good. I didn't say a word. The doctor came in. It was his third time in the ring. I knew the cut was bad. It was bleeding really bad. . . . I just kept fighting. . . . I don't have to prove myself. I'm a proven warrior just like this guy is. . . . I think the fight should have been called a no-contest. But I'll fight him anytime again."

Blood streamed down the right side of Leija's face as he spoke. The doctor had made the right decision to stop the fight. The cut seemed at least as bad as the one Micky suffered against Vince Phillips. It was a safety issue, and the doctor used the proper amount of precaution. Still, both fighters were upset by what had just transpired, and how it might affect their careers.

"I had a feeling it could have been stopped," Micky said. "I wasn't sure. It's hard to tell. They put that Vaseline on it. I couldn't really see how bad it was. It's unfortunate for both of us, not just for me taking the loss. I think it should have been called a technical draw. No one deserved to win the fight. I wanted a great fight. Nothing away from Jesse. He's a great warrior just like myself. I don't want to go out this way. No one does. Shit, I think it should have been a no-contest. We're two warriors. I'd rather lose it on my back than this way."

As the fighters made their way back to their dressing rooms, Ron Borges walked over to Joe Souza and challenged him about the cut.

"Jesus Christ, Joe, I've seen you take care of cuts where the guy needed a transfusion. You weren't trying too hard," Borges said accusingly. "The only thing you didn't do was put your foot in there."

Souza responded dejectedly, "Ah, come on, it was a bad cut."

Meanwhile, Sal was running around like a raging animal. He was sprinting from the dressing room and back, shouting for someone to find Dick Cole, the boxing commissioner. He wanted to file a protest as quickly as possible. Sal's body was drained. He was sweating and hyperventilating. He felt like he might pass out. Finally, he grabbed Al Valenti and, breathing heavily, said, "Oh my God! What did I do to his career? I threw his belt in against Diaz. We lost to Leija. All the pieces are falling apart, Al!"

"This is worse than the Texas Chainsaw Massacre," Valenti stated flatly.

Even in his panic, Sal could notice Lou DiBella walking calmly over in his direction. Sal was nervous. In order to prevent DiBella from telling him it was all over, Sal started rambling frantically.

"Lou, you know this is bullshit! I'm filing a protest. We'll get this thing overturned. C'mon, Lou. You know this was their game plan all along. You heard them say all week this fight wouldn't last long. This is what they meant. Lou, really, we're in Texas. That's all. We're in Texas. Micky would have won that fight. It's just bullshit!"

Lou smiled. If Sal weren't so tormented, he might have enjoyed letting him drift in the wind for a moment. Instead, when Sal ran out of words, Lou put his hands on his shoulders, leaned in, and said, "I still want to work with you."

"You're not giving up on me?" Sal said with great surprise.

"No. This was beautiful. This was absolutely beautiful. I'm gonna make the Arturo Gatti fight for Micky Ward."

Sal was confused. DiBella began to walk away, but Sal was determined not to let him out of his sight. The limousine arrived, and as DiBella started to climb in, Sal put his hand on DiBella's ass and pushed him into the car. Sal jumped in right after him. There was no way he was going to let DiBella get away from him until he explained what was going on.

DiBella told Sal that boxing can be a funny game. Sometimes you have to lose to win. If Micky had beaten Leija and looked good doing it, Gatti and his people wouldn't want anything to do with him. Micky had always been the kind of fighter who made opponents wonder, "Why am I putting myself through this, fighting this guy?" But by losing to a soft puncher like Leija, Micky looked vulnerable. Gatti would have no doubt that if Micky couldn't beat Leija, he certainly couldn't beat him. Gatti would go where the money was, and the money would be better with Micky, because styles make good fights. And style-wise, Gatti–Ward was better than Gatti–Leija. DiBella knew that the way the fight went down wouldn't affect the attractiveness of a Gatti–Ward fight.

"Leija got fucked," Borges explains. "He thought it was a done deal that the winner would get Gatti next. And it would have been a done deal if Micky had looked better. But the dollars were there because Micky didn't look good against Leija. So, Gatti can get some credit for beating a tough guy without taking too much risk. Micky looked closer to done."

But Micky wasn't done. In fact, he was just beginning.

CHAPTER NINETEEN

Just about the same time that Micky had his very first fight, the one in the rain outside the Lynn Harbor House when he was seven years old, a baby was born on the other side of the ocean. Giovanni and Ida Gatti decided to name their fourth child Arturo. The family emigrated to Canada, and young Arturo Gatti grew up on Joliette Street in the heart of Montreal's "Little Italy." Arturo played soccer and hockey as a child, but he quickly developed a passion for boxing. As Micky had done, Arturo followed his older brother into the gyms and began boxing when he was seven.

Arturo won three Golden Gloves titles, two Canadian titles, and fought in the World Championship in Peru. As a nineteen-year-old, he lost in the Olympic trials for the 1992 Barcelona Olympics and decided to turn pro. He moved to Jersey City, New Jersey, and began his professional career by winning twenty-nine of his first thirty fights, picking up the USBA and IBF super featherweight titles along the way. But he went winless in three fights in 1998, and it looked like his career could be headed in the wrong direction. He was a champion at twenty-four and an ex-champion at twenty-six, and word was that he was partying a little too hardy. After going zero for three in 1998, Gatti fought only one round in 1999, but it was a first-round knockout of Reyes Munoz, and Munoz was taken from the ring on a stretcher. Gatti, already dubbed the "Human Highlight Film" for his ability to withstand and dish out punishment, was still a very marketable commodity. Boxing fans loved to see this guy fight, but in an effort to give the people what they wanted, Gatti was putting his career in jeopardy.

"Arturo was a great boxer, but he played to the crowd a little bit," Gatti's manager, Pat Lynch, said. "He had these wars and he forgot about what a great boxer he is, and he'd just brawl. Those wars are so memorable, everybody figured it to be a short career if he continued like that, but he just kept going."

Those wars included his 1997 bout with former world champion Gabriel Ruelas. On that October night, Ruelas peppered Gatti with seventeen unanswered power shots in the fourth round, and it looked like Gatti would be going down in defeat. Somehow he managed to stay upright, and then he floored Ruelas with a vicious left hook to the jaw in the fifth round. Ruelas rose before the count of ten, but he couldn't continue. That fight and his 1998 battle with Ivan Robinson were both dubbed "Fight of the Year" by *Ring* magazine.

But how many grueling toe-to-toe brawls does a fighter have in him before he's hit in the face by the end of his career? That may have been the question surrounding Gatti before he knocked Munoz out and then destroyed Joey Gamache in February 2000. As Gatti was making the move up to the junior welterweight division, he won four consecutive fights, three of them by knockout in the first two rounds, the other a unanimous decision over previously unbeaten Joe Hutchinson. So Gatti was able to convince people in boxing that he still had plenty left in his tank and, in fact, as he got heavier, he got stronger, and therefore he still deserved big paydays. Now, however, the big question around Gatti involved steroid allegations.

"Steroids?" Sal LoNano wondered out loud. "It didn't ring true to me. Dickie was saying he was taking steroids and novocaine in the face. But nobody's gonna cover this shit up with those urine tests before and after a fight."

Still, Gatti's demolition of a talented fighter from Lewiston, Maine, not only raised eyebrows, it also initiated significant changes in pre-fight weigh-ins. Gatti was supposed to weigh 141 pounds for the fight against Gamache, and on the day before the fight, he stepped on the scale in full view of a hundred witnesses, but as soon as the slide was pushed across the bar to the 141-pound mark, he stepped off. There was immediate question as to whether he had actually made weight or not, but there was no protest. The next day, HBO unofficially weighed both fighters again, and this time Gatti weighed 160 pounds. Gamache was 145. Gatti had apparently gained some twenty pounds in twenty-four hours. "Too much pasta," his handlers first joked. Later, Lynch questioned the validity of the second weigh-in, claiming that it was done on a bathroom scale on an uneven floor.

As it was when Micky fought Mike Mungin, the additional fifteen pounds and Gatti's six-inch reach advantage proved to be too much for Gamache. Gatti punched through Gamache's defense, wobbling him with nearly every blow. Gamache, a former champion with a 55–3 record, went to the canvas twice in the first round and nearly died in the second round. Gatti hit him with a thunderous left hook and a dynamic right uppercut that put Gamache out before he hit the floor. Gamache was lifeless for seven minutes. He slipped into a coma and spent two days in the hospital. Gamache ultimately survived, but with serious neurological damage and near-constant headaches for years after the beating. He never fought again.

Gamache first sued the New York Boxing Commission for 5.5 million dollars and later filed suit against Gatti, his manager, Top Rank, Main Events, and the New York State Athletic Commission's executive director, Anthony Russo, for ten million dollars. The second suit claimed that all of those parties knew that Gatti was overweight but made sure that the fight went ahead anyway. In 2010 a judge ruled that Gatti was not weighed properly but that this didn't cause a premature end to Gamache's career. As a result of the controversy, fighters are now officially weighed a second time on the day of the fight.

Gatti earned three hundred thousand dollars for less than six minutes of work against Gamache, and after beating a couple of lesser known opponents, he was ready for another big payday against Oscar De La Hoya—at least he thought he was ready.

On March 24, 2001, De La Hoya opened up a gash under Gatti's right eye in the first round of their fight at the MGM Grand in Las Vegas. Seconds later, a combination sent Gatti to the deck in a fetal position. He managed to get up, but was beaten up for four more rounds before his corner finally threw in the towel during the fifth round.

"I could have kept going, but I respect my corner," Gatti said after the fight. "Oscar had a pretty good defense. I never really hit him flush. He was faster than I thought."

So, much like Micky and a preponderance of other boxers, Gatti was once again in the position in which he needed to give his career new direction by rebounding from a loss. He glanced in Micky's direction, but Gatti wanted a million dollars for the fight and Micky's camp believed that he deserved at least half that, and HBO wasn't willing to foot 1.5 million dollars for a non-title fight between junior welterweights. So, Gatti chose an easier path and knocked out Terron Millett in four rounds. That was in January 2002. It was then time to make the Micky Ward fight.

"Now, who was Gatti gonna fight where he was gonna make any money?" Valenti remembers asking. "Who's he gonna fight to make some money and win? Gatti had run his course. He had won a title at 130 pounds, but he was having trouble making those weights. He had lost to Ivan Robinson twice and got destroyed by De La Hoya. He didn't have a real good win until he beat Terron Millet a couple of weeks after the Ward–Leija fight. Now, he thinks he's all that. And we'll let him think that in order to get him in the ring. We know it's gonna be a great fight and that Micky can win it. And if he wins it, there are a lot of directions he can take to make that big payday."

The deal came together very quickly. By mid-February 2002, Micky agreed to receive a 435,000 dollar purse to fight Gatti at Mohegan Sun Resort and Casino in Connecticut on May 18. Gatti's share would be one million dollars. The purse was the richest of Micky's career, and he could have made even more if he'd agreed to fight in Gatti's hometown of Montreal. But Micky gave up a few thousand dollars in order to fight closer to home where he would be more comfortable. "I'm ecstatic that we're finally going to get it on," Micky said. "It's the fight I wanted, and I think it's the fight the fans wanted, too. Gatti's one tough fighter. . . . To win, I'm going . . . to come out fighting from the start. I have to stay close to Gatti—the closer the better—to stay away from his power. I don't want to be on the end of his punches, I want to be under 'em."

But as Micky had come to expect in his tumultuous and unpredictable career, the fight was in danger of being called off.

The problem wasn't so much between Micky and Arturo as it was between DiBella and Gary Shaw, the CEO of Main Events.

"Shaw and DiBella had a feud like you wouldn't believe," Valenti recalls. "It was the Hatfields and McCoys."

Just to stick it to DiBella, Shaw told Team Ward that they wouldn't be receiving any hotel rooms, food, or tickets to the fight. In essence, Micky and his camp would be frozen out of several common courtesies extended to fighters involved in fights of this magnitude. "They're treating Micky like he's a four-round fighter," DiBella shouted. "We told Main Events if they don't want to give us what's normal for a co-main event fighter, the fight is off."

Once again, money was the great peacemaker. HBO ponied up another twenty-five thousand dollars to cover Team Ward's expenses, including rooms, food, and tickets for a small entourage over at the nearby Foxwoods. At the press conference before the fight, Micky and Arturo shared a respectful embrace while DiBella and Shaw yelled profanities at one another from across the room.

"It was like the wrong guys were preparing to get in the ring with each other," Valenti says.

But the right guys were ready for battle. Arturo trained in Vero Beach, Florida, and Micky trained at the World Gym in Tewksbury, Massachusetts, about five miles from his home. He adopted a training style in which he sparred several rounds, but only allowed himself thirty seconds instead of the standard one minute to rest between rounds. He hoped that these shorter rests would make it easier for him on fight night when he was given those extra thirty seconds. His primary sparring partner was then-unbeaten Providence middleweight Peter Manfredo Jr. Micky was as prepared for this fight as he had ever been. It was the biggest night of his life. He and Arturo both knew that they defined what boxing should be all about. They had very similar styles and similar skills. "It's going to be a great fight," Micky said days before the bout "Arturo's a great fighter, a warrior, and a great guy. It's been a long road for me. I take each fight like it could be my last. I'm going to fight my butt off."

May 18 arrived quickly. Micky put in six weeks of intense training, drove down to Uncasville, Connecticut, a few days before the fight, and turned into his ordinary irascible self. He could get real testy before a fight. It was Sal's job to walk the tightrope between helping Micky, catering to his every need, and getting the hell out of his way. Dickie was involved in all of the training sessions, but then Sal would manage to find a convenient excuse to pull Micky away—and that suited Dickie just fine. He was content to go off on his own and do his own thing. Nobody knew exactly what that was, but they all had their suspicions.

Team Ward came together in the locker room a few hours before Micky would enter the ring. Micky was already done with his pre-fight workout. He had worked up a good sweat and his heart was pounding when Sal called everybody together. Each man kneeled as Sal prayed. He asked God to bless Micky, to give him strength, and to please give the corner strength as well. Then he added:

"And take care of his hands, Lord. He's had a lot of problems with his hands."

Micky blessed himself and jumped to his feet. Team Ward was ready. Micky entered the ring wearing white trunks with an insignia across the cheeks that read, "Lowell Spinners." He also wore a Spinners uniform jersey with the number 38, and a Spinners baseball cap. The "38" represented the number of career victories Micky would have, presuming he beat Gatti. And there was a charitable reason for his specially designed wardrobe that night. Similar trunks were being sold at the Spinners baseball park, and the proceeds would be donated to Kids in Disability Sports.

Gatti stood across the ring in the red corner wearing a big smile. He was 34–5 and seven years younger, but he had much more experience than Micky had in this type of fight. He'd already made millions many times over. He'd been the main event on HBO. This wasn't just how he made his living: this was fun. And he was enjoying every moment of it.

"You were both given your instructions in the dressing room," referee Frank Cappuccino said at the center of the ring. "I want you to be careful in each of your corners where you might be a little wet. So just be careful into the corner. Now, both of you touch gloves. I leave it with you."

Moments later, as Micky jogged in place, the bell sounded. He sprinted to the center of the ring and landed a solid left hook to Gatti's head. Gatti was not nearly as quick as Zab Judah, but he was every bit as fluid. There was tremendous rhythm in his footwork. He appeared to be bouncing on pockets of air. Halfway through the first round, Gatti landed a roundhouse right and a good left hook. A few seconds later, he did it again. This time, a cut opened over Micky's right eye.

"It does look like a bad cut," HBO's Larry Merchant observed.

Gatti began target practice on the cut. Micky absorbed an especially violent combination late in the round, and he pounded his fists together as if to tell himself that he better get going. The round belonged to Gatti.

In the corner, Al Gavin was quick through the ropes. He inspected the cut, "No problem, it's on the outside. Relax." The cut was not directly over the eye so it wouldn't impair his vision. Gavin squeezed the area of the cut hard for several seconds and then jammed a Q-tip into it, filling the hole with Vaseline.

Gatti came out in the second round and landed a rapid flurry of punches. Instead of defending himself or countering, Micky took the shots and waited for the onslaught to end. When it did, Micky threw just one punch.

"Micky is very predictable right now," HBO fight analyst Emanuel Steward correctly stated.

Gatti continued to punch from all directions and with both hands. He threw a quick jab and a straight right and followed those with a left hook, each one landing. Micky was once again getting off to a slow start.

"You can punch on him all day long, but you're just standing there," Dickie bellowed with exasperation between the second and third rounds. "Head movement. Double jab. Head movement. Double jab. The overhand right, but you've got to keep your right hand up. All he's looking for is a hook or an uppercut on you. C'mon, deep breath. Use your thirty-second rest."

"C'mon Mick. You hurt him that round," Sal lied.

The fight was only six minutes old, but the wear and tear created by thirty years of boxing showed on Micky's face. He was already tired and bloody. But he stood up, adjusted his red belt, the one that read WARD in big, white lettering, and prepared for the next battle. Across the ring, Buddy McGirt, Gatti's new trainer, told him how well he was doing.

"All right now, listen," McGirt said. "When he gets close, keep your hands up. He's trying to get that body shot. When he gets close to you, just keep him turning. Okay? You're boxing beautifully. Just keep using the speed. Okay? Straight right hands."

In round three, Micky set up camp inside and wailed away at Gatti's midsection. The punches seemed to take some life out of Gatti.

"What are you doing?" McGirt yelled incredulously. "You got his respect. Listen to me, when you get him inside, don't take that body shot, Arturo. Listen to me, you finished beautiful. You don't have to take that shot. Don't take it. As soon as you get inside, go to your left. Look at me. Look at me. I'm over here. Stay focused, Arturo. Listen to me. You're boxing beautiful. Don't take that shot."

Arturo won the first three rounds, but now he was slumped ever so slightly on his stool. His eyes were glazed over, and he was having trouble focusing on McGirt's words. The body shots hurt so much, he couldn't move like he wanted to, and Micky had tagged him with a hard right hand just before the bell. Gatti stood and tried to clear his head, telling himself to get back to boxing.

"Stick and move," he told himself. "Stick and move."

Gatti did that for the first minute, and would have continued sticking and moving, but the punch seemed to come from nowhere. *Bam!* Micky landed a straight right hand with full force. Gatti's head flung backwards from the sheer force of it. Gatti was hurt, but not in trouble. He bounced away quickly.

Then HBO's Jim Lampley exclaimed, "What a body shot!"

But Lampley wasn't marveling at Micky's patented left hand. It was a hard left thrown by Gatti that sent Micky to his knees. And it was low. It was below the belt. While Micky was down on his knees, he pounded the canvas with one of his best combinations of the night. He was clearly frustrated and quite possibly hurt. Gatti tried to tell Cappuccino the punch was good, but the correct call was made. Cappuccino had scolded Gatti in the previous round, reminding him to keep his punches up, but there was no warning issued.

This time he said to Gatti, "You keep doing it, fella. You keep doing it. You know it's happening."

The punch landed with twenty-seven seconds to go in the round, and time should have been called immediately. With the clock stopped, Micky would be given up to five minutes to recover from the low blow. But the clock never stopped. So, while Micky was pacing and trying to shake off the discomfort, the bell sounded to end the round. That meant the fifth round would start in one minute, and Micky would have to be ready to go. A mistake by the timekeeper cost him his five-minute recovery period.

"He should have more time," Gavin complained. But Micky interjected, "I'm all set. I want to go."

Dickie shoved the green mouthpiece back in its place, the bell sounded to begin round five, and Micky was there. He touched gloves with Arturo, and they began their dance once again.

The final thirty seconds of this round epitomized both fighters. Gatti hit Ward no fewer than eleven times. Micky didn't throw a single punch in retaliation. Gatti stepped back again to catch his breath. Instead, he took no fewer than twelve punches. The first several blows were a quick flurry of short lefts and rights. Micky fired a straight right that sent Arturo into the ropes. Once there, Micky landed a left to the body that made Gatti visibly wince. An uppercut and two hard left hooks later and Gatti was backpedaling to the adjacent ropes. Now, Gatti was bleeding and again looking for a breather. Instead, he took perhaps Micky's best right hand of the night and a left for good measure. The bell sounded.

"This is becoming Micky Ward's fight," Lampley shouted. "They're fighting in a phone booth, and that's the way he wants it."

Gatti's right eye was bleeding, and Micky was an absolute mess. The blood from above his eye had smeared all over his face. His nose and his lip were bleeding as well. Lampley was right. This was becoming Micky's fight.

"Just aim your punches," Gavin said while working diligently on Micky's cuts. "You've got this guy. Give me your head. Let me work on you."

"How you feeling?" Dickie asked. Micky nodded, indicating that he felt a lot better than he looked.

In the opposite corner, McGirt was shouting his instructions.

"Punch him. Punch him. And turn out. You're staying inside taking unnecessary body punishment. Don't take it. You've got to suck it up like a champ now. Listen to me. He's in the same fight you're in. Okay? He's feeling the same tired as you are, if not more tired. Nice and smart. Okay, when he gets close to you, listen to me, if you don't feel like punching, move your upper body. He's not going to do anything. Okay? Then go back to the jab. He's seen you on the ropes, and it's touch, touch, touch. Keep doing that until you get that second wind. Take a deep breath. Now, we're boxing like Arturo Gatti. Listen to me. Look at me, baby. You've got this fight. You can rest all day tomorrow. You understand? This is for all the marbles, baby. You understand me? Box!"

Micky entered the center of the ring to start the seventh round with the cut above his eye still bleeding. Gatti snapped off a couple of shots that opened it up even more. But Micky was fortunate: the blood trickled down the side of his face, not into his eye. He was fine, barely aware of the wound.

"I wonder what kind of brains and heads are on both these guys," Steward commented. "They're getting hit with shots right on the chin, and it seems like it just stimulates them."

"Through six rounds," Lampley offered as evidence, "Gatti landed more than two hundred punches, most of them on the face of Micky Ward."

"To this stage," Steward continued, "Micky has been outdone in terms of talent, and skill, but not in heart."

Gatti boxed well in round seven, picking up another win on the judges' scorecards. He was picking up momentum and fighting a strategically sound fight. He was not repeating his earlier mistake of brawling with Micky along the ropes. Instead, he moved well around the ring and engaged only when he saw an opportunity to land a punch or two and then move away. The style McGirt demanded was working.

"Listen to me, baby. When he gets close to you, Arturo, if you don't want to punch, have your hands up. Just move. He don't want to fight no more. He's looking for the one shot."

This entire night was Micky's one shot. He was on HBO. He was making big money. He was thrilling the crowd all around him and around the world. But he was tired, and he was frustrated. Micky sat in his corner with Dickie squeezing his sides and Gavin twisting his head this way and that. Sal was offering encouragement. The crowd was buzzing and so was Micky's head. The one minute he was given between rounds was not the best time or place to focus on a singular thought, but Micky found one.

"I'm all right," he said to no one in particular. He wasn't even sure he said it out loud.

"Are you?" Gavin asked, looking for affirmation.

Micky looked up at him for a moment before it registered in his brain that Gavin's question was in response to something he had just said. What was it? Oh, yeah, "I'm all right."

"Yeah," Micky said. He was breathing heavily and in some significant pain, but he gave Gavin what he wanted to hear. "Yeah, I'm all right."

With that established, Dickie cut in. "You're doing everything with your left now, Mick. Everything with your left. Bang the shit out of him. Mick, don't be a punching bag. If you're going to be a punching bag, I'm not gonna let this go like this. Fight hard. Deep breath."

"You've got to be busier," Gavin agreed. "You've got to punch."

Micky entered the eighth round behind in the fight. HBO's unofficial scorekeeper and fight analyst Harold Lederman had Gatti ahead 67–65, and he had it that close primarily because he gave Micky a 10–8 round in the fourth because of the low blow by Gatti. It was going to be tough for Micky to win this fight by decision. He needed a knockout, and he went for it.

With forty-five seconds to go in the eighth, Micky landed a hard uppercut that snapped Gatti to attention. Micky stalked Gatti across the ring, landing a couple of sharp right crosses. Gatti was in trouble. So he threw two of his angriest punches of the night. They landed flush, but Gatti was surprised to learn they weren't nearly enough to regain control of the fight. Micky brushed them off as if they were nothing, and then blasted Gatti with a sharp left, landing squarely on his chin. It staggered Gatti just a bit. Most spectators wouldn't even have noticed it because it occurred while Micky was being hit, too. Gatti threw his punches with a flourish and a force that were impossible not to notice. Furthermore, Micky was bleeding profusely and looked like the more beaten man. But Micky ignored the assault, stepped inside, and landed effective, less flamboyant punches.

But as Gatti walked toward Micky and landed several hard shots, Micky stopped him in his tracks with one laser-sharp, accurate punch. Gatti stopped walking forward and start walking backward. Micky approached him with only ten seconds to go in the round. He heard the loud clap indicating how much time was remaining and gave it everything he had.

Bam! Micky started his barrage with a left. *Bam! Bam!* A right and a left found their mark. *Bam!* Another right. Then a body shot and an uppercut. Gatti had no response. He backed into the ropes and prayed for the bell to ring. He knew he could withstand the attack for a few seconds longer. Just three seconds to go in the round, two . . . *bam!* Another shot to the top of the head. *Ding!* Gatti stumbled toward his corner, obviously dazed.

"Oh my gosh! Oh my goodness! What a fight!" Lampley said.

Dickie jumped into the ring and brought Micky to the corner. That was a huge round for Micky, perhaps the turning point of the fight.

"Mick, come here. You've got him going," Dickie said. "I swear you've got him going."

Meanwhile, McGirt saw this fight suddenly slipping away. Gatti was probably still ahead on points, but if he didn't right himself quickly, this fight might never get to the scorecards.

"You've got to suck it up!" McGirt screamed. "You're taking too many shots inside, Arturo. Throw the right hand to the body, Arturo. Listen to me. You've got six minutes. Give me the six minutes."

Micky was on top of Arturo immediately in round nine.

"When the ninth round started," Micky would say later, "I knew I had to go out there and get right on him. He was still hurt. He was probably ahead at that time. I knew I had to either drop him, stop him, or do something."

Thirteen seconds into the round, Micky got in close, tapped Arturo to the head, and then shot the left to the body. Classic Micky. Gatti felt it immediately. He took two steps backward and dropped to one knee. It's the kind of blow most fighters don't get up from.

"His money punch," says Lampley.

"He hit me to the body," Gatti explained after the fight. "I'm a man, but I couldn't take that body shot. It was an accumulation of punches. I just had to go down."

"Jesus, thank God," Micky was thinking as Cappuccino sent him to a neutral corner. "Don't get up."

Micky initially went to the wrong neutral corner, so Cappuccino pointed to another corner, and Micky ran over to it. Excited. Anticipating this could be the end. Gatti was still grimacing in obvious pain. Cappuccino turned toward Gatti, who was still on one knee, and began counting. ". . . six, seven, eight, nine . . ." and Gatti rose. He was still wincing, still very much in pain. Cappuccino rubbed Gatti's gloves on his own shirt and stepped away. Micky came in for the kill. Keep in mind, the devastating punch landed at the thirteen-second mark of the round. There were still over two and a half minutes to go. Could Gatti survive?

Adrenaline coursed through Micky's veins. He was losing this fight on the scorecards, but he could still taste victory. It was for all his years of hard work, for Lowell, for Dickie, for his family, but most of all, it was for Micky. He deserved this, and he would get this, damn it!

As soon as Cappuccino signaled that the fight would continue, Micky pounced. He threw twenty-three consecutive, unanswered power shots, starting off at the body where the damage was originally done. Then he landed a hard left hook that staggered Gatti and sent him reeling to the other side of the ring. With his victim helpless against the ropes, Micky landed another body punch. Gatti winced again. There were still two minutes to go in the round. How had Gatti lasted this long?

"I was tagging him, but he wasn't going nowhere," Micky explained later. "Well, he was going somewhere, but he wasn't going down where I wanted him to go. I couldn't get back to the body. So, I had nowhere else to go, but to the head. He took it."

"He is me. He's everything I am," Gatti told *Friday Night Fights* in the days leading up to this brawl. "He's a true warrior."

Now Gatti was demonstrating again what kind of warrior he was. He refused to go down again. He wasn't able to defend himself with anything but his feet, and he kept them moving. He hoped Micky would punch himself out. That was his only chance, so he waited. He took more punches and waited some more. Finally, Micky took a moment to inhale deeply. Gatti stared at Micky and his head was clear; it was his turn now.

Bam! Bam! Gatti landed two hard shots to Micky's belt. A slow uppercut missed, but a left hook found Micky's ear. Two big rights and another left bounced off the top of Micky's head. The energy inside the ring had transferred from Micky to Gatti.

"It wasn't looking too good, but I got my second wind," Gatti said after the fight.

Gatti backed Micky up with a barrage of body shots, each one landing on Micky's belt. They were not low, but they were close, especially for a man who had already been penalized for such tactics.

"Vicious body shots by Gatti," Lampley exclaimed. "Ward nods as if to say 'C'mon. C'mon! C'mon! Let's fight!'"

Now Micky had backed into a corner and Gatti was standing in front of him, looking for his best chance to land the fatal blow. Micky's head moved left and right, barely eluding some of the harder shots. His hands were low, but he rattled off a flurry of harmless lefts and rights as if he was attacking a speed bag. But five or six of those is all he had left. He needed to catch his breath. Gatti pummeled him with a series of body shots. These were full-speed, full-contact blows to Micky's midsection, and there had been dozens of them throughout this fight. Micky took them, thankful that he hadn't met an opponent who threw them as well as he does. As Micky tried to bull his way out of the corner, Gatti fell on him and pushed him back, using Micky to help himself stay on his feet.

"Stop! Stop!" Cappuccino barked his command and separated the fighters. One minute remained in the round.

"When we were hanging on each other, I was trying to save some time," Gatti admitted later. "There was a minute left. I was just hoping the bell would ring. I'm just trying to survive that round."

The brief pause in the action was an opportunity for both fighters to take a moment. But as soon as Cappuccino indicated that they could continue, they landed shots simultaneously. Micky's was a big right hand. Gatti went with his left to the body. After the punches landed, the men found themselves chest-to-chest. Here, Micky stepped to the side and threw that left hand into Gatti's body. It hurt him again. Gatti stepped away, again in obvious pain. Micky moved in and landed an uppercut on the chin and a hard left hook. He went to the body and to the head again. Gatti was hurt again. He was tired. He had very little left. Micky, who took the last minute off, only to be punched repeatedly, now felt up to getting off a rapid-fire succession of punches. The energy had transferred again.

"I knew I had to come back and take control over that ninth round," Micky explained. "I just wanted to throw straight hard punches. One, two, three, four. Nice and hard. Bang, bang, bang, bang! *Bang, bang, bang, bang!*"

Micky pushed Gatti up against the ropes and started to tee off. He landed one huge right hand that turned Gatti sideways in the ring. As Gatti attempted to escape, he was throttled by Micky's left hand on his throat. It wasn't so much a punch that landed there, but an attempt by Micky to shove Gatti and keep him from getting away. Then he landed another big right hand that should have put Gatti on the canvas. There were nine clean blows to Gatti's head. Each one should have knocked him down. None of them did.

"Stop it, Frank. You can stop it any time," Lampley said rhetorically to referee Frank Cappuccino. "Arturo Gatti's out on his feet."

"I thought the fight could have been stopped right there," Micky said after the fight. "I'm thinking, 'What the hell does he have in his head?' I know he's a very tough guy, but that's a lot of punishment for somebody to take."

Still thirty seconds to go in the round. Gatti wrapped his arms around Micky and was quickly pushed away by the referee.

"Frank Cappuccino's gonna let them keep going!" Lampley exclaimed.

With ten seconds to go, Gatti whiffed with a hard left and Micky responded with four quick punches, but they were tired punches, unable to add to the damage already done.

"Less than ten seconds to go in the round," Lampley announced. "Gatti's gonna survive the round!"

"This should be the round of the century," Steward observed.

Micky had met his match, someone who possessed his same resolve, someone who refused to go down or stay down. Micky was tired. Gatti was hurt. It was an unbelievable three minutes of violence near the end of an incredible boxing match.

"They have struck the courage nerve and the nostalgia nerve," Merchant observed. "In boxing, this is the equivalent of those forensic cop shows that show you open hearts beating and pumping. Open-heart prize-fighting. Nostalgically, this fight sort of brings back to us a very visceral time when the sons and grandsons of European immigrants were fighting their ways off the farms, out of the mines, and out of the factories."

In the ninth round alone, Gatti landed forty-two of sixty-one power punches, and Micky landed sixty of eighty-two. Each fighter took more than forty power shots to his head and body, and not only kept going, but kept throwing. It was an unbelievable display of valor. Gatti managed to find his way over to his corner with some assistance from McGirt. Gatti flopped onto his stool and an ice bag suddenly appeared on his forehead. The corner was quick to action.

"Listen to me," McGirt said attempting to get Gatti to focus on him. "I'm not going to let you take this punishment."

Gatti looked up. He could barely see through swollen eyes. His head remained unclear. The crowd was roaring, but he couldn't hear them. His head rolled slowly to his left, and he appeared to be looking down at something.

"Look at me!" McGirt yelled to no avail. "Look at me, Arturo! Tell me something."

Gatti didn't say a word. His mind was someplace else, and he probably wished his body was, too.

In the other corner, Gavin said with conviction, "Micky, this guy's done." Then Gavin threw a wet towel over Micky's head and grabbed him hard with two hands alongside both of Micky's cheeks. He leaned in close, going eye-to-eye with Micky and said, "You've got him, Mick!"

Dickie followed with additional words of encouragement. He was watching his brother do what he himself had never done. Micky was giving everything he had. He was living up to his utmost potential. Micky simply possessed an uncommon internal strength. Micky's mind was what made him extraordinary, while Dickie's mind had betrayed him, causing him to give in to weakness, temptation, and greed. Although Dickie wanted to be where his brother was now, he never succumbed to the dark sides of envy.

"I know it's your toughest fight, Mick," Dickie said. "You've got it in you."

As he said this, Micky rose from his stool and saw a commotion over in Gatti's corner. There were several people in the ring, and Micky saw one of the people in Gatti's corner waving the fight off. Gavin saw it, too, and gave Micky a big hug around his head. Micky raised his hands in victory.

"This fight's going to be stopped," Lampley said and then quickly added, "Nope, it's not!"

"No, no. The fight ain't over. Fight ain't over," Cappuccino bellowed to both sides of the ring. "No. Last round."

Cappuccino told both fighters to get back in their corners and wait for the word. The bell had already sounded to start the final round, and by the time everything was cleared up, extraneous people cleared out of the ring, thirty seconds had passed. The tenth and final round of this amazing battle would only be two and a half minutes long.

Thinking it was over, Micky recalled, "I was like 'Thank God.' It was a huge sigh of relief. I was like, 'Oh, yeah!' I mean, I can't say how much that meant to me. And then somebody says, 'Oh, no. The fight's not over.' So, I was like, 'What the hell?' I had to get remotivated. What the fuck! Now you got to get back up again. I only had seconds to get back. I was flat after that. No excuse. He won the tenth. No doubt about it."

Micky was flat because in boxing, unlike other sporting events, a fighter is glad when it's over. Whether he won or lost, he's simply glad it's over. So, it's extremely difficult to restart.

Gatti's corner didn't stop the fight, although the fight could have been stopped by rule during the ninth round when McGirt climbed onto the ring apron a few seconds too early as Gatti was getting pummeled at the end of the round. McGirt considered having the fight stopped and even went over to Pat Lynch before the start of the tenth and said, "I'm telling you right now, if he starts taking some shots, I'm stopping it."

The ninth round, considered by many to be the "Round of the Century" was a display of the best and worst boxing has to offer. It was the best because it showed how much courage and valor man can possess, but it was the worst because man is not supposed to have that much courage and valor. It's not healthy.

Gatti did win the tenth round, and he did it almost miraculously. He came out bouncing around as if the previous round had never happened. He was refreshed. He quickly landed a hard body shot and three more to the head. Two straight hands and a big left hook opened up Micky's cut. Micky had lost his momentum and was waiting for the fight to end. It was a potentially disastrous mistake on his part, because the decision of the judges was very much in doubt. In a rare moment of inactivity, Micky and Gatti leaned against one another. They did not hold each other. They did not clench. They did not throw punches. They merely leaned against one another, each man's chin resting on the other man's shoulder. They were essentially holding each other up.

"I am humbled by watching these two guys take the punishment they are taking," said Merchant.

With twenty seconds left, both fighters just kept throwing punches with reckless abandon. In ten seconds, they threw what seemed to be a hundred punches. In reality, it was only forty, but the flurry was exciting to watch.

"This is the way it has to end," Merchant said.

"We told you this would be a candidate for Fight of the Year," Lampley added. "We didn't know it would be a candidate for Fight of the Century."

With ten seconds left, a few final blows were landed in the center of the ring until, finally, Gatti stumbled forward and hugged Micky. Both men staggered up against the ropes. Before Cappuccino could separate them, the bell sounded, and the fighters who had just tried to pummel each other into submission, embraced in a moment of mutual respect.

"Arturo Gatti, Irish Micky Ward, two of the most honest fighters in the sport of boxing," Lampley summarized. "Circa 2002, a fight straight out of the 1950s, a throwback to the golden era of the ring."

Dozens of people crowded into the ring. Micky paced and continued to bleed. He managed to smile as he awaited the decision that would change his life. A win meant he would get another big-money fight, perhaps his first million-dollar payday. A loss meant he might retire.

"Ladies and gentlemen, we have a majority decision," the ring announcer said into the microphone. Micky shrugged as if to say, "Of course. Nothing ever comes easy."

"Judge Frank Lombardi scores the bout 94–94, a draw. Judge Richard Flaherty scores it 94–93. Judge Steve Weisfeld sees it 95–93. All to the winner by majority decision . . ."

Sal held his breath. Dickie clenched his fists. Micky prayed.

". . . Irish Micky Ward."

Micky heard his name. Then he heard it again.

"Ward!" the announcer repeated.

Micky exhaled hard, the way a man might when he's trying not to cry. There was so much emotion, so much relief, so many people looking to share in the moment. Sal bear-hugged Micky, lifting him several feet off the ground. Micky raised his fist in victory, but allowed himself to celebrate for just a few seconds. He jumped down from Sal's embrace and rushed over to congratulate Arturo. They shook hands and knew at that moment that they would be forever linked. They had just made history. The question asked almost immediately was, "Would history repeat itself?"

Larry Merchant posed the idea of a rematch during his post-fight interview with Micky and Gatti.

"Thank you, guys, for giving us a memorable night at the fights," Merchant began. "Was this as tough as anything you've been through, Micky?"

"Most definitely," Micky responded. "Arturo's a gentleman. He's a great fighter. He didn't have to prove nothing to no one tonight. He's proved over the years what he can do. He's a great man. He's a great warrior. I have nothing but total respect for him. This fight was a very close fight. This fight could have gone either way in my mind. I take nothing from Arturo. He's a great man."

Gatti offered similar praise, "He's a really tough guy. You know, I hit him with some good shots. He kept getting stronger every round, and I've got to give it to him. It was a tough fight, close fight. It could have gone either way. I just thought that I shouldn't have got a point taken off for a low blow, because it was not intentional. But that's all right."

It was the point deduction in the fourth round, and Micky's 10–8 round as a result of the knockdown in the ninth that pushed Micky over the top on two of the judges' scorecards.

"At the end of the ninth round was your trainer trying to stop the fight?" Merchant continued with Gatti.

"Not at all. He told me if I wanted to keep going, keep going. He said it's a close fight, you can win this fight. This is the last round. If you take this round, you have the fight. I wanted to keep going. You know he hurt me to the body. He's a strong guy."

"Were you almost out in that ninth round?"

"Actually, I was trying to take my breath back and he kept punching me, but no, I'm all right. I know I seem gone, but I'm not."

Merchant turned to Micky, "Did you think he was finished in that ninth round?"

"Oh, yeah! To be honest with you, I did. I did. But you can't take nothing for granted with Arturo. He's a rock. He's like granite. I don't know how to explain it, man. He's like granite. I've never hit anyone with shots like that. My hand's killing me, and my elbow. I don't know. What the hell's he got in his head? I don't know. I almost punched myself out. When he started coming back, I said, 'Damn!' I just had to keep throwing. One-two, one-two, one-two. Straight punches."

Finally, Merchant asked the question on everybody's mind.

"Do you guys want to do this again?"

"I would love to," Gatti said, extending his hand to Micky. "I would love to get a rematch."

Micky shook Gatti's hand and said, "If we can do it, we'll do it. We can talk. It's a great fight between two warriors. It's honesty."

Gatti's manager, Pat Lynch, heard the words, and his heart dropped to the floor.

He walked Gatti back to the locker room wondering all the while if a second fight with Micky Ward was a good idea. Yes, there would be very good money for both guys, but to repeat the utter brutality could jeopardize both men's careers, and even the quality of their lives.

After a combined 521 power punches, 296 for Gatti, 225 for Ward, the combatants were willing to clash again—for the right money.

CHAPTER TWENTY

The hard-luck loser was on top of the world. Micky Ward, who had lost nearly every big fight of his career, had just won his biggest. Before Gatti, he was a journeyman fighter. Now, everyone in the boxing community, the money men on the inside and the fans on the outside, knew who Micky Ward was. He was a brave, gutsy, honest, blue-collar worker who just happened to do his work inside a square ring. He was old school. So was Gatti. From now on, when people talked about the greatest fights of all time, Gatti–Ward would be in the conversation. For now, however, the conversation centered on how to get them to do it again.

This time, however, Micky was more involved and more demanding about what kind of money he'd be making for a rematch with Gatti.

"I want a million dollars," he said. It was a number that commanded instant respect. Micky had been abusing himself for the pleasure of others for thirty years, and he figured it was time he got paid for it. DiBella and LoNano believed that Micky should get his million bucks, so that was the starting-off point for the negotiations.

But Micky asked for his million before he knew how much money was in the fight. As it turned out, there was more than 2.1 million dollars earmarked for Team Ward.

So, DiBella and LoNano can pat themselves on the back for holding true to their word about getting Micky his million-dollar payday. But for Gatti–Ward II, DiBella received six hundred thousand dollars. Sal got three hundred thousand dollars. Al Valenti got one hundred thousand dollars. And Dickie got one hundred thousand dollars, too. Add it up with Micky's million, and it shows that Lou picked up 30 percent of Micky's total purse, Sal 15 percent, and Al and Dickie each walked away with 5 percent.

"We're all making this fight," Sal explained. "I'm going for the gusto. I could have very easily said to Micky, 'You're gonna fight Arturo for six hundred grand,' but I said 'No.' I took my management fee beyond that, so that he got his purse every time."

Micky's family suggested to him that he should just cut DiBella out of the deal entirely. After all, he never signed a contract with DiBella, and Kathy Duva and Main Events had taken the lead in promoting the fight. So why should DiBella be entitled to such a large chunk of change?

"There's a real sort of mobster sense to the whole thing," Ron Borges explains, "where if you forget me now, I'll forget you later."

But this time Micky wouldn't listen to his mother or Dickie. DiBella had been loyal to him after he lost to Leija, and now Micky would be loyal to DiBella. Micky holds no grudges, but he is aware that Lou and Sal grabbed a bigger slice for themselves than they should have. But in the moment that he received that one-million-dollar check with his name on it, nothing else mattered. "When I got that check with all the zeroes on it, it was like Woo-woo! Mr. Magoo!"

Now, since Micky won the first fight, his people should have been promoting the second fight. The upside was enormously high because the boxing community was buzzing with anticipation of the rematch. But DiBella wasn't in the financial position to take all the risk, so Main Events took over.

"For all his knowledge, Lou had very little experience on this side of the desk," Valenti explained. "There was no rematch clause in the original contract, so Lou is supposed to take the upper hand. I told Lou, 'Look, you can make a deal tomorrow for Fox-woods, but it's a smaller venue, so you're gonna have a PR prob-lem. You had seven thousand at the last fight, you're gonna have twenty thousand who want to see the next fight. If you go to Fox-woods, you're gonna be in a four-thousand-seat bingo hall. You know what? It's gonna sell out. So what? You're in control. That's all that matters.'"

But DiBella wasn't in control. He and Duva agreed that they would both go out and shop for the best site deal they could get. Whoever came back with the best deal would get the fight at their desired location. Because Gatti fought out of New Jersey, Duva wanted the fight in Atlantic City, and she got an offer from Bally's. DiBella wanted the fight closer to Micky's home, so he pursued an offer from Tom Cantone, the vice president of entertainment at Foxwoods. Cantone's offer of five hundred thou-sand dollars was slightly higher than Bally's. So, by the original agreement, Foxwoods would get the fight. But Duva wasn't ready to give up.

During a conference call with DiBella and Cantone, Duva announced, "There's another bid. My company's bidding."

Main Events put up the money, assumed all the risk, and cut a side deal with Bally's to have the fight at Boardwalk Hall which seats 11,500 people. The fight sold out, and Main Events cashed in.

"It was driving me crazy that this fight was going to go into a bingo parlor with four thousand seats," Duva said. "It just seemed wrong."

Valenti, who thought the fight should have been staged either in Boston or at Foxwoods, was disappointed, both in the outcome and in DiBella.

"He dropped the ball," Valenti says critically. "In the final analysis, we had a deal with Foxwoods. And in fairness to Lou, he buckled. But it was a good day for everybody. There were some bumps in there. I don't like that we had a deal with Foxwoods and walked away. I don't like the idea that Kathy Duva treated us like second-class citizens. We won the first fight, and we're looking to have the lead in the second fight. But bygones are bygones. Everybody made money."

And although it was true that Duva was trying to gain a home "ring" advantage by bringing the fight to New Jersey, Micky wasn't concerned. Atlantic City was like his second home anyway. In fact, he had fought in Atlantic City more times than Gatti had.

"The crowd can't be any more hostile than when I fought Jesse James Leija in San Antonio or Shea Neary in London," Micky told reporters at a pre-fight news conference. "And I won the crowd over in that fight."

And Micky was already winning people over. That news conference was held at McSorley's Old Ale House just off the Bowery, and while the gathered media remained impartial, the patrons were squarely on Micky's side. It helped that McSorley's was an old Irish saloon. It first opened its swinging doors in 1854, and its list of customers included everyone from Abraham Lincoln to John Lennon and now Micky Ward and Arturo Gatti.

"So this is what a real Irish bar looks like," Valenti said as he shuffled across the sawdust-covered floor. "I'd always wondered."

Micky was also finding new friends closer to home. In the weeks leading up to the rematch, Micky was honored by supporters at the Somerville Good Times Sports Emporium. After a big night of drinking and celebrating, Sal presented Micky with a brand-new blue Corvette, which George Kimball of the *Boston Herald* reported, "Micky was in no condition to drive."

There was also a big send-off rally at the John F. Kennedy Plaza outside Lowell City Hall. And on Veterans Day, an organization of former U.S. Marines known as the Semper Fidelis Society gave Micky its first Ted Williams Globe and Anchor Award. The honor recognized the "commitment and dedication to excellence" that baseball Hall of Famer Ted Williams showed as a marine fighter pilot and for the rest of his life on and off the baseball field.

"For me to be even mentioned in the same breath as Ted Williams is an incredible honor," Micky said.

This was a new life for Micky. Honors and accolades were coming from all directions. His rematch with Gatti was among the most anticipated fights in recent years, and he was becoming a star. No longer driving down to Atlantic City with Mickey O'Keefe or with Richie Bryan scrounging for gas money along the way, Micky was going to and from press conferences in stretch limos.

All he ever did was work hard and stay straight. He remained loyal to his brother, keeping Dickie by his side all the way to the top of the mountain. He remained loyal to Lou DiBella who he never had a contract with, but felt obligated to. He never forgot who his friends were, and he was never fooled by the hangers-on who only pretended to be his friends. It was also never lost on Micky how incredibly fortunate he was. He knew that hard work guaranteed nothing. Other boxers had worked hard, maybe just as hard or harder. But they weren't about to step into the ring for a million dollars. They were forgotten warriors, guys who had fallen long before they ever reached the dizzying heights to which Micky had climbed. They were equally deserving, but not nearly as lucky.

There was Ray Oliveira of nearby New Bedford, Massachusetts. Oliveira beat Charles Murray twice and Vince Phillips once. Micky lost to both those fighters, but he was cashing in and Oliveira was having trouble finding fights. There was David Rivello who battled Micky to a split decision, and never fought again. Rivello was a talented fighter with a lot of heart. Where was his million-dollar payday? There was Reggie Green, who battled Micky evenly for ten rounds and then fought only four more times, twice against guys with losing records for short money. When Green lost to Zab Judah, it was the last time he ever fought. When Micky lost to Judah, his career was just starting to take off.

Years of hard work, countless hours in lonely, dusty old gyms, thousands of times caught on the receiving end of punches that would make most men cry, and still there are no guarantees. The night of November 23, 2002, as he stepped into the ring in front of nearly twelve thousand boxing fans and millions more watching at home, Micky knew that he had made it as a boxer.

Gatti was actually the first to step into the ring that night wearing a baseball cap of the Port Authority Police. He bounced around and jabbed while Micky made his entrance to the rock sounds of Whitesnake singing, "Here I Go Again." The lyrics seemed especially appropriate. "I don't know where I'm going, but I sure know where I've been. . . . Here I go again on my own. Going down the only road I've ever known. Like a drifter I was born to walk alone. And I've made up my mind. I ain't wasting no more time."

Micky had the number 9 on his white trunks, in honor of Ted Williams. He was wearing blue sneakers. Gatti was wearing just the opposite, blue trunks with white sneakers. They both waited in their respective corners as the ring announcer, Michael Buffer, momentarily silenced the crowd.

"Main Events in association with DiBella Entertainment and the King of Beer, Budweiser, along with HBO Sports, are proud to present the featured bout of the evening. The rematch. Ten rounds of boxing for the undisputed, never-surrender, blood-and-guts championship of the world!"

HBO had begun broadcasting fights in 1973 when heavyweight George Foreman fought Joe Frazier in Kingston, Jamaica. This would be the network's five hundredth fight, and it promised to be one of the best.

"Wearing white," Buffer continued. "The fighting pride of New England, never-quit, never-surrender, former junior welterweight champion of the world, Irish Micky Ward."

The crowd erupted in applause. Gatti was fighting close to home, but it offered him no advantage.

"From Jersey City, New Jersey," Buffer announced, "the ultimate blood-and-guts warrior, the former junior welterweight champion of the world, Arturo 'Thunder' Gatti."

Again the crowd applauded enthusiastically. It was as though the spectators were less concerned about who won the fight. They just wanted it to be a great fight.

Following the referee's instructions in the center of the ring, the bell sounded and the rematch began. Gatti's manager, Pat Lynch, sat in his seat and prayed, "Just don't let these guys get hurt."

DiBella sat down next to Sal and said, "Can you imagine if Gatti wins this one? There'll be a third."

"That's history, huh, pal?" Sal responded.

"Yup, that's history, but we gotta get by this one."

Gatti's game plan for the second fight was to be in better condition and to box more. He didn't expect to be able to knock Micky out. This was Micky's fiftieth professional fight, and the only time he ever lost on a stoppage was the time he was cut against Vince Phillips. Gatti believed that he needed to box and win by decision; however, perhaps in an effort to conserve energy, he didn't come out moving laterally as much as he did in the first fight. Meanwhile, Micky was snapping off more jabs than was his custom.

"Both guys better realize this is a brand-new fight," HBO analyst George Foreman cautioned. "Don't try to continue something that ended months and months ago."

"Ward is as tough as you can be as a boxer," Foreman added. "Gatti's got no right but to do anything but box this man."

A single punch in the third round changed the course of history. With 2:17 to go in the round, Micky stepped forward, and Gatti tagged him with a short right. He was in good balance. Micky was leaning in. And the punch landed flush. Micky dropped instantly, falling face first into the turnbuckle. While referee Earl Morton motioned Gatti to a neutral corner, Micky bounced up, but stumbled like a drunk. He struggled to find his footing. Morton came over to give him a standing eight-count, but Micky interrupted.

"I'm fine. I'm fine." He repeated the words to convince both the referee and himself that they were true. But Micky was not fine. He was far from it.

Arturo went in for the kill, but somehow Micky's defense remained solid. His arms were out in front of him, and Gatti's punches couldn't find their mark. Still, he attacked. Finally, a hard right connected. Gatti's forward movement put him right on top of

Micky, and Micky wrapped his arms around him. He was clearly hurt now. His eyes were unable to focus.

"Micky Ward is very wobbly. He has no legs," Lampley said.

There was still 1:42 left in the round. As Morton separated the fighters, Micky moved to his right. He wanted to move to his left, but he was unable to right himself. Finally, he took the fighting posture. As Gatti took a moment to appraise the situation, Micky tapped his belly with his gloves as if to say, 'Give me more.' Gatti explained to Lynch after the fight that Micky's gesture and his overall fortitude caused Gatti to stop and reconsider going for a knockout at that time.

"I was not going in there and shooting everything I had at him just to try to get him out of there," Gatti told Lynch. "I know if I did, he was coming back and then I'd have a problem. He was a wounded animal, and that's dangerous."

Since the knockdown, Micky was merely trying to survive. He sensed that Gatti would not be able to finish him. But Gatti fired off a few more shots, and then Micky countered with a short left and a big overhand right. That one hurt Gatti.

"He's still dangerous," Gatti thought.

The final thirty seconds was an exchange of single shots by each fighter. Micky bounced up and down as if to shake the cobwebs from his head. As the bell sounded, he pounded his gloves together. He was determined, not frustrated, not angry. Nonetheless, he needed help from Dickie to find his way back to the corner.

"They're doing it again in Atlantic City!" Lampley shouted. "Gatti–Ward II already living up to expectations."

The fight doctor raced up to Micky's corner and asked, "Micky, are you okay? Do you feel good?"

Micky gave him a quick authoritative reply, "Yeah, I'm fine."

That would suffice for the time being. Even though Dickie struggled to get the mouthpiece out of Micky's mouth, the doctor was satisfied that the brutality could continue.

"Ice, ice, ice! Fucking ice!" McGirt yelled in an uncharacteristically chaotic corner. Gatti's side was excited and sensing the fight could end very soon.

"Listen to me. This is yours," McGirt told Gatti. "Go out and use the jab. Go back downstairs. Your right hand over the top is going to work, baby!"

Micky's resolve and resilience in the fourth round was nothing short of amazing, even heroic. The punch that knocked him down also knocked off his equilibrium. "He caught me good. It happens," Micky said after the fight. "He caught me behind the ear. And he just caught me. He threw my equilibrium off. I don't know how I stood up. Jesus!"

He not only stood up, he also managed to stand and fight. And he came out in the fourth round even more aggressive, appearing somewhat refreshed. Gatti was on his toes, and it looked as if neither fighter had just battled for nine violent minutes. By the middle of the round, Gatti's left eye was beginning to swell shut, and by the time the round was over, Gatti was bleeding from a cut over the left eye. It was essentially an even round.

"This is not about money. This is a fight," Foreman said with respect. "This is about pride and dignity. This is telling the other guy, 'This is the family I'm from. This is the country I'm from. This is who I am.'"

Micky bounced back to his corner at the end of the round. He was still trying to tell himself and his corner that he was fine, but in truth, he was still trying to regain his equilibrium.

"You all right?" Dickie asked without need of an answer. "That was a much better round. That's it. He's done. You took his best shots, and now it's time for you to retaliate. Let's go! Don't let him hit you low. Hit him back, Mick. He's dead tired."

"He's going down right now," Al Gavin said, speaking for the first time between rounds. "Aim the punches, Mick."

Each round developed very much like the previous one. Gatti bounced on his toes, threw a few punches, and then backed up. Micky approached, and once he was back in range, Gatti stopped his retreat and threw clean combinations, often to the body, sometimes just a bit low.

"You know what I like about Micky Ward?" Foreman asked rhetorically. "He's been hit below the belt I don't know how many times tonight, and he hasn't looked to the ref or complained or looked for any excuses. That's what you call a man."

But the man was losing, and it was getting worse with time.

The fight was exciting, but unlike the first fight, it was lopsided. Micky had lost every round, and he hadn't landed a punch with any real force in four rounds. For a moment in the seventh round, Dickie began looking around for the towel. Dickie had seen just about enough. He was ready to have the fight stopped. But the round ended.

"I'm gonna tell 'em," Dickie threatened in the corner.

"Don't tell 'em. I'm good," Micky lied.

"Look at me! Wake up!" Dickie demanded as he slapped Micky twice on the cheek. "Listen to me. Keep those hands up and fight back. You've got to go for it, Mick. Go for it!"

Gatti continued to execute his plan perfectly. His patience was being rewarded. He was easily winning every round, and he wasn't paying a price. He was avoiding Micky's power, and he only needed to do it for nine more minutes.

"If I'm in Micky Ward's corner," Foreman predicted, "I'm thinking if he doesn't pick things up this round and get going, I'm not going to allow him to get totally wiped out like things are going for him right now."

Round eight went to Gatti, too.

"Don't get careless," McGirt cautioned. "He's gonna get desperate. Okay? Arturo, don't look for the knockout. Let's just keep piling up points. Keep piling up points."

And, in truth, there was some desperation in Micky's corner along with some positive thinking.

"You can win this fight," Gavin told Micky. "It ain't over yet. You're in better shape."

"Micky, bend down," Dickie commanded. "Throw the uppercut and a hook. Bend down! You're not doing it. You said you were gonna do it. I'm gonna stop it."

Dickie didn't mean it. He only said the words to piss Micky off, to get him fighting mad.

"I'm all right, Dickie. C'mon," Micky said with both determination and annoyance.

"You're not all right! Uppercut hook! Push him the fuck off you!"

Micky was just as angry and frustrated as Dickie was, but fatigue and poor balance made it difficult for him to do anything about it. In the closing seconds of round nine, Gatti fired seventeen punches at Micky. Micky blocked and ducked most of the punishment. Then, as the bell sounded, Gatti landing another solid right, sending Micky wobbling back to his corner.

"The first fight was like a head-on collision," Merchant deadpanned. "This fight is more like a one-car accident."

Before the tenth and final round, both corners attempted to inspire their fighters. Dickie and Gavin had seen Micky rally from behind in the past. They knew he was capable of landing the unexpected late-round knockout, and they wanted him to know it, too.

"He's ten times tireder than you could ever be," Dickie said. "Whatever you are, he's deader. His legs can't move. You're dead, but he's ten times deader."

"He's dead tired," Gavin agreed. "If you can walk through him, then you've got him."

But Gatti was gearing up for the final round, determined to find whatever he had left and give it all.

"Listen to me," McGirt began. "Don't fall into his trap. You understand?"

"Yes," Gatti responded.

"Three minutes. Can we do three minutes?"

"Yes, sir!" Gatti shouted this time.

"Let's go, baby. Give it to me. Jab. Don't get caught in a slugfest."

Micky and Gatti walked to the center of the ring at the start of the tenth round, their twentieth overall, and hugged momentarily. Then they stepped back and came forward at each other again. In the final thirty seconds, both fighters swung nonstop and wildly at each other. Both fighters took additional and unnecessary shots, damage they could have avoided if they were so inclined. They were not. When it was over, Micky looked down in resignation, and Gatti raced over to his corner, jumped on the ropes, and began to celebrate.

"You're a fucking man!" Lynch shouted in Gatti's face.

"Gatti may have won that fight so decisively that there wouldn't be a reason for a third fight," Merchant said, adding, "It was a worthy sequel."

Micky and McGirt shared an embrace. Gatti and Micky hugged again, too. There was mutual respect and admiration all over the ring. Micky consented to pose for a few pictures with Gatti, each man holding up one glove. Gatti's eye was bleeding, and McGirt stopped the picture-taking for a moment and said, "I don't want him looking bruised up."

That made Micky smile just a bit. A few moments later, the smile was gone, and reality set in. Two judges, George Hill and Luis Ramirez, scored the fight 98–91 in favor of Gatti, and the third, Joseph Pasquale, scored it 98–90. The scores accurately reflected the one-sided nature of the fight. So, did the punch stats. Gatti landed 276 punches to Micky's 180.

"I was listening to my trainer," Gatti explained. "I boxed the way I was supposed to box the first fight. . . . Tonight I used my legs, but I stayed in front of him and moved my head real good. We worked on staying low. When I was close to him, he had a hard time landing his body shot because I was low. It gave me an opportunity to move around him. I was in great shape. I think I landed more punches than the first fight. Micky Ward's got a very strange defense. His hands never move. They're like two pillars right in front of his face. So, I had to take my shots this time."

Micky knew he was beaten badly in the rematch, but he didn't shy away from the possibility of a rubber match.

"He fought a good fight," Micky acknowledged. "Not gonna take anything away from him. No excuses. He fought a smart fight and a good fight. He's a good guy and a great fighter. It was his night tonight. Plain and simple. The better man tonight beat me; that's all. If we can get together again, I'll give it one more shot. If not, I don't know."

"It's 1–1," Gatti interjected. "So, a third one, I wouldn't mind."

"Sounds good," Micky concluded.

It was time for Gatti–Ward III: The Final Chapter.

CHAPTER TWENTY-ONE

The wars inside the ring between Micky and Gatti were brutal, but respectful. The wars outside the ring between their management teams were nearly as brutal but without nearly as much respect. As usual, the battle lines were drawn around the money. For a third fight between Micky and Gatti, there was a big pile of money, enough so that everyone should have been happy. But even after a deal was struck, Micky wasn't happy. He was bitter.

"I've seen a lot of things in boxing that weren't pretty," Micky told the *Boston Globe*. "I've been at this for thirty years. A lot of things happen that aren't right. After I beat him, I gave him a rematch for even money. I don't regret that. I respect him. If he don't respect me, there's nothing I can do about that. I know I did what was right. Let them live with what they did to me on this."

With 3.2 million dollars already on the table before a single ticket had been sold, Micky was offered only eight hundred thousand dollars. Granted, it would be the second-largest payday of his career, but he'd still have to pay everyone on his management team.

"Why did they want to make me feel like a creep in my last fight?" Micky wondered. "What keeps people like that motivated is beating people down. Getting over on people. We're one to one. Why not even money again or maybe sixty-forty? I'm bringing in as many people as he is."

Micky was right. Fighters don't get paid based on who's better. Who can sell the most tickets is what matters. And certainly, the reason a third Ward–Gatti fight was in such high demand was because the public wanted to see the trilogy completed. For that to happen, both fighters were of equal value. Therefore, it stood to reason that they should be paid equally.

"But I know why it went like this," Micky added. "If I told them I'd dump Lou DiBella, they would have given me the extra 250,000 dollars that would have made it fair. But I wouldn't do it. I've seen a lot of disloyal things in boxing, but I ain't going to abandon the people who helped me get where I am for money. If I didn't get the fight, I didn't get it. In my heart, I knew what was the right thing. So do they, but they didn't do it. If it never happened, I could live the rest of my life knowing I did the right thing. I would have gone back to work. I'd sit back on the roller and roll away. Paving season's on! Why do people have to be so greedy?"

It was a rhetorical and naïve question in the world of boxing to be sure. In the end, Main Events raised Micky's purse to 1,075,000 dollars plus 25 percent of the net on the gate. After paying DiBella, Sal, Dickie, Al Gavin, and assorted other expenses, Micky stood to take home about 725,000 dollars. "I was fair with them after Micky beat Gatti, but they wanted to tear us apart when they got the upper hand," Sal told the *Globe*. "They got a problem with DiBella, but why should Micky have to pay for it? People have told me we should just dump DiBella and we'd get paid. Too many people in the fight game forget about loyalty. The first fight they screwed us. The second fight we were fair. We split fifty-fifty when we had the leverage because we thought it was right. So why do we get called pigs?"

Kathy Duva from Main Events said her first responsibility was to Gatti, and that after the amount he'd be paid was determined, there wasn't enough left over for everyone on Team Ward to get the amounts they wanted, but she added accusingly about Sal and DiBella, "If they were more concerned with what their fighter gets paid instead of what they get paid, there wouldn't have been a problem."

But Main Events offered something closer to a seventy-five–twenty-five split, which could have been an indication that they really didn't want the fight. They figured that Gatti was younger and ranked higher and he could have made a million dollars-plus fighting several different fighters. Micky's best chance at one last payday was to fight Gatti. Micky had learned over the years that most of what happened outside the ring was out of his control. Fate and people with varying interests and varying degrees of integrity were in charge. But Micky could deal with being nickel and dimed, because he was getting out with millions. The poor kid from the bad town announced that he'd be retiring after his third fight with Gatti. Micky made nearly three million dollars in his last three and a half years in the ring. It was an amazing accomplishment for a man with an uneven 38–12 record, especially when you consider it was done in the so-called twilight of his career. Micky found the fights because he had an audience who appreciated his heart. He was proud to have made the money, and he was dead set on getting out of the dangerous game while he could still count it.

"After our last fight, I considered retiring," Ward admitted. "My family wanted me to stop. I was worried about my health, so I took a CAT scan to be sure everything was all right. It didn't show nothing wrong. Then I started to feel better, and I thought, 'Two out of three and that's it.'"

Of course, when a fighter knows he's retiring, the reasonable belief is that the fight has already left him. So there were plenty of doubters who thought Micky was only fighting Gatti for one last sizeable paycheck.

"If they say that, then they don't know me," was Micky's response to such conjecture. "Until Sunday morning, I'm a fighter. I wanted this fight to redeem myself and then walk away from boxing. For me, it's to get revenge on Gatti for the last fight. Maybe he got more of the money, but I want to get the upper hand on him in the fight. The way we fight, we both know what's coming. I can't take the heart out of the guy and he can't take the heart out of me. . . . But I can beat him."

Micky had already proven that he could beat Gatti, but the second fight put Gatti's superior boxing skills on display, and most boxing observers assumed that Gatti would be able to repeat the strategy in the third bout. Micky vowed to move his head more to avoid taking as many punches. He promised not to fall into Gatti's traps by following him around the ring. And he pledged to let Gatti be the aggressor, so that he could win the fight by counterpunching.

Micky repeated his assertions several times before Buddy McGirt finally scoffed, "Micky Ward isn't going to come out and box like Sugar Ray Robinson."

Micky's best chance of winning was to land his paralyzing body shot to the liver, and his best chance of doing that was to work his way to the inside. It's the style that brought Micky to the big stage, and it was very likely the style that he would go out with. The only thing Gatti's team had to worry about was their own fighter's predisposition to do the same.

"Micky says this is his last fight, so I expect him to fight his best," Gatti said. "I have to stay smart and stick to my plan. But, you know me. I want to box, but if I have to fight, I'm not afraid to fight."

"This is it," Micky explained, "and I want it more than anything else. It's okay that nobody thinks I can win. They didn't think I could win the first fight either. I'll go out giving my best because that is what I love to do."

The knowledge that both fighters would give their all twice inspired the expansion of Boardwalk Hall's seating capacity. By the time Micky and Arturo were ready to step into the ring, the arena accommodated fifteen thousand people, an astronomical number of fans to see a non-title fight between non-heavyweights. All of those people were anxious to see a repeat of Ward–Gatti I, which was recognized as the 2002 Fight of the Year from the Boxing Writers' Association.

Micky drove down to Atlantic City in the first week of June 2003, prepared to finish what he had started, an epic trilogy with Arturo Gatti and a successful career. His first boardwalk fight had been against Chris Bajor in January 1986. Bajor's career ended eight months later. Seventeen years later, Micky was still going strong.

The opportunities were there, but Micky was vehement in his resolve not to be lured by money into another fight. There were reports that IBF lightweight champion Paul Spadafora wanted to move up to junior welterweight, and since Spadafora was considered a light puncher, there were also growing whispers among boxing people that Micky could earn a big but low-risk HBO payday. And there was also the possibility that an impressive win by Micky over Gatti could put him in line to fight Kostya Tszyu. A fight such as that would be worth millions and a title that Micky had always coveted. But Micky professed to have no interest in additional fights.

"Nope," he said. "Not for two and a half million. Not for *five* million. This is it. I don't want to hear about another fight. I did all I could do in boxing, and I did it the way you should. I've gone farther than anyone thought I would. I have enough money to set myself up, and I'm still healthy. How many fighters can say that? I'm satisfied with everything I did, and how I did it."

Micky remembered how he felt in the days leading up to and during his first retirement. He felt like a loser, a quitter. He felt empty inside, like there was something left undone. He didn't anticipate feeling like that this time. Everything was different now, from his bank account to his overall mindset. This time his decision to walk away was final, and it was comforting.

"I'm kind of relieved it's almost over," Micky said. "I'm glad to be done with 'Drink this. Don't drink that. Eat this. Don't eat that. Sleep now, not later.' I won't miss the limelight or the headaches. It's time to stop. Sure, it's kind of sad, but I'm glad it's almost over. A lot of people thought I was done a long time ago. I even thought I was done, but I decided I ain't done until I'm done."

Win or lose to Gatti, Micky was going out a winner. He'd won the respect of millions. The boxing public loved him. He was a champion of the people. Ron Borges was able to explain why in a story written the day before Micky's last stand.

> *A fighter faces the question often asked by revolutionaries and warriors in moments of crisis. "Would you rather die on your feet or live on your knees?"*
>
> *In a boxing ring, that question has a literal side because men die there with far too much frequency and great warriors like Ward and Gatti are mindful of that, yet keep that sad reality at arm's length like an opponent who's too strong on the inside.*
>
> *They parry the thought. They jab at it, slip under it, always respecting it but refusing to give in to it. At times, they ignore the stark possibilities and fight on through bleary eyes or a bloodied face. That is why the public has fallen in love with Ward. It is why it will cheer him madly as he walks down the aisle for the last time tomorrow night in an odd venue for boxing.*

On June 7, 2003, ring announcer Michael Buffer got the evening started, "Ladies and Gentlemen, by way of Bally's Atlantic City, Main Events is proud to present the third and final chapter of the Gatti–Ward boxing trilogy. Ten rounds of boxing for the unofficial but undisputed blood-and-guts championship of the world! Let's get ready to r-r-r-r-umble!"

The last word rolled off his tongue as Micky shuffled his feet from side to side. He was flanked by Dickie, Sal, and his nephew Sean Eklund. Micky was wearing a Lowell Spinners jersey with the number 39 on it, representing what he hoped would be his thirty-ninth career victory.

Buffer went on, "Tonight, he enters the ring for his final fight. Tonight he vows to end his eighteen years in the ring with a victory. Ladies and gentlemen, the fighting pride of Lowell, Massachusetts, the former super lightweight world champion, Irish Micky Ward!"

The crowd erupted dutifully. Fans there knew that they were part of something special.

Gatti stood in the red corner as the crowd noise died down enough for Buffer to continue.

"Gatti is a former 130-pound champion. Over his career he has become recognized as a fighter of unchallenged valor and courage with his never-surrender, never-quit style. Ladies and gentlemen, from Jersey City, New Jersey, the former junior lightweight world champion, the ultimate blood-and-guts warrior, Arturo 'Thunder' Gatti!"

On cue, Gatti began bouncing on his toes as Buffer dramatically announced his name. The crowd was equally enthusiastic in their reception of Gatti, and he responded by kissing his right glove and waving it high in the air. History was about to happen.

True to his word, Micky was more aggressive, especially with his jab. He landed the first punches of any real consequence, and he moved well to his left and right. He was quicker with his counters and more willing to finish with flurries of his own than he had been in the second fight. It was a good first round for Micky, but he returned to his corner with a cut in the middle of his left eyebrow. It was not yet of any great concern.

"Be active," urged Dickie. "It's the last fight of your career, Mick. Fight hard, baby! Hands up!"

Dickie encouraged Micky to throw more right hands because that was the punch that knocked him on his ass during a recent sparring session with his little brother.

Gatti began landing an inordinate number of body shots in round two. He bounced well around the ring, moving with rhythm and grace. He was able to make Micky swing and miss a lot and then land a few quick shots before backing up again.

"Micky Ward doesn't look too good at this point in time," Emanuel Steward observed.

"No. Arturo's beating him up," Jim Lampley added. "He's beating him in every way, power punches, boxing, ring generalship, seems to have more spirit."

Gatti landed twenty-three of thirty-four power punches in the third round. By the end of the round, Micky's nose was bleeding. He had a cut over his eye, and he was taking a beating to the body. The round could have been scored 10–8 it was so dominating.

"Listen, very beautiful," McGirt praised. "Just go back downstairs again. Just go back downstairs to the body. . . . It's your show."

It was much quieter on the other side of the ring. Micky was getting two Q-tips shoved up his nose to stop the bleeding, and Dickie was less vocal than usual. Gatti was fighting a brilliant fight again. Micky needed something to change the momentum and direction of this fight, or he could wind up getting hurt on his way out of the fight game.

"If Micky Ward wants to get back into this fight, he's going to have to return to his shock-and-awe style of fighting," Merchant said flatly.

Twenty-six seconds into the fourth round, Micky caught a break. Gatti fired a hard right hand that landed on Micky's left hip. Gatti immediately backed away writhing in pain. Micky knew what that meant, because he'd been in the same position. He immediately went after Gatti with a left hook to the head. Gatti was either unable or unwilling to block it with his painful right hand. Micky landed a few more shots, and now it was Gatti who wasn't firing back.

"It appears almost certain at this point that Arturo Gatti feels as though he's broken his right hand," Lampley said. "And Micky Ward is taking advantage to pound him!"

Gatti didn't throw his first right hand for a full minute after he felt the pain shoot up his arm. When he finally tested his right hand again, the punch was not thrown with its usual violence, but it was a minor victory that he threw it at all. He winced again.

"No question Gatti has hurt his right hand," Lampley observed. "That's gonna change the fight."

Gatti's pain energized Micky. He closed in on Gatti in the center of the ring and delivered five-straight left hooks and uppercuts. Gatti had no answer. He merely stepped around Micky and backed away.

"Ward's back in it now. Back in it in a big way!" Lampley said excitedly.

Gatti was almost defenseless. For the better part of the fourth round, his right was useless and his left was lifeless. Finally, he started throwing more forceful lefts, but he only tapped Micky with his right. Meanwhile, Micky favored the uppercuts. He threw several, landed some, but it was a big overhand right that wobbled Gatti in the final thirty seconds of the round.

"No question the hand is hurt," Steward said. "They may end up having to stop the fight. That's what makes boxing so different from all other sports. In any other sport, you could call a time-out, substitute another athlete. You can't do it in boxing. The whole team is Gatti."

"Arturo wants to throw his right hand, but just can't!" Lampley interrupted. "Micky Ward landed a haymaker shot!"

Fighting with sudden desperation, Gatti disregarded his pain and began fighting back, not wildly, but with precision. After hurting his hand, then being hurt by Micky's blows, Gatti was in danger of being stopped. Now fans were witnessing an incredible turnaround. Gatti was retaking control of the fight. He threw seven straight left hooks, mixing in just one straight right, thrown instinctively. That's what a fighter does. After thousands of combinations in the gym and in the arenas, a fighter follows up a series of lefts with a right. Gatti did it despite the pain. And he fought back valiantly in the final seconds of round four.

"Gatti showing great courage as he tries to get Ward off of him with one hand," Lampley announced. "High drama in Atlantic City. Crowd on its feet."

"This is what they came for," Larry Merchant added.

Gatti survived the round and returned to his corner with the crowd still on its feet. Gatti slumped on to his stool and laid his head on McGirt's shoulder.

"My hand," was how Gatti began the conversation.

"Huh?"

"My hand."

"What do you want me to do?"

"My right hand."

"What do you want me to do?" McGirt repeated.

"I'm gonna keep going."

Of course, he was going to keep going. That's what Micky did when he lost his equilibrium in the third round of the second fight. "Okay, listen," McGirt said confidently. "Here's what you've gotta do. Use that jab. Keep that jab working. Don't stay inside and take no body shots. Okay? . . ."

Micky and Dickie knew Gatti's hand was hurt. His hand may have been broken, but he wouldn't know that until the fight was over. Since he had made the decision to keep fighting, Gatti continued with reckless regard for his body. He began the fifth round throwing with both hands. It was intended to demonstrate to Micky that he wasn't hurt. Micky stalked him anyway, but Gatti kept him at a distance.

Midway through the round, Gatti landed a hard right to Micky's chin. It was a good thing for Micky that Gatti pulled it just a bit. Soon, the cut opened above Micky's left eye. He ignored the blood rolling down his face and landed a hard left hook, but Gatti shrugged it off as if it were nothing. Gatti began using his right hand more and more as the round progressed. It had gone numb. No pain. No problem. With fifteen seconds to go in the fifth, both fighters went after each other with haymakers. Two solid straight rights from Micky. Two huge left hooks from Gatti. And the bell sounded. It was becoming a brawl not unlike their first encounter. Micky was prepared to go out in style, and Gatti was willing to accommodate.

The ring doctor, Dominic Coletta, paid a visit to Micky's corner to inspect his cuts. There was one on the bridge of his nose, another one on his cheek, and a third above his left eye. Occasionally, his nose bled as well. He was a mess. His face looked worse than in any of his previous fifty fights. The cut on his eyebrow was as wide as a coin slot, but Gavin seemed to have the bleeding under control.

"It's all right," Gavin assured Coletta. "It's above the eye."

"Yeah, it shouldn't trickle down. All right, I'll let it go."

Then after the doctor had left, Gavin leaned in toward Micky and told him, "He's fighting with one hand."

Dickie heard it and added, "Don't let a one-handed fighter beat you."

But Arturo was becoming less and less of a one-handed puncher. Whatever the extent of his injury, whatever the extent of his pain, Gatti was dealing with it. Micky had to remain cautious and not forget about Arturo's right.

Round six was a relatively inactive round for Micky. But he was certainly throwing more punches in this fight.

"Down goes Arturo on a wide swinging right hand!" Lampley said attempting to hide his astonishment. "The bell sounded and round six has come to a close. Micky Ward who was behind on points, now has a leg up to get back into the fight."

The knockdown came suddenly and unexpectedly, when Micky landed a big right hand, and Gatti simply stepped away. He wasn't hurt, so he reengaged. This time he was met with a short left and a hard overhand right to the top of his head. And that's what put him down. Gatti rose immediately as the bell sounded to end the round. He was still given a standing eight-count before he was sent along to his corner.

"He's trying to come over the top with that right hand, Arturo," McGirt said, maintaining the calmness and control in his voice. "You've got to move to your right a little more, because he's not using that left hand. Keep the left out in front of you."

Dr. Coletta made his way over to Gatti's corner this time, and asked, "Arturo, how are you feeling?"

"Fine."

"You fine?"

"Yeah."

That was all, and that was enough. The bell sounded for the start of round seven, but Micky wasn't ready to come out of his corner. Dickie couldn't get the mouthpiece in for Micky, and Micky couldn't get a handle on it while wearing the gloves, so the referee, Earl Morton, had to call time-out. Dickie dropped the mouthpiece, but picked it up off the canvas and shoved it into Micky's mouth. Micky stood there unperturbed, and then playfully punched Dickie in the belly.

Micky and Gatti jumped to the center of the ring and resumed trading big shots. Gatti landed a hard left to the body that forced Micky to take a step back. Micky hiked up his shorts and took a deep breath. Gatti, either admiring his handiwork or taking a breather of his own, never saw the short left and the hard right combination.

"He hurt Gatti with the right hand, hurt him badly!" Lampley reported. "And here comes Gatti trying to fight his way off the ropes."

Gatti's left eye had opened up and was bleeding as badly as Micky's.

"Look at Arturo firing that broken right hand," Lampley said. "Ward waits for him to finish and then stages his own assault."

It was another incredibly punishing round for both fighters. They seemed to take turns hitting each other. Micky took more time and punishment, but each time Gatti stopped punching, Micky started.

"I knocked him down at the end of the sixth," Micky explained. "Usually I'd come out in the seventh and get right on top of him. But when I came out for the seventh, I knew right then and there, I had nothing. I was a shell of myself. My legs felt like they were in quicksand. My body was dead tired. That's when I knew I was done. That confirmed my retirement."

Halfway through the seventh round, Micky's exhaustion caused him to make a mistake. He fought his way inside, but when he got there, he had nothing left. He took a moment to rest when he was at close range, and Gatti made him pay for it. He wobbled Micky with a stinging left hook.

"Can Gatti follow up?" Lampley wondered aloud.

"I never thought I would see anything as exciting as their first fight," Steward said, adding, "This is equaling it, maybe even more so for power punches."

The round was reminiscent of the ninth round of their first fight. Power punches landing cleanly. Both fighters taking and giving everything they had. Both fighters weakened, but still determined. It was brutal, and it was beautiful.

"There has been nothing like this in boxing since Bowe–Holyfield a decade ago," Merchant said referring to the three fights between heavyweights Riddick Bowe and Evander Holyfield in 1992, 1993, and 1995.

"This is better," Steward said with the highest of praise. "This is better, and you get more action in ten rounds than you normally get in a fifteen-round fight."

Micky kept coming forward, stumbling forward actually, while Gatti backed up, waiting for him to get in range. It was another very active round that Gatti was winning with dozens of hard power shots. Micky had no answer.

"Ward almost seems like he's ready to go," Merchant said with thirty-five seconds still to go in the round.

As the bell sounded, Steward stood and applauded with the rest of the fifteen thousand witnesses. Gatti had just thrown 176 punches in that round, more punches than he had ever thrown in a single round before, and he landed 61 power shots. Imagine 61 hard punches to the head and body. Micky took them all and headed back to his corner, his face a bloody mess. But his biggest problem was that his vision was severely impaired.

"I can't see," Micky told his brother.

"What do you mean you can't see?"

"I mean my eyes are all fucked up. Everything's blurry. I'm seeing three of him out there."

"Then hit the one in the middle," Dickie instructed without sympathy.

Meanwhile, it was Gavin who entered the ring now instead of working from behind the ropes and over Micky's shoulder. He needed to get in there to get a good look at the damage Gatti had inflicted. He couldn't do anything about the eyesight, so he ignored it. Instead, Gavin squeezed down hard on the cut above

Micky's eye. And for the first time all night, Micky acknowledged the pain.

It was obvious that Gatti has trained hard for this fight. He routinely ran ten miles a day, and his endurance was evident as he came out on his toes in the eighth round. Micky was able to land a couple of hard rights, but Gatti simply kept bouncing and moving, looking for another angle to throw from. The action from the seventh round had carried over to the eighth. Lampley admitted to hating the word *incredible* when describing sporting events, but added, "This is incredible."

"It's as if they're not even human," Steward agreed.

"It's because they're human that makes this such a compelling drama," Merchant interjected. "It's definitely not normal. Even other fighters are moved by the great toughness and resilience of these two fighters, qualities that are every bit as rare as great boxing ability."

Again, it was nearly silent in Micky's corner. His cuts were tended to for the full minute allotted. Then, when it was time to rise from his stool, Micky heard, "Hands in close." Micky couldn't be sure if it was Dickie or Gavin who said it. His mind was fuzzy, his eyes had been bothering him for the past two rounds, and he was not sure what was happening. He looked across the ring and still saw three Gattis, and wondered how he could beat all three of them. He was so tired. Just two rounds to go in his career. He would keep fighting until the end, "But what's the matter with my eyes?" he wondered.

The ninth round seemed to go more quickly than most for Micky. It was a blur. A round he doesn't remember as clearly as many others he fought, yet it was very much like most of the rounds he fought with Gatti. Gatti had the advantage in punches thrown and punches landed, while Micky remained in a steady march toward his opponent. Micky used his instincts and experience to get through the round.

"I fought seeing double for three rounds," Micky explained later. "I saw four or five of him. It was weird. It was upside down.

Three Gattis on top of each other. It was weird. I was telling Dickie in the corner, 'I can't see.' He was like, 'What do you want me to do?' And I said, 'I'm not gonna stop.'"

Gatti had a broken right hand, and he kept going. Micky was seeing double and triple, and he kept going. There was no championship on the line. The money would be paid whether the fight went the distance or not, but they kept going anyway. And they weren't just going through the motions. They were fighting hard, determined to not go down at all or go down in a blaze of glory, and that's why they are wrapped in glory to this day.

"It never crossed my mind that I should quit on the stool," Micky said. "Despite being told that I could have gone blind during the Green fight, and now not having proper vision in this fight. I didn't think of not fighting the last three rounds. I figured, 'Hell, I've fought three hundred rounds, I can go three more.'"

Now, he only had one more to go. Three more minutes of a boxing life that had lasted three decades. From a seven-year-old boxing in the rain to a thirty-eight-year-old who reigned as the king of the working man. Micky felt the water pouring down over. His head was down and the cool water dripped down his face and into a bucket below him. He kept his eyes closed and his mind blank. He couldn't focus on the magnitude of the moment. It was too big, and he was too tired. The only thought that registered for him was that he should turn to the other bucket and spit out some blood.

"Last round of your career, Micky," Dickie said. But whether it was the last round or not, it felt like every other round. Time for Micky to go out and give it all he had.

"Last round," McGirt reminded his fighter and then cautioned him, "Use your legs, but let your hands go. Box him, but move your hands. We're gonna close this show big, but no slugfest. You understand."

The tenth round began with a hug at the center of the ring.

Clearly, only Micky and Arturo knew what was inside the other man, and they truly respected each other for it. They had earned each other's respect, and in so doing they had found something that is sometimes even more elusive than the respect of others. They found the respect of self. To watch what Arturo was capable of, and to realize that he was capable of the same courage and greatness gave Micky what he had fought so long to achieve—self-respect.

Thirty seconds later, Micky wobbled when Gatti caught him with a hard left. For the last three minutes of his career, Micky would need to stand up in the face of adversity and find a way to survive.

Gatti threw flurries and then got on his bike. He gave the impression that he was fresh, but midway through the round, Micky stunned him with a great left hook to the head. Gatti was forced backward, and Micky pursued him, landing a hard right. Gatti looked like he might go down. His rear end was pushed between the ropes as he bent over to avoid another blow. He was able to stand up and uppercut his way out of the predicament when Micky took a moment to rest.

"That may have been the last hurrah of Ward," Merchant uttered.

In the final thirty seconds of Micky's career, he engaged in a battle befitting his epic trilogy with Gatti. Both men finished their three-battle war by landing hard shots to the head.

"Oh my God!" Steward said in awe.

Micky and Gatti repeated the violence until the final bell sounded, and then they hugged again, the product of mutual respect and sheer exhaustion.

"They're done," Lampley punctuated the moment. "What Arturo Gatti and Micky Ward share together, only they know, only they can touch it, only they can feel it."

Dickie was among the first to enter the ring, and he lifted Micky high in the air so that all the spectators could salute his brother, the valiant warrior. When Dickie was in jail, he had promised himself and Micky that he would get out someday and make him a champion. He kept that promise. Micky was a champion of the people. Part of the subtext of Micky's career is that he gave Dickie a chance to walk with him toward something better than what they had known as kids growing up in Lowell. Micky's career was a beacon in Dickie's life, a light that he could follow out of the darkness of his drug addiction. Micky had stayed straight on his path, and Dickie had stayed straight on his. Together they had arrived at this moment.

The ring filled up with people very quickly, but Micky was able to find some solitude in his corner. Only Dickie was there helping him remove his gloves. Micky wore a big smile. He knew it wasn't likely that he had won the fight, but he was happy nevertheless. He was relieved, not only that his career was over, but that this especially difficult fight was over.

"Are you hurt?" someone asked.

"Just my hands," Micky said.

"Probably from hitting him on the head," Dickie said, and Micky laughed. He was exhausted. He was hurt. He stood there with a fat lip, a swollen left cheek, blood leaking out of three different cuts on his face, and triple vision. But he was retired. And that was something to feel good about.

"After thirty grueling rounds, a round of applause for two warriors who gave it everything they had in this ring," Buffer rallied the crowd. "We now go to the scorecards for the final chapter of the Gatti–Ward trilogy. Joseph Pasquale scores it 96–93. George Hill, 96–93. Luis Rivera, 97–92. All for the winner by unanimous decision. Arturo 'Thunder' Gatti!"

Micky didn't seem to listen to the announcement. He was preoccupied with trying to get his gloves off. He made one final tug as Gatti raised his arms in exultation. Immediately, Gatti looked around the ring to find Micky, and they embraced again. It was a proper ending to one of the greatest trilogies in boxing history, and it was a proper decision by the judges. In the end, Gatti outlanded Micky 349 to 128. Of those 349 punches, Gatti only landed 98 jabs. The rest were power shots. "I know what type of man Micky Ward is," Gatti told Merchant in the ring after the fight. "I knew he was coming in tonight to fight the best fight of his life. If it had been anybody else, he would have quit. And Micky Ward hurt me in the fourth round. I hurt my hand in the fourth round, but Micky Ward is unbelievable. He's got a heart. And for someone who wants to retire, he fought a helluva fight."

Then Merchant turned to Micky and asked him how he felt about going through one last incredibly difficult fight. Micky responded, "He caught me with some good shots early that stunned me. It threw my equilibrium off. He fought a great fight. He hurt me early, not really bad, but enough to get me a little dizzy. I just couldn't get untracked after that. He fought a great fight. He fought his fight. I take my hat off to him. No excuses. I was in great condition. Things happen in the ring, you always have a game plan, but sometimes you have to go to something else if that doesn't work, and that's what happened."

Merchant was curious about what happened when Gatti hurt his hand, especially the conversation with McGirt in his corner. Gatti explained that he just wanted McGirt to know that he had hurt his hand, so that McGirt would understand what was going on and alter the strategy as he saw fit.

"How soon did you know that you were fighting a one- or one-and-a-half-handed fighter?" Merchant asked Micky.

"I knew as soon as he hit me. I could see it in his face. I could tell. He wasn't throwing with the power that he caught me with earlier. I knew it, but he's got balls like you wouldn't believe. He's got heart. I told you he's like Jason. He doesn't stop. You can't stop him. That's his nickname, not Thunder.

"He caught me earlier in the fight with a good right hand that discombobulated me," Micky continued. "I just couldn't get my legs under me like I wanted to. I knew he'd come back from it. That's what he's about. He comes back. All the time I hurt him was at the end of the round, never at the beginning."

The post-fight interview is an odd occurrence, because it happens so soon after the two fighters have been beaten about the head. How can they be expected to give well-thought-out answers to questions involving events that transpired during the heat of battle? Their minds are racing, and their bodies are drained. Still, Micky was eloquent in his praise of Gatti, his message to young kids, and in his acknowledgment of his own legacy.

"It's mutual respect," Micky explained. "I want to beat him more than anything in the world, but outside he's a human. He's a beautiful guy. That's what it's about. It's about respect. It's not about who's tougher. We're both tough guys. It's about respect, and that's what all the kids in the world should have is respect for each other. I gave it my all. I always gave it my all, a hundred percent. I'd tell any kid, don't get into it unless you're serious, because it's a serious sport."

"Is this series going to be with you and identify you for the rest of your life?" Merchant inquired.

"Yeah, probably, most definitely. And I'll stay friends with him for life. That's just the way it is."

Friends for life with the man who hit you a thousand times in thirty rounds of magnificently violent boxing. Near the end of the HBO broadcast, Emanuel Steward tried to explain how earning another boxer's respect is the first step toward everlasting friendship.

"It's respect, and to some degree you even learn to love each other. When you hit a person with the best punch you've got, and they just come right back to you, first of all, you respect them, and after a certain time you actually have to say, 'I love this person.' Somebody can be this tough, to come back and fight and the anger becomes respect."

As Steward spoke, Micky was being helped out of the ring. His arm draped around Dickie's shoulder. They were brothers who came to this point in their lives from vastly different directions. They would leave in different directions as well. Dickie really didn't know where to go from here. He was forty-five years old and had yet to hold a steady job, an ex-con without a high school education. What choices did he have? He was undoubtedly on his way back to a gym in Lowell where he could find more fighters to train. Wouldn't they all want to be trained by the guy who once fought Sugar Ray Leonard, and who brought Micky to the top of the mountain?

"Sure they would," Dickie thought.

Micky would also be heading home to Lowell, eventually. But the first place Micky was headed was to the hospital—where he would meet up with Arturo Gatti.

CHAPTER TWENTY-TWO

Micky and Arturo were both rushed to the Atlantic City Medical Center after the fight. Charlene sat in the front seat of Micky's ambulance while Sal stayed in the back, holding an ice pack to Micky's head.

When Sal tried to put the oxygen mask over Micky's face, Micky stopped him and said, "Sal, I needed that thing in the third round. I don't need it now."

Within minutes, Micky was in the trauma room. Doctors quickly determined that he was dehydrated and needed stitches in his cheek and above his eye. He was placed on a heart monitor and left alone for a few minutes. His double vision was making it difficult for him to keep his eyes open without adding to his headache, so he closed his eyes and tried to rest.

Suddenly, the curtain separating him from another patient swung open, and Micky heard, "I think we should get paid more money for this."

It was Arturo offering the best smile he could through his swollen face and busted-up lip.

"How you feeling?" Arturo asked with genuine concern.

"I'm hurting," Micky answered truthfully.

"Me too," Gatti admitted.

They didn't talk about the fight or their places in history. They talked about mundane things, about their fiancées waiting for them in the lobby and about playing together in an upcoming golf tournament at Foxwoods. At one point, Micky looked down and realized that he wasn't wearing anything on his feet.

"Somebody stole my shoes," he blurted. "I don't know who the hell stole my shoes!"

Micky noticed Gatti was wearing sneakers that were just like his. He knew they weren't his, but he teased Gatti anyway.

"Hey, those are my sneakers," he charged. "What are you doing with my sneakers?"

"These aren't yours," Gatti protested. "What size do you wear?"

Micky wore a size 8. Gatti wore a size 10.5. The mystery of what happened to Micky's shoes was never solved. Micky and Arturo laughed about that, and they laughed some more when they traded stories about how beat-up they felt. They were the happiest patients at the hospital that night.

"We were laughing our asses off," Micky recalls. "His lip was all cut up, and my eyesight wasn't for shit. I had to get stitches, too, but it was fun!"

The fun was interrupted when the doctor came in to sew up Micky's cuts. At that point, the curtain separating Micky and Arturo was closed again. While the doctor tended to Micky, Ron Borges stayed to observe and to continue his post-fight interview with Micky.

"Well, now you're the best kind of fighter there is," Borges told Micky. Then, while Micky was still trying to figure out what that meant, Borges added, "You're an ex-fighter."

"Yes, I am." Micky confirmed.

"A year from now, just remember that's what you are," Borges advised. "You're an ex-fighter."

"I will," Micky promised.

"They might throw a lot of money at you to fight Kostya Tszyu or somebody else," Borges said. "Everybody could use an extra million. How are you going to say no to that?"

"I have nothing left," Micky responded. "I can't keep going."

At three o'clock in the morning, after Micky had been given IV fluids, a complete physical, and a CAT scan, it was time to return home to Lowell. A limo arrived to take Micky back to the hotel, and he was given a substantial amount of painkillers.

"What are you gonna do with those?" Borges asked.

"Not give them to my brother. I can promise you that," Micky answered.

Before he left, Micky went over to Gatti.

"You be careful," Micky said.

"You be careful, too. It's dangerous out there," Gatti offered, referring to Atlantic City and the world in general.

"Yeah," Micky said. "It's dangerous where we go, too."

Stooped over, walking gingerly, and wincing occasionally, it was hard to imagine these were the same men who only two hours earlier had been willing to endure pain and fatigue beyond the limits of most people. Their minds had taken them to a place where it was okay to fight with a broken hand or with nauseating double vision.

When Arturo left the hospital, he was thinking about his next fight. He had spent that last year of his career preparing for, and fighting, Micky Ward. He had made more than a million dollars for each of the three fights, and since he had looked very impressive winning the last two encounters with Micky, Arturo figured he was ready to fight for a title. He did that six months later. In January 2004, he beat the previously undefeated Gianluca Branco for the vacated WBC light welterweight title. Micky was in his corner that night.

Arturo successfully defended the title twice, knocking out Leonard Dorin and Jesse James Leija. Both fighters retired after their losses to Gatti.

Then Gatti was knocked out by Floyd Mayweather Jr. trying to defend his title a third time. Later, fighting for the seventh consecutive time at Boardwalk Hall in Atlantic City, Gatti won the IBA welterweight title from Thomas Damgaard of Denmark. Again, Micky was there to lead Arturo out of the dressing room and into the ring. Their friendship is still going strong.

Arturo's career still had plenty of life in it after his trilogy with Micky. He was well-respected and well-known before those three fights, and he continued to entertain fight fans long after Micky had retired to Lowell. But Arturo's legacy, like Micky's, will always be tied to the thirty rounds they spent together.

"Micky solidified Gatti's place," Kathy Duva explains. "He took him to a whole other level. I don't know that Gatti would be where he is today. Together, their sum is greater than the parts. That made both of their careers. They're icons. They both are, and neither of them would be, without the other."

As Gatti continued to make millions, Micky began to pay for his. As Micky ages, he'll have to worry about pugilistic dementia. The thousands of punches he took to the head and his occasionally abusive alcohol consumption are conspiring against him in that regard. But his first physical challenge after retiring was his double vision.

"Arturo hit me in the head hard," Micky remembers. "I could feel it, but I didn't really get dazed. But soon I started seeing double. I saw two or three Gattis the rest of the night. I kept trying to shake it off, but it didn't go away. I wasn't complaining, I was just telling Dickie because it was so amazing. It was weird . . . and it never did go away. The doctors at the hospital after the fight couldn't do anything for me. They thought maybe I had taken a thumb to the eye, but I knew that wasn't it. So I went to see Dr. Francis Sutula and he tells me that when I got hit, my brain shifted in my skull. That was causing the problem."

And Micky fought with his brain in the wrong place for at least three rounds, and he continued to live in that condition for fifteen months after the fight. After seeing a series of doctors who correctly diagnosed his problem but hoped it would correct itself over time,

Micky was referred to Dr. Sutula by Harvard boxing coach Doug Yoffe, whose wife, Patti, had been the ring doctor in Micky's fight against Vince Phillips. And in the words of Dr. Sutula, an oculoplastic surgeon at the Massachusetts Eye and Ear Infirmary in Boston, "Micky was really screwed up."

"This was acute trauma," Dr. Sutula said. "Micky didn't have any of this double vision before that fight. If the brain or head has been knocked around a little bit, and it's sort of shifting around in the cerebral spinal fluid, you get hit in the front part of your head, but your brain moves back against the skull and then moves forward again. Micky's brain moved inside his skull. The back part of the brain hit the skull. That messed up his fourth nerve. When fourth-nerve injuries occur, which happens in cases of trauma, you would see it on one side, but he had it on both sides, and he had it asymmetrically. Seeing it bilateral and asymmetrical was really kind of odd. Having it on both sides suggests the trauma happened at least twice. When this occurred, it must have been very hard for him to fight. The only thing that would have saved him is if one of his eyes was swollen shut. That would have gotten rid of the double vision."

The most obvious result of all this brain shifting and nerve damage was that Micky's eyes didn't move together. Sometimes treatment for Micky's type of injury involves simply putting a patch on one eye. It's a familiar and common practice. When one muscle is gone, what doctors try to do is to weaken the other muscle to create balance. Micky chose not to wear a patch.

Instead he learned to live with vertical double vision. Certain gazes were worse than others for him. If he looked up and to the left, it was impossible for him to tell which was the correct image and which was the double. He simply got in the habit of tilting his head toward one shoulder and keeping his head down. That kind of body posture and head position began causing bad neck pain and headaches. When it became intolerable about six months after his fight with Gatti, he consulted Dr. Sutula for the first time.

"You could see the problem just in the physical exam," Dr. Sutula said. "We used prisms, tilted his head, and watched how his eyes were moving. It was obvious."

Initially, Dr. Sutula recommended the same course of action that the previous doctors had: do nothing and see if the nerve injury would heal itself over time. But almost a year after first seeing Dr. Sutula, there was no change. So, on September 16, 2004, Micky underwent surgery to get his eyes to move together again. After enduring the frustration, inconvenience, and pain caused by double vision, Micky came out of surgery, once again with a singular focus. He had to thank Kathy Duva and Carl Moretti of Main Events.

Fighters commonly receive a one-year limited-liability insurance policy to cover themselves in case of injury during a fight. But because so much time had passed between the injury and the surgery, Micky's policy had lapsed. His insurance company refused to pay the ten thousand dollars in medical expenses. Moretti learned of the situation, talked to Duva, and Main Events paid the bill. Micky, who had brought the best out of Arturo Gatti, also managed to bring the best out of others. Main Events did themselves proud, and Micky could now walk with his head held high, too.

"When I saw him the day after the surgery," Dr. Sutula said, "his wife, Charlene, said to me, 'He doesn't have his funny head position anymore.' He still had some double vision in extreme conditions, but that went away. And he still has excellent uncorrected visual acuity, twenty-twenty in both eyes."

For the first time in fifteen months, Micky could see things clearly. He knew he had friends at Main Events. He knew Lou and Sal were men he could trust. Micky had finally figured out who the good guys were. They were his friends Richie Bryan and Tony Underwood. They were men like Skeets Skioli, Cleo Surprenant, and Al Gavin. And Micky knew that when it came to good guys, there was none better than the man he had left behind.

"I'm here because someone likes me for who I am," Micky told the audience at his retirement party at Foxwoods in the fall of 2003. "Someone who was with me from the beginning." There Micky paused. He waited until he knew he had everyone's attention. Maybe he waited just to tantalize Sal and Lou and Dickie and Alice and anyone else who thought he was talking about them.

"Mickey O'Keefe," he said finally.

The name hung in the air for a moment. Not everyone at the retirement party knew who Mickey O'Keefe was, and many of the people who did know him weren't happy that Micky had singled him out for such high praise. Sal expected to hear his name. After all, he was the one who invested his own money in the Hampton Beach fights and who made the connections with Al Valenti and Lou DiBella. Lou figured it might be him since he was the one with the HBO dates that made Micky his millions. Dickie assumed it would be him, because he was the one who introduced Micky to boxing as a seven-year-old, and who trained him for his most lucrative fights. And of course, Alice was his mother and his first manager. She'd been with him every step of the way. How dare Micky put that cop ahead of her when doling out credit.

"I just about fucking cried," O'Keefe recalls. "It meant a lot to me to hear him say that in front of those people. But all I did was get him doing push-ups, pull-ups, and dips. He did the rest."

The more Micky did, the further he moved along his journey, the more he learned. He learned that nearly everyone involved in his boxing career took a little piece of him. First, it was his mother and Top Rank who guided the first half of his career. Then it was his brother who made a better living than most ex-cons because Micky was willing to go through torturous workouts and masochistic fights. Then it was Sal and Al and Lou who enjoyed huge paydays each time Micky got his. That's what made guys like Cleo, Richie, and Mickey so special.

"Mickey didn't want control," Micky says of the cop who began the journey with him only to be dropped off in the middle of the climb. "All he wanted was what was best for me. . . . I know if it weren't for Mickey O'Keefe, there'd be no Micky Ward. People might not want to hear it, but it's the truth. . . . When I look back, it hurts that Mickey wasn't there at the end."

O'Keefe's friend Danny Gilday agreed with Micky Ward and took it a few steps further.

"If it wasn't for Mickey O'Keefe," Gilday says, "Micky Ward would never be back fighting. Dickie Eklund will tell you it was him. Alice Ward will tell you it was her. Sal LoNano will tell you it was him. But it was Mickey O'Keefe. If Mickey O'Keefe doesn't get involved with Micky Ward, he's a street person in Lowell. He'd be an alcoholic and an addict like his brother. I have no respect for Dickie. He's a thief. He's been a scumbag his whole life."

Those were harsh words concerning Dickie, but for a time, Micky might have agreed. While Micky was training for the third Gatti fight, Dickie showed up at the gym one day with several pieces of paper.

"Here, Micky," Dickie said as Micky was stepping into the ring for one of his sparring sessions. "You need to sign this."

"Sign what?"

"It's a movie contract," Dickie explained. "They want to make a movie about my life, and they just need you to sign this so you can be in it."

"Can't we talk about this later?" Micky asked. "I can't sign anything with my gloves on anyway. Just show it to me later."

Dickie returned a few nights later with the same demand: "Sign this, Micky." Again Micky turned him away. He was busy training for the last fight of his career, and he didn't have time to read over some document.

"Why do you keep bringing this to me here?" Micky asked. "I don't want to be bothered with this shit when I'm in here. I certainly ain't gonna take the time to read it when I'm working."

"C'mon, Mick," Dickie implored. "You don't have to read it. It's just a release. Everybody who's gonna be in the movie has to sign one."

Micky didn't respond. He simply began pounding the heavy bag, and he kept pounding away until Dickie finally got the message and walked away. The conversation repeated itself on two other occasions.

Finally, Micky and Dickie met Dorothy Aufiero, a principal of Scout Productions and Edgartown Ventures at Aufiero's office where she confirmed for Micky what Dickie had been saying. They wanted Micky to play a small role in the film, and for that, they needed his name on some documents. Micky left Aufiero's office that day with a five-page legal agreement and a one-thousand-dollar check. He didn't sign the document, nor did he read it, but he cashed the check.

A week later, Dickie badgered him again about the movie deal. It was now three weeks before the fight with Gatti, and Micky was getting a little testy. He pulled the document out of his gym bag, quickly scribbled his name on the dotted lines, and threw the document at his brother.

"There! Are you happy now?" Micky shouted. "Take the fucking thing and get out of my face!"

What Micky didn't know at the time is that he had just been duped into giving away the rights to his own life story.

Micky didn't realize what had happened until two months later, in July 2003, when several Hollywood producers began negotiating with Sal and Lou to make a separate movie about Micky. Actor Mark Wahlberg, a Massachusetts native, was involved in those negotiations, and he had already agreed to let Dickie train him to play the part of Micky.

Scout Productions got wind of the plans for a movie about Micky, and their attorneys quickly issued cease and desist orders. After all, they believed that they had the rights to Micky's life story. They even had a five-page legal document signed by Micky that verified it.

Micky hired a high-powered attorney and filed suit in Middlesex Superior Court asking a judge to declare the contract void. Micky didn't sue Dickie directly, but his lawyers contended in the lawsuit that Dickie was involved in the deception.

"These people defrauded Micky Ward," said attorney Harry Mannion, of the Boston law firm Cooley, Mannion, Jones. "They knew exactly what they were doing, and they used his own brother to perpetrate that fraud. What was done to Micky Ward by these people is worse than anything that was done to him in the ring."

"It was unconscionable," Mannion continued in the *Boston Globe*. "We have investigated this thoroughly. Micky had no idea what he was signing. There was no way he could have understood the legal language in that contract. He was purposely misled to believe he was only agreeing to be in a film about his brother."

This one hit Micky in the gut. People had been willing to sell Micky's body, one piece at a time, for years. Now, his own brother was willing to sell him out for one more payday. Micky couldn't deny it, and he couldn't defend it, but he certainly could explain it. When asked why his brother would be willing to scam him, Micky said directly, "Because they threw money at him."

Scout Productions hired BWR, a public relations firm, which issued a statement claiming, "There were no misrepresentations or false statements made to Mr. Ward . . . and numerous witnesses can corroborate that no false statements were made, including his brother."

Ultimately, the lawsuit was dismissed in November 2003 when Micky and the production companies reached an agreement that was financially beneficial to Micky. The new deal included option payments and percentages of the movie's gross, and Lou and Sal were added to the project as technical consultants. Once again, they had helped negotiate a lucrative deal for Micky in which they would also be paid.

"The story of Micky and Dickie has the potential to be a great film," Lou said. "I'm happy we're all on the same page. Micky is happy his whole team is involved."

But Micky wasn't happy. He remained estranged from his brother, no longer truly able to trust him. As Micky was approaching retirement, Dickie was back on the streets. On May 20, 2006, some believe Dickie fought twenty-eight-year-old Dennis Bilodeau outside Captain John's tavern on Westford Street in Lowell. The fight took place in the dark shadows of the bar just after 1:00 a.m. Bilodeau, described as a loving father, was later found unconscious with severe head wounds. He was flown by medical helicopter to Brigham and Women's Hospital in Boston, where he died the next day of blunt-force trauma to the head. His death was ruled a homicide.

Two days after the bar fight, on a sunny Sunday afternoon, Dickie was arrested outside of his house at 217 Wilder Street in Lowell. He was picked up on an outstanding warrant for allegedly beating his girlfriend. While in custody, police asked Dickie what he knew about Bilodeau's death. Dickie told the cops a variation of what he told the *Lowell Sun* prior to the third Gatti fight.

"I turned my life around in prison," Dickie defended himself. "I haven't had a beer, and I've been off the cocaine for eight years. There was a time when I never thought I'd be able to tell anyone that. I just thank Holy God.

"The fact I'm off the booze and drugs doesn't mean I'm a better person than somebody who can't beat their addiction," Dickie added. "The only person I'm better than is the guy Dickie Eklund used to be."

But that wasn't true. He was forced to stay clean for nearly five years in prison, and he kept himself clean and mostly sober for nearly five more after his release, but by 2005, the dubious star of *High on Crack Street* was starring in another self-destructive role. He was back on crack.

Police questioned Dickie about Bilodeau's death for several hours, before finally releasing him. They described Dickie as either a suspect or a witness, but they didn't have enough evidence to charge him with anything. Instead, police arrested thirty-three-year-old Heather Jaynes and charged her with perjury. Jaynes is the daughter of former championship boxer Beau Jaynes and the niece of both Micky and Dickie. She was at Captain John's the night of the fight, and police believe that she was protecting someone, probably Dickie. Jaynes was released after her father posted a one-thousand-dollar-cash bail.

On July 2, 2006, Dickie was arrested by Lowell vice detectives and charged with possession of crack cocaine.

According to the police report, Dickie made a call from a phone booth on the corner of Dover and Branch Streets. It was a phone booth known to detectives as one frequently used for drug activity. Dickie and an unidentified woman then got into a cab that took them to a nearby location on Lincoln Street. There, Dickie walked with an Asian male and made what appeared to be a drug transaction. It was twelve o'clock in the afternoon.

Dickie returned to the cab, and when police pulled it over, they say they could smell freshly burning crack. They searched Dickie and found a glass tube, still warm and with crack residue on it. Police believe Dickie swallowed the rest of the crack he purchased when they pulled over the cab. The woman with Dickie and the cab driver were not taken into custody, but Dickie was arrested for possession and released on forty-dollars bail. A free man once again, Dickie returned to the gym where he was training some of Lowell's young fighters, impressionable teenagers who looked up to Dickie and hoped that he could do for them what he claimed to have done for Micky.

In June 2007, 25-year-old John Morrell of Chelmsford was indicted on one count of manslaughter for the beating death of Dennis Bilodeau.

CHAPTER TWENTY-THREE

Finally, Micky's hard work had been rewarded with good fortune. He had fought long and hard and had pocketed more than three million dollars. He walked away from boxing a winner.

Jim Lampley said it succinctly at the end of Micky's last fight—thirty rounds with Arturo Gatti. "It has to be the most thrilling and entertaining thirteen-loss career."

True, Micky lost thirteen of his fifty-one professional fights, which qualifies him as better than average, and he never won a major world title, his WBU light welterweight title not withstanding. But he became a working-class hero, an underdog with an over-sized heart.

In the days leading up to his second and final retirement, Micky told the *Boston Herald,* "I'll probably work, but I'd do that no matter how much money I had. I figure I'll take a month off, but don't be surprised to see me driving the paver again before the summer's over. It's not like I started throwing money around once I started making it. I invested most of it. I did buy a house in Lowell, but I have a mortgage like anybody else. I can honestly say my lifestyle didn't change once I started making money, and it won't now."

Well, his lifestyle did change a little bit. Although he went back to paving streets and parking lots in Lowell and living in a house on Upham Street, about two hundred yards from his childhood home on Stevens Street, he now worked when he wanted to, not because he had to.

Micky kept his word about retirement, never once looking back. He married Charlene at the Viva Las Vegas Chapel on May 27, 2005.

"An Elvis impersonator sang," Micky recalled. "It was pretty cool."

Then he and his wife settled down with his four dogs, Buddy, Bruno, Bubba Booey, and Ernie, a St. Bernard, an English mastiff, an English bulldog, and a Pekinese, in that order.

Micky and Charlene bought a tanning salon, Caribbean Sun Tanning, on Middlesex Street in Lowell. And Micky began training a small stable of fighters, including his nephew Sean Eklund, who had the talent, the courage, and enough poor judgment to follow his uncles into the world of boxing. Eklund had his first professional fight up at the Hampton Beach Casino in New Hampshire, the same place where Micky's career took a definitive upward turn. Eklund lost that night.

A life of leisure isn't something Micky had ever known, and he wasn't looking for an introduction at the age of thirty-eight. But whether he was comfortable with it or not, Micky was a celebrity, and he had time on his hands. He attended dinners in his honor. He accepted awards. He played in charity golf tournaments, even though his double vision made it impossible for him to see the ball for more than a year. He dropped the ceremonial first puck at a Lowell Lock Monster's hockey game where fifteen hundred fans received Micky Ward bobblehead dolls. He signed autographs, and he raised money for the Lowell-based Kids in Disability Sports, Inc.

Micky even kept himself in good-enough shape to run the Boston Marathon, though he didn't take his training quite as seriously as he had when he was still a professional boxer. When other runners spent the evening before the marathon carbo-loading on pasta, Micky was getting drunk. He showed up at the starting line in Hopkinton with a pounding headache, and by the time he reached the finish line in Boston, he felt even worse. Still, he finished the 26.2 miles. He knew about hard journeys, and he always went the distance.

"Micky Ward belongs to that great upper middle class of prize-fighters," Larry Merchant said. "He's not in the elite, but he's never cheated the fans or the public. Too often, the top fighters' bouts are performances—concerts, if you will. But in terms of competition, action, and drama, guys like Micky Ward are the heart and soul of the sport."

Micky did things in the ring that showed more courage than talent. His comebacks and knockouts against Alfonzo Sanchez and Reggie Green showed people less about what kind of boxer he was, and more about what kind of man he was, and they began rooting for the man. So, despite losing three of his last four fights, Micky remained a hero of the people.

It was an uncommon success story. At one point, the kid from Lowell was being promoted by a guy who couldn't promote fights in his home state, managed by a novice manager, and trained by his brother, a former crack addict. Meanwhile, any one of his seven sisters could barge into his locker room drunk at any time. Yet, inside this maelstrom was a calm but violent fighter.

Luck was involved. Talent had something to do with it. And the will to win kept Micky moving forward in the ring and upward outside of it. It didn't hurt that he was a white Irish kid who could fight, either. He was given opportunities, and he failed. He was given second chances, and sometimes he failed again. But he finished every fight on his feet, and walked out of the ring with his head held high.

Micky Ward was not a saint or an innocent. He was imperfect as a man and as a fighter, but as both, he was dependable and respectable. He lived in two worlds—boxing and the real one—and in both there are right roads and wrong roads to travel, pitfalls ready to devour anyone who missteps. In the worlds where Micky resided, there were hundreds of ways to screw up, and only one way to succeed. You have to fight. You don't always have to win, but you have to keep fighting. Micky kept fighting. And the low-key, strangely humble, and honest Irish kid who could fight did more than that, he became a legend.

INDEX